Writing Dialogue for Film and Television

Andrew Parry

Published by Andrew Parry, 2024.

WRITING DIALOGUE FOR FILM AND TELEVISION

First edition. November 28, 2024.

Copyright © 2024 Andrew Parry.

ISBN: 979-8230724711

Written by Andrew Parry.

Table of Contents

Introduction

Welcome to this book, your comprehensive guide to mastering one of the most crucial aspects of screenwriting. Dialogue, the spoken words of your characters, is not just a means of communication but a powerful tool that shapes the story, reveals character depth, and immerses audiences in the world you've created. In this book, we delve deep into the art and craft of writing dialogue that resonates, engages, and leaves a lasting impression.

Dialogue is more than just exchanging information. It's the heartbeat of your screenplay, driving the narrative forward and breathing life into your characters. Whether it's the sharp repartee of a high-stakes confrontation, the quiet introspection of a character's moment of realization, or the subtle hints of hidden motives, dialogue is the lens through which your audience experiences your story.

This book adopts the philosophy of starting with the end in mind. By focusing on how dialogue functions in the climactic moments and working backwards, we gain insight into its fundamental role throughout the screenplay. Each chapter is designed to explore a specific aspect of dialogue, offering practical advice, techniques, and examples to help you craft dialogue that is not only believable but also impactful.

We'll begin by examining the role of dialogue in key moments like the climax, resolutions, and the final scene, exploring how it can resolve conflicts, deliver emotional payoffs, and cement character arcs. As we move through the chapters, we will also cover essential elements like voice, subtext, deception, and the use of language, demonstrating how these components work together to enhance the overall narrative.

Additionally, we'll delve into how dialogue can establish setting, reflect themes, and balance with action. Each chapter will provide you with the tools to handle various dialogue types—be it witty banter, dramatic revelations, or suspenseful exchanges—ensuring you can tackle any genre or scenario with confidence. I explore each concept within each context and provide you with examples as ideas to spark your own imagination.

Ultimately, this book aims to equip you with the skills to create dialogue that is not only functional but memorable. By understanding and mastering the nuances of dialogue, you will be able to craft stories that captivate your audience and stand the test of time. Whether you're an aspiring screenwriter or a seasoned writer looking to refine your craft, I hope this book will serve as your essential guide to writing dialogue that truly sings.

Welcome to a journey through the art of dialogue—where every word matters and every conversation counts.

Crafting the Climactic Dialogue

Crafting climactic dialogue requires a delicate balance of tension, revelation, and emotional payoff. The climax of your screenplay is where all your plot threads come together, and the dialogue in this scene must be impactful and memorable. To achieve this, start by considering the final confrontation or resolution. What are the characters' goals in this moment? How do their desires clash or align? Understanding these dynamics will guide you in writing dialogue that feels organic and powerful.

In the climactic scene, your protagonist and antagonist often face off in a battle of wits or physical confrontation. The dialogue here should reflect their inner struggles and the stakes at play. The protagonist's dialogue should convey their determination, growth, and the lessons they've learned throughout the story. For instance, in "Die Hard," John McClane's climactic dialogue with Hans Gruber encapsulates his journey from reluctant hero to determined savior.

The antagonist's dialogue, on the other hand, should reveal their motivations and flaws. This is their moment to either justify their actions or show their true colors. The climax of "The Dark Knight" features the Joker's chaotic philosophy clashing with Batman's sense of order, making their dialogue rich with thematic depth.

One effective technique is to use callbacks to earlier scenes. If a character mentioned a significant belief or catchphrase earlier in the story, bringing it back in the climactic dialogue can create a powerful resonance. This not only rewards attentive viewers but also highlights character development and thematic continuity. For example, in "The Lord of the Rings: The Return of the King," Aragorn's line, "For Frodo," before charging into battle, echoes his earlier conversations about bravery and leadership.

Subtext is crucial in climactic dialogue. Characters often say one thing while meaning another, adding layers to the conversation. This can be seen in "Inception," where Cobb's dialogue with Mal in the climactic dream sequences is laden with subtext about guilt, love, and letting go. The surface conversation about dreams and reality hides a deeper emotional struggle.

Emotional honesty in dialogue can elevate the climax. Characters may finally voice truths they've been hiding, leading to cathartic moments for both them and the audience. In "Good Will Hunting," the climactic scene where Sean tells Will, "It's not your fault," repeatedly, is a raw, emotional breakthrough that changes Will's trajectory.

The pacing of climactic dialogue should match the tension of the scene. Short, sharp exchanges can heighten the sense of urgency, while longer, more reflective lines can give weight to revelations. Consider the rhythm of your dialogue and how it complements the action. In "The Matrix," the climactic dialogue between Neo and Agent Smith is a blend of quick retorts and philosophical musings, perfectly matching the escalating stakes.

Incorporating rhetorical devices can make climactic dialogue more impactful. Repetition, metaphors, and rhetorical questions can emphasize key points and add a poetic quality. For example, in "Gladiator," Maximus's line, "What we do in life echoes in eternity," uses metaphor to underscore the film's themes of legacy and honor.

As you craft your climactic dialogue, think about the voices of your characters. Each should speak in a way that is true to their personality and background. Consistent voice ensures that the dialogue feels authentic and maintains the integrity of your characters. In "Breaking Bad," Walter White's climactic dialogue retains his blend of scientific precision and growing arrogance, making his final confrontation with Jesse Pinkman all the more compelling.

Finally, consider the thematic resolution in your dialogue. The climax is where your story's themes should come to a head. Use dialogue to encapsulate the central message of your screenplay. In "The Lion King," Simba's climactic dialogue with Scar ties back to themes of responsibility, family, and reclaiming one's destiny.

To write compelling climactic dialogue, immerse yourself in the characters' journeys, let their voices shine through, and ensure that every word carries weight. This scene is the heart of your screenplay, where everything comes together in a powerful, unforgettable moment. By focusing on these elements, you can create dialogue that not only serves the story but also resonates deeply with your audience.

Resolutions and Revelations: Dialogue in the Final Scene

The final scene of your screenplay is where all the storylines converge, conflicts are resolved, and characters reveal their true selves. Crafting dialogue for this crucial moment requires a deft touch, ensuring that every line serves the purpose of tying up loose ends and delivering emotional satisfaction to the audience.

At the core of the final scene's dialogue are resolutions. This is where characters reflect on their journeys and acknowledge the changes they've undergone. Consider how your protagonist has evolved from the beginning of the story to this point. Their dialogue should reflect newfound insights or a sense of closure. For example, in "Forrest Gump," Forrest's final dialogue at Jenny's grave reveals his enduring love and the simplicity of his wisdom, bringing his journey full circle.

Revelations in the final scene can be powerful tools to leave a lasting impact. These revelations can pertain to plot twists, hidden truths, or character motivations that were hinted at but never fully explained until now. In "The Sixth Sense," the final scene's dialogue reveals Dr. Malcolm Crowe's realization of his own death, which recontextualizes the entire narrative and provides a profound resolution.

Thematic closure is essential in the final scene's dialogue. This is where you drive home the central message of your story. Whether it's a lesson learned, a moral stance, or a philosophical viewpoint, your dialogue should encapsulate the essence of your screenplay. In "The Shawshank Redemption," Red's final words about hope and redemption provide a thematic closure that resonates with the audience long after the credits roll.

The dialogue in the final scene should also address any remaining questions or unresolved subplots. This doesn't mean spoon-feeding the audience every detail, but rather giving enough information to provide a sense of completion. In "Harry Potter and the Deathly Hallows Part 2," the final scene's dialogue wraps up the fates of the main characters while leaving room for the audience's imagination about their future.

Emotional resonance is key. The final scene is often a cathartic moment for characters and viewers alike. The dialogue should tap into the emotions that have been building throughout the story, offering a release or a poignant reflection. In "Toy Story 3," the final dialogue between Andy and his toys is laden with nostalgia and farewell, striking an emotional chord that is both heartfelt and bittersweet.

When writing the final scene's dialogue, consider the dynamics between characters. Relationships often reach a pivotal point in the conclusion. Dialogue can showcase the resolution of conflicts, the deepening of bonds, or the acceptance of losses. In "Casablanca," Rick's final dialogue with Ilsa at the airport exemplifies their complex relationship and the sacrifices they make, emphasizing the theme of selflessness and duty.

Subtext remains crucial even in the final scene. What characters say on the surface may carry deeper meanings, reflecting their internal states and unspoken emotions. This layered dialogue adds depth and keeps the audience engaged, prompting them to think beyond the literal words. In "Lost in Translation," the final whispered words between Bob and Charlotte are never revealed, leaving their true sentiments to the audience's interpretation.

Pacing the dialogue in the final scene requires careful consideration. Unlike the rapid exchanges of the climax, the final scene often benefits from a more measured pace, allowing characters and audiences to savor the moment. Reflective pauses and thoughtful lines can enhance the gravity of the resolution. In "The Godfather," Michael

Corleone's final words and the slow closing of the door on Kay signify his complete transformation and the end of his moral struggle.

Revisiting earlier dialogues can provide a satisfying sense of closure. Echoing lines or phrases from previous scenes can highlight character development and thematic continuity. In "The Lord of the Rings: The Return of the King," Sam's reflection on their journey and the repetition of "Well, I'm back" bookends his character's arc beautifully, emphasizing his growth and the cyclical nature of their adventure.

The final scene is also an opportunity to leave a lasting impression with memorable lines. Crafting dialogue that lingers in the audience's mind can elevate your screenplay. Think of iconic closing lines like "After all, tomorrow is another day" from "Gone with the Wind," which encapsulates Scarlett O'Hara's resilience and optimism.

In conclusion, dialogue in the final scene is a delicate blend of resolutions and revelations. It should encapsulate the characters' journeys, resolve key conflicts, and deliver emotional and thematic closure. By focusing on these elements, you can craft a final scene that leaves a profound impact, ensuring your screenplay resonates with audiences long after the story ends.

Unveiling the Truth: Dialogues That Resolve Conflict

Dialogue that resolves conflict is a pivotal element in any screenplay, bringing closure to the story and often revealing deeper truths about the characters. This type of dialogue not only settles disputes but also uncovers motivations, secrets, and personal growth. Crafting such dialogue requires an understanding of the characters' arcs, the underlying themes, and the emotional stakes involved.

The essence of conflict resolution dialogue lies in its ability to reveal hidden truths. This is the moment where characters often confront their deepest fears, acknowledge their flaws, or confess their secrets. Consider the emotional weight of these revelations and how they impact the characters involved. For instance, in "A Few Good Men," the courtroom scene where Colonel Jessup exclaims, "You can't handle the truth!" is a powerful moment of revelation that resolves the central conflict while exposing the moral complexities of the characters.

To write effective conflict resolution dialogue, start by identifying the core issues at play. What are the characters truly fighting about? What are their underlying motivations and desires? Addressing these questions can help you create dialogue that goes beyond surface-level arguments and taps into the deeper, more resonant themes of your story. In "Good Will Hunting," the climactic confrontation between Will and Sean about Will's potential and fear of failure serves as a powerful resolution to their conflict.

Character voices play a crucial role in these dialogues. Each character should speak in a way that is true to their personality and background, maintaining consistency while also reflecting any growth or change. The protagonist's dialogue might shift from defensive and closed-off to open and vulnerable, while the antagonist's dialogue could reveal hidden vulnerabilities or a surprising moral stance. In "The Dark Knight," the dialogue between Batman and the Joker during their final confrontation showcases their contrasting philosophies and resolves their conflict while leaving room for thematic exploration.

Subtext is a valuable tool in conflict resolution dialogue. Characters may not always state their feelings outright, but their words can carry deeper meanings and implications. This layered dialogue can add richness to the scene, making the resolution more satisfying. In "Silver Linings Playbook," the final argument between Pat and Tiffany is laden with subtext about trust, love, and healing, making their eventual reconciliation more poignant.

Emotional honesty is essential. Characters should express their true feelings, even if it means being vulnerable or admitting mistakes. This authenticity can lead to powerful, cathartic moments that resonate with the audience. In "The Pursuit of Happyness," Chris Gardner's heartfelt plea to his son about never giving up is a raw, honest moment that resolves their struggles and reinforces the film's themes of perseverance and hope.

The pacing of conflict resolution dialogue is crucial. It should build tension, reach a peak, and then gradually ease into resolution. Quick, sharp exchanges can heighten the sense of urgency, while slower, more reflective dialogue can give weight to the resolution. In "Pulp Fiction," the diner scene where Jules confronts Ringo is a masterclass in pacing, with the dialogue shifting from tense confrontation to a reflective monologue that resolves the conflict in an unexpected way.

The setting can also influence the effectiveness of conflict resolution dialogue. The environment in which the conversation takes place can reflect the characters' states of mind and the nature of their conflict. In "Inception," the final confrontation between Cobb and Mal takes place in a dreamscape that symbolizes their fractured relationship, adding a layer of symbolism to their dialogue and its resolution.

Revisiting earlier conflicts in the resolution dialogue can create a sense of closure and continuity. Characters might reference past arguments, misunderstandings, or moments of connection, tying the resolution back to the story's development. In "The Avengers," the final battle scene is peppered with dialogue that calls back to previous conflicts and character dynamics, reinforcing their growth and unity.

Thematic resolution is another key aspect. The dialogue should not only resolve the immediate conflict but also reflect the overarching themes of the screenplay. This can provide a deeper, more satisfying resolution for the audience. In "The Godfather," Michael's final dialogue with his family members encapsulates the themes of power, loyalty, and the corrupting influence of ambition, providing a fitting resolution to the film's conflicts.

Finally, ensure that the resolution feels earned. The dialogue should reflect the characters' journeys and the stakes involved. Avoid easy or contrived resolutions; instead, strive for dialogue that feels authentic and true to the characters' experiences. In "Breaking Bad," the final conversation between Walter White and Skyler is a culmination of their long-standing conflict, with Walter's admission of his true motivations providing a deeply earned and impactful resolution.

In conclusion, crafting dialogue that resolves conflict involves a careful balance of revealing truths, maintaining character voices, utilizing subtext, and ensuring emotional honesty. By focusing on these elements, you can create powerful, memorable scenes that bring your screenplay to a satisfying and meaningful conclusion.

The Power of the Last Words

The final words in a screenplay carry immense weight. They are the audience's lasting impression, the final echo of your story's themes, and the culmination of your characters' journeys. Crafting these last lines requires precision and an acute understanding of your narrative's essence.

The last words should encapsulate the story's core message. Whether it's a line of dialogue or a reflective narration, these words need to resonate with the audience, offering closure while often leaving something to ponder. Consider the ending of "Casablanca," where Rick's line, "Louis, I think this is the beginning of a beautiful friendship," not only closes the narrative but also hints at future possibilities, embodying the theme of personal sacrifice for the greater good.

To create impactful last words, reflect on the protagonist's journey. How have they changed from the beginning to the end? Their final lines should reflect this transformation. In "The Lord of the Rings: The Return of the King," Samwise Gamgee's simple line, "Well, I'm back," speaks volumes about his character's growth and the completion of his epic journey. It is a quiet, yet powerful affirmation of his return to normalcy after an extraordinary adventure.

Antagonists, too, can deliver memorable last words. These lines can reveal their final thoughts, regrets, or defiance, offering a deeper insight into their character. In "Blade Runner," Roy Batty's poignant monologue, "All those moments will be lost in time, like tears in rain," provides a profound reflection on life and mortality, humanizing him in his final moments.

Thematic reinforcement is another key function of last words. They should echo the themes explored throughout the screenplay. In "The Shawshank Redemption," Red's final words, "I hope," tie back to the film's overarching theme of hope and redemption, leaving the audience with a sense of optimism and resolution.

Subtext can elevate the last words, adding layers of meaning. What the characters say on the surface may carry deeper implications, allowing the audience to derive multiple interpretations. In "Lost in Translation," Bob's whispered words to Charlotte are never revealed, allowing viewers to project their own meanings onto the moment, making it deeply personal and evocative.

The emotional impact of the last words is crucial. They should evoke a strong emotional response, be it joy, sorrow, hope, or contemplation. In "E.T. the Extra-Terrestrial," Elliott's heartfelt farewell, "I'll be right here," leaves a lasting emotional imprint, encapsulating the bond between the characters and the bittersweet nature of their parting.

Context is essential in determining the tone and content of the last words. The setting, the characters' state of mind, and the events leading up to this moment all influence what is said and how it is delivered. In "The Great Gatsby," Nick Carraway's reflective closing lines, "So we beat on, boats against the current, borne back ceaselessly into the past," resonate with the novel's themes of aspiration and the relentless passage of time, providing a fitting end to the story.

Simplicity often enhances the power of the last words. Overly complex or verbose dialogue can dilute the impact. A concise, well-chosen phrase can leave a stronger impression. In "Gone with the Wind," Scarlett O'Hara's declaration, "After all, tomorrow is another day," is both simple and profound, capturing her indomitable spirit and resilience.

Last words can also provide a twist or reveal, adding a final layer of intrigue or surprise. This technique can leave the audience with a sense of wonder or curiosity. In "The Sixth Sense," the revelation, "I see dead people," is not the final line, but it reverberates through to the end, reshaping the audience's understanding of the entire film.

In ensemble films, the last words can reflect the collective journey of the characters, offering a sense of unity or shared destiny. In "The Breakfast Club," the closing narration, "You see us as you want to see us," speaks to the collective identity and the stereotypes each character has confronted and transcended.

Moreover, the delivery of the last words matters as much as their content. The actor's performance, the tone, and the pacing all contribute to the effectiveness of the final lines. A well-delivered line can linger in the audience's mind, enhancing its impact.

Finally, consider the visual and auditory context accompanying the last words. The imagery, the music, and the overall atmosphere can amplify the emotional and thematic resonance. In "Schindler's List," the haunting visuals and John Williams' evocative score underscore Oskar Schindler's final words, "I could have done more," adding layers of poignancy and regret.

In summary, the last words in a screenplay are a crucial element that demands careful consideration. They should encapsulate the story's themes, reflect character development, evoke strong emotions, and leave a lasting impression. By focusing on these aspects, you can craft final lines that resonate deeply with your audience, ensuring your screenplay is remembered long after the credits roll.

Building to the Climax: Dialogue that Leads to the Final Scene

Building dialogue that leads to the final scene involves creating a gradual escalation of tension, stakes, and emotional intensity. The dialogue must drive the narrative forward, deepen character relationships, and foreshadow the impending climax. This process requires a balance of pacing, subtext, and thematic reinforcement to ensure a seamless and impactful transition to the climactic moment.

As you build towards the climax, the dialogue should reflect the increasing stakes and urgency. Each conversation should push the characters closer to the pivotal moment, revealing more about their motivations, fears, and desires. In "The Dark Knight," the dialogue between Batman and the Joker escalates the tension, with each exchange revealing deeper philosophical conflicts and setting the stage for their final confrontation.

Foreshadowing is a crucial element in building to the climax. Subtle hints and clues embedded in the dialogue can create anticipation and suspense. These can be direct references or more oblique mentions that become significant in retrospect. In "The Sixth Sense," Dr. Crowe's conversations with Cole contain subtle hints about his own condition, which are only fully understood during the climax.

Character development through dialogue is essential. As the story progresses, characters should reveal more about themselves, allowing the audience to connect with their journeys. This deepens the emotional impact of the climax. In "Rocky," the conversations between Rocky and Adrian build their relationship and highlight Rocky's insecurities, making his final fight emotionally resonant.

Conflict is a driving force in the build-up to the climax. Dialogue should reflect the internal and external struggles of the characters, heightening the tension. In "A Few Good Men," the escalating verbal confrontations between Kaffee and Jessup build to the explosive courtroom climax, each exchange increasing the stakes and emotional intensity.

The pacing of dialogue is crucial. Early in the narrative, conversations can be more leisurely, allowing for character exploration and world-building. As the climax approaches, the dialogue should become sharper and more focused, reflecting the tightening plot and escalating stakes. In "The Matrix," the shift from philosophical discussions early on to rapid, urgent exchanges in the lead-up to the climax mirrors the escalating action.

Subtext adds depth to the build-up. Characters often say one thing but mean another, creating layers of meaning that enhance the narrative complexity. This subtext can hint at unresolved conflicts or foreshadow future events. In "Breaking Bad," Walter White's conversations with Jesse are filled with subtext about power dynamics and trust, adding tension that culminates in the series' climax.

Dialogue should also reflect the thematic elements of the story. As you approach the climax, reiterate the central themes through conversations, ensuring they resonate with the audience. In "Inception," the recurring discussions about reality and dreams build the thematic foundation that the climax ultimately resolves.

Relationships between characters are pivotal in the build-up. Dialogue should explore and challenge these relationships, adding emotional stakes to the climax. In "Star Wars: The Empire Strikes Back," the evolving dialogue between Luke and Darth Vader, culminating in the revelation of their relationship, adds immense emotional weight to the climax.

Exposition through dialogue needs to be handled delicately. While building to the climax, it's essential to provide necessary information without slowing down the pace. This can be achieved through natural, engaging conversations that reveal critical plot points. In "Jurassic Park," the dialogue between Dr. Grant and the others about the park's dangers builds tension and provides vital information leading to the climax.

The tone of the dialogue should align with the overall mood of the narrative. As the climax approaches, the tone often shifts to reflect the rising tension and impending conflict. In "Jaws," the shift from light-hearted banter to serious, urgent dialogue mirrors the escalating threat of the shark.

Incorporating callbacks in dialogue can create a sense of continuity and build emotional resonance. Referencing earlier conversations or events can add layers of meaning and highlight character development. In "The Lord of the Rings: The Return of the King," Sam's reminder of their earlier discussions about home and hope strengthens the emotional impact as they approach the climax.

The protagonist's dialogue should reflect their internal journey, showcasing their growth or struggle. Their conversations leading up to the climax should reveal their evolving mindset and set the stage for their ultimate challenge. In "Gladiator," Maximus's dialogue about honor and vengeance evolves, culminating in his final confrontation with Commodus.

Antagonists also play a crucial role. Their dialogue should challenge the protagonist and escalate the stakes, making the climax more intense. In "Silence of the Lambs," the chilling conversations between Clarice and Hannibal Lecter build tension and add psychological depth, leading to the climactic resolution.

In conclusion, building to the climax through dialogue involves careful pacing, character development, conflict, and thematic reinforcement. Each conversation should add to the narrative tension, deepen emotional connections, and foreshadow the climactic events. By focusing on these elements, you can craft dialogue that leads seamlessly and powerfully to the final scene, ensuring a compelling and satisfying resolution for your screenplay.

The Turning Point: Pivotal Dialogue in the Third Act

The third act of a screenplay is where the story reaches its crescendo, and pivotal dialogue during this phase can make or break the narrative's impact. This is the moment where characters are pushed to their limits, conflicts come to a head, and crucial revelations occur. Crafting effective dialogue for this act requires a deep understanding of the characters, the stakes, and the thematic core of the story.

At the heart of the third act is the turning point— a moment of irreversible change for the protagonist. This dialogue should reflect the culmination of the character's journey, embodying their growth, realizations, or decisions. In "The Matrix," Neo's conversation with Agent Smith in the climactic battle is a turning point where Neo fully embraces his role as "The One," transforming the stakes of the conflict.

Pivotal dialogue often carries the weight of revelation. These revelations can be about the plot, characters, or underlying themes. In "Star Wars: The Empire Strikes Back," the iconic line "I am your father" delivered by Darth Vader to Luke Skywalker not only serves as a shocking plot twist but also fundamentally alters Luke's understanding of his identity and destiny.

Character dynamics are at their most intense in the third act. The dialogue should highlight these tensions and shifts in relationships. In "The Shawshank Redemption," the conversation between Andy and Red about hope and escape reflects a significant turning point, as Andy reveals his plan and Red's skepticism begins to crumble, setting the stage for the film's resolution.

Conflict resolution through dialogue in the third act must be precise and impactful. This is where characters confront their deepest fears, resolve misunderstandings, or make critical decisions. In "Good Will Hunting," the pivotal therapy session where Sean tells Will, "It's not your fault," serves as a cathartic moment, breaking down Will's emotional barriers and facilitating his path to healing.

Subtext plays a crucial role in third act dialogue. Characters often express deeper truths and emotions indirectly, adding layers of meaning to their words. This can heighten the tension and emotional resonance. In "Inception," the climactic dialogue between Cobb and Mal in the dream world is fraught with subtext about guilt, loss, and acceptance, making their final confrontation deeply poignant.

Thematic reinforcement is essential in the third act. The dialogue should echo the central themes of the story, providing clarity and closure. In "The Dark Knight," the final conversation between Batman and the Joker underscores the film's exploration of chaos versus order, with the Joker's philosophy clashing with Batman's sense of justice in a final ideological showdown.

Pacing is critical in third act dialogue. As the story accelerates towards its climax, the dialogue should reflect this urgency. Quick, sharp exchanges can convey a sense of desperation or immediacy, while more reflective dialogue can provide a moment of pause before the final push. In "The Lord of the Rings: The Return of the King," the dialogue during the Battle of Pelennor Fields balances urgent commands with brief, reflective exchanges about bravery and sacrifice.

Emotional intensity peaks in the third act, and the dialogue should capture this. Characters are often at their most vulnerable or determined, and their words should reflect the high stakes and emotional weight of the moment. In

"Titanic," the final dialogue between Jack and Rose as the ship sinks encapsulates their love and desperation, leaving a lasting emotional impact.

The resolution of subplots through dialogue in the third act can provide a sense of completeness. Addressing lingering issues or secondary characters' arcs can add depth to the main narrative. In "Harry Potter and the Deathly Hallows Part 2," the dialogue between Harry and Voldemort during their final battle resolves numerous subplots and character arcs, bringing the series to a satisfying conclusion.

Foreshadowing and callbacks in third act dialogue can create a sense of unity and coherence. Referencing earlier conversations or themes can enhance the impact of the climax. In "The Godfather," Michael's final words to Carlo, "Don't tell me you're innocent. Because it insults my intelligence," echo back to earlier themes of power and betrayal, solidifying Michael's transformation.

The antagonist's dialogue in the third act is just as important as the protagonist's. It should challenge the protagonist and reveal the antagonist's true motivations or final gambit. In "Die Hard," Hans Gruber's calm, calculated dialogue during the final showdown with John McClane highlights his cunning and ruthlessness, heightening the tension of their confrontation.

Clarity and resolution are paramount in third act dialogue. While maintaining the complexity and depth of the characters and themes, the dialogue should bring a sense of closure to the narrative threads. In "The Avengers," the final dialogue during the Battle of New York resolves the team's internal conflicts and solidifies their unity, paving the way for the climactic battle.

In summary, pivotal dialogue in the third act is a delicate balance of revelation, conflict resolution, thematic reinforcement, and emotional intensity. By carefully crafting these elements, you can ensure that your screenplay reaches its climax with maximum impact, leaving a lasting impression on your audience.

Dialogues that Deliver Emotional Payoff

Delivering an emotional payoff through dialogue is one of the most satisfying elements of screenwriting. This is the moment when the audience's investment in the characters and their journey is rewarded with a powerful emotional experience. Crafting such dialogue requires a deep understanding of character arcs, emotional stakes, and the narrative's thematic core.

Emotional payoff dialogues often come at pivotal moments in the story, such as the climax or resolution. These dialogues should encapsulate the characters' growth, the resolution of their conflicts, and the thematic essence of the story. In "Toy Story 3," the final conversation between Andy and his toys is a poignant example. Andy's heartfelt speech as he hands over his beloved toys to Bonnie is laden with nostalgia, love, and a sense of closure, delivering a profound emotional payoff for both the characters and the audience.

For a dialogue to deliver an emotional payoff, it must be authentic and true to the characters. Forced or unnatural dialogue can break the emotional connection. The characters' words should feel genuine and resonate with their established personalities and journeys. In "Good Will Hunting," the therapeutic breakthrough between Will and Sean, where Sean repeatedly tells Will, "It's not your fault," feels deeply authentic and earned, leading to a powerful emotional release.

Subtext is a powerful tool in crafting emotionally resonant dialogue. Often, what characters don't say is as important as what they do say. This indirect communication can add layers of meaning and enhance the emotional impact. In "Lost in Translation," the final whispered words between Bob and Charlotte remain unknown to the audience, but the emotion conveyed through their interaction speaks volumes about their connection and the impact they've had on each other's lives.

Timing and pacing are crucial in delivering emotional dialogues. Allowing moments of silence, pauses, and the right pacing can give weight to the words and allow the emotions to sink in. In "E.T. the Extra-Terrestrial," the pause before Elliott says, "I'll be right here," gives the audience a moment to feel the depth of their bond, making the farewell more impactful.

The context in which the dialogue takes place also influences its emotional power. The setting, the circumstances, and the build-up to the moment all contribute to the emotional resonance. In "The Fault in Our Stars," the dialogue during the eulogy scene is made more poignant by the context of Hazel and Gus's shared experiences and the impending sense of loss, heightening the emotional impact.

Dialogues that deliver emotional payoff often involve vulnerability and honesty. Characters are typically at their most open and truthful during these moments, revealing their deepest fears, hopes, and regrets. In "A Beautiful Mind," when John Nash speaks at the Nobel Prize ceremony, his heartfelt acknowledgment of his wife's support and his struggle with mental illness provides a touching and sincere emotional climax to his journey.

Relationships are central to emotionally charged dialogues. The interaction between characters who share a deep bond can create powerful emotional moments. In "The Pursuit of Happyness," the final exchange between Chris Gardner and his son, where Chris's pride and relief are palpable, encapsulates the film's emotional journey and the strength of their relationship.

Conflict resolution through dialogue can also deliver an emotional payoff. When long-standing conflicts are resolved through honest and heartfelt conversations, the emotional release can be significant. In "Silver Linings Playbook," the final reconciliation between Pat and Tiffany, where they confess their feelings and understand each other's struggles, brings a satisfying emotional closure to their tumultuous relationship.

Reflecting on past events through dialogue can enhance the emotional depth. Characters reminiscing about shared experiences or significant moments can create a powerful connection with the audience. In "The Lord of the Rings: The Return of the King," the final moments between Frodo and Sam, where they reflect on their journey and their bond, bring a poignant end to their epic quest.

Dialogues that tie into the thematic core of the story often carry the most emotional weight. When characters articulate the story's central themes in a personal and meaningful way, it can resonate deeply with the audience. In "Dead Poets Society," John Keating's final words to his students, "O Captain! My Captain!" encapsulate the film's themes of individuality, inspiration, and the impact of a great teacher, delivering a powerful emotional payoff.

Finally, the performance of the actors can significantly enhance the emotional impact of the dialogue. The delivery, tone, and expressions of the actors bring the words to life and can elevate the emotional resonance. In "Forrest Gump," Tom Hanks's portrayal of Forrest's simplicity and earnestness in his final dialogue with Jenny adds layers of emotional depth to their farewell.

In conclusion, dialogues that deliver emotional payoff require authenticity, subtext, timing, context, vulnerability, and a strong connection to the characters' relationships and the story's themes. By focusing on these elements, you can craft dialogues that resonate deeply with the audience, providing a satisfying and memorable emotional experience.

Confrontation and Catharsis: Dialogue in the Climactic Battle

The climactic battle in a screenplay is where the stakes are highest, and the emotional and narrative tensions reach their peak. Dialogue in these moments must be charged with intensity, delivering both confrontation and catharsis. This dialogue not only propels the action but also provides deep emotional and thematic resolution.

In a climactic battle, confrontation is inevitable. The protagonist and antagonist face off, often revealing their deepest motivations and inner conflicts. This is the time for characters to voice their truths, challenge each other, and assert their positions. In "The Avengers," the dialogue between Loki and the Avengers during the Battle of New York is filled with confrontation, where Loki's arrogance clashes with the resolve and unity of the Avengers, highlighting their respective ideologies.

The language used in these confrontations should be sharp and impactful. Characters are often under extreme pressure, and their words should reflect the urgency and gravity of the situation. In "Harry Potter and the Deathly Hallows Part 2," the final battle between Harry and Voldemort is marked by terse, powerful dialogue that underscores the high stakes and the culmination of their long-standing conflict.

Subtext is crucial in climactic dialogue. Characters might say one thing but mean another, adding layers of complexity and heightening the emotional impact. In "The Dark Knight," the final confrontation between Batman and the Joker is rich with subtext. The Joker's taunts and Batman's responses reveal their fundamental ideological differences and the personal stakes involved, making their battle more than just a physical one.

Catharsis in the climactic battle is about emotional release and resolution. This is where characters often confront their fears, confess their secrets, or resolve their internal conflicts. In "Star Wars: Return of the Jedi," Luke's dialogue with Darth Vader during their final duel brings about catharsis. Luke's appeal to his father's goodness and Vader's eventual redemption provide a powerful emotional release for both characters and the audience.

Thematic reinforcement is vital. The dialogue should echo the central themes of the story, providing clarity and closure. In "The Lord of the Rings: The Return of the King," the dialogue during the Battle of the Black Gate reflects themes of hope, sacrifice, and the struggle against overwhelming odds. Aragorn's rallying speech, "For Frodo," encapsulates the film's themes and motivates the characters for the final push.

Personal stakes are at their highest during the climactic battle. The dialogue should reflect the personal journeys of the characters, highlighting their growth and the culmination of their arcs. In "Gladiator," Maximus's final confrontation with Commodus is steeped in personal stakes. Maximus's dialogue about his family and his desire for justice brings his arc full circle and adds emotional weight to their duel.

Incorporating callbacks can enhance the emotional impact. Referencing earlier dialogues or moments can create a sense of continuity and reinforce character development. In "Avengers: Endgame," Tony Stark's final line, "I am Iron Man," is a powerful callback to his declaration in the first "Iron Man" film, bringing his character arc to a poignant conclusion.

The antagonist's dialogue is crucial in the climactic battle. It should challenge the protagonist and reveal the antagonist's motivations, providing depth to their character. In "Die Hard," Hans Gruber's dialogue during his final confrontation with John McClane showcases his cunning and determination, making his eventual defeat more satisfying.

Emotional honesty is essential. Characters should be raw and open, expressing their true feelings and motivations. This honesty can lead to powerful moments of catharsis. In "The Pursuit of Happyness," the final confrontation with Chris Gardner and the job interviewer is emotionally charged, as Chris's honesty about his struggles and determination leads to his eventual triumph.

The pacing of dialogue in the climactic battle should match the action's intensity. Quick, sharp exchanges can convey the urgency and high stakes, while longer, more reflective lines can provide moments of emotional depth amidst the chaos. In "The Matrix," the rapid-fire dialogue between Neo and Agent Smith during their final battle is interspersed with moments of philosophical reflection, enhancing the scene's impact.

Setting and context also play a role. The environment in which the climactic battle takes place can influence the dialogue. The setting can reflect the characters' internal states or the broader themes of the story. In "Inception," the final confrontation within the dream layers adds complexity to the dialogue, as characters grapple with the nature of reality and their subconscious fears.

In summary, dialogue in the climactic battle should deliver both confrontation and catharsis, driving the action forward while providing emotional and thematic resolution. By focusing on sharp, impactful language, subtext, thematic reinforcement, personal stakes, and emotional honesty, you can craft dialogue that heightens the intensity of the climactic battle and delivers a satisfying conclusion to your screenplay.

Reflective Dialogue: Characters' Final Thoughts

Reflective dialogue at the end of a screenplay offers characters a moment to process their journeys, providing the audience with insight into their inner thoughts and emotions. This type of dialogue is often contemplative and introspective, allowing characters to voice their growth, realizations, and the lessons they've learned. Crafting such dialogue requires a balance of authenticity, thematic resonance, and emotional depth.

Reflective dialogue is a window into a character's soul. It should feel genuine and true to the character's voice and experiences throughout the story. In "Forrest Gump," Forrest's simple yet profound reflection, "I'm not a smart man, but I know what love is," encapsulates his journey and the depth of his understanding, despite his simplicity. This line resonates because it is authentically Forrest, capturing his essence.

Thematic reinforcement is crucial in reflective dialogue. This is an opportunity to highlight the central themes of your story, offering closure and clarity. In "The Shawshank Redemption," Red's final reflection about hope, "I hope I can make it across the border. I hope to see my friend and shake his hand. I hope the Pacific is as blue as it has been in my dreams. I hope," ties together the film's theme of hope and redemption, leaving the audience with a sense of optimism.

Emotional honesty is essential. Characters should speak from the heart, expressing their true feelings and thoughts. This honesty can lead to powerful, cathartic moments. In "Good Will Hunting," Will's letter to Sean, "Sorry, I had to go see about a girl," is a simple yet deeply honest reflection on his growth and decision to pursue happiness, resonating with the audience on an emotional level.

Reflective dialogue often involves a degree of vulnerability. Characters are typically at their most open and unguarded, sharing their fears, regrets, and hopes. In "The Fault in Our Stars," Hazel's final reflection, "You gave me a forever within the numbered days, and I'm grateful," reveals her deep gratitude and the impact of her relationship with Gus, providing an emotional and thoughtful conclusion to her journey.

Subtext can add depth to reflective dialogue. What characters say on the surface may carry deeper meanings, reflecting their internal conflicts and resolutions. In "The Godfather," Michael Corleone's final words, "Just when I thought I was out, they pull me back in," are rich with subtext, reflecting his internal struggle with power and the inescapable nature of his family's legacy.

The pacing of reflective dialogue should be measured and deliberate, allowing the audience to fully absorb the character's thoughts. Pauses and silences can be as powerful as the words themselves, giving weight to the reflection. In "Lost in Translation," Bob's final whispered words to Charlotte are less about the specific dialogue and more about the emotional resonance of the moment, enhanced by the contemplative pacing.

Relationships play a key role in reflective dialogue. Characters often reflect on their relationships and the impact others have had on their journeys. In "The Lord of the Rings: The Return of the King," Frodo's final thoughts about Sam, "You cannot always be torn in two. You will have to be one and whole for many years. You have so much to enjoy and to be and to do," reflect on their deep bond and the sacrifices they've made, providing emotional closure.

Reflective dialogue can also serve to resolve lingering questions or uncertainties. Characters might offer insights or explanations that bring clarity to the narrative. In "Titanic," Rose's final words about Jack, "He saved me in every way that a person can be saved," provide a clear and heartfelt acknowledgment of his impact on her life, resolving the emotional arc of the story.

The setting and context of the reflective dialogue can enhance its impact. The environment can mirror the character's internal state or the broader themes of the story. In "Blade Runner," Roy Batty's final monologue, "All those moments will be lost in time, like tears in rain," is set against the backdrop of a dystopian future, reflecting the film's themes of memory, mortality, and humanity.

Reflective dialogue should also tie back to the character's arc, showcasing their development and transformation. In "A Beautiful Mind," John Nash's final reflection on his life's work and his acknowledgment of his wife's unwavering support encapsulate his journey from brilliance through madness to redemption, providing a powerful emotional payoff.

Incorporating a sense of hope or forward-looking perspective can leave the audience with a sense of optimism. Characters reflecting on their future or expressing hope can provide a satisfying and uplifting conclusion. In "The Pursuit of Happyness," Chris Gardner's reflection on achieving his dreams and looking forward to a brighter future is both inspiring and emotionally fulfilling.

In conclusion, reflective dialogue that captures characters' final thoughts should be authentic, thematically resonant, emotionally honest, and deeply reflective of their journeys. By focusing on these elements, you can craft dialogue that offers profound insight into your characters, providing a meaningful and satisfying conclusion to your screenplay.

Unmasking the Villain: Antagonist's Final Monologue

The antagonist's final monologue is a powerful tool in storytelling, offering a chance to reveal hidden motivations, deep-seated beliefs, and the true nature of the villain. This monologue can provide context to the antagonist's actions, evoke sympathy, or cement their role as the story's ultimate foe. Crafting this dialogue requires careful attention to character development, thematic resonance, and emotional impact.

The antagonist's final monologue often serves as a moment of revelation, unmasking the deeper layers of their character. This is the time to explore the antagonist's backstory, their motivations, and the driving forces behind their actions. In "The Dark Knight," the Joker's final monologue to Batman about the nature of chaos and his desire to bring Gotham to its knees reveals his philosophy and gives the audience a deeper understanding of his chaotic nature.

This monologue should encapsulate the antagonist's core beliefs and worldviews. It's an opportunity to showcase the philosophical or ideological differences between the antagonist and the protagonist. In "Gladiator," Commodus's final words to Maximus reveal his insecurities and desperate need for approval, highlighting the stark contrast between his corrupt ambition and Maximus's honor and integrity.

Emotional depth is crucial in the antagonist's final monologue. This is a moment to humanize the villain, showing their vulnerabilities and perhaps evoking a sense of pity or understanding from the audience. In "Blade Runner," Roy Batty's final speech about his experiences and impending death, "All those moments will be lost in time, like tears in rain," offers a poignant look into his humanity, creating a complex and sympathetic character.

The monologue should also reflect the themes of the story, reinforcing the narrative's central messages. In "Harry Potter and the Order of the Phoenix," Voldemort's final confrontation with Harry highlights themes of power, fear, and the corrupting influence of the quest for immortality, reinforcing the story's exploration of good versus evil.

Tension and drama are essential in the delivery of the final monologue. The antagonist's words should be charged with emotion, whether it's anger, despair, pride, or resignation. This heightened emotional state can intensify the scene and make the monologue more impactful. In "Star Wars: Return of the Jedi," Emperor Palpatine's final taunts to Luke Skywalker are filled with malicious delight and confidence in his victory, heightening the tension of the climax.

Subtext adds layers of meaning to the monologue. The antagonist might reveal more through what they don't say directly, using implications and insinuations to convey their true thoughts and feelings. In "Skyfall," Silva's monologue to M is laden with subtext about betrayal, revenge, and his twisted sense of justice, revealing the depth of his obsession and the personal nature of his vendetta.

The setting and context of the monologue can enhance its impact. The environment in which the antagonist delivers their final words can reflect their inner state or the culmination of their plans. In "Die Hard," Hans Gruber's final moments as he falls from the Nakatomi Plaza are underscored by his last desperate attempts to kill John McClane, reflecting his relentless nature and the high stakes of their confrontation.

The antagonist's final monologue should provide closure to their arc, tying up any loose ends and explaining their ultimate fate. Whether they meet their end, achieve a temporary victory, or escape to fight another day, their final words should bring a sense of resolution. In "The Silence of the Lambs," Hannibal Lecter's chilling final words to Clarice, "I'm having an old friend for dinner," provide a darkly humorous closure to his arc while leaving the door open for future encounters.

A memorable antagonist's monologue often includes a twist or a revelation that changes the audience's understanding of the story or the character. This can be a shocking confession, a hidden motive, or a last-minute manipulation. In "Se7en," John Doe's final revelation of his plan and its horrifying implications completely upend the protagonists' sense of victory and deliver a devastating emotional blow.

The tone of the monologue should be consistent with the antagonist's character and the overall mood of the story. Whether it's sinister, reflective, defiant, or tragic, the tone sets the stage for the final moments of the antagonist's arc. In "The Godfather Part II," Michael Corleone's cold, calculating demeanor during his final confrontation with Fredo reflects the film's dark, tragic tone and Michael's complete transformation into a ruthless leader.

In summary, the antagonist's final monologue is a critical moment that unpacks their motivations, reinforces the story's themes, and delivers emotional and dramatic impact. By focusing on authenticity, thematic resonance, emotional depth, and dramatic tension, you can create a powerful and memorable monologue that enhances the climax of your screenplay and provides a fitting resolution to the antagonist's journey.

The Protagonist's Final Speech

The protagonist's final speech is a crucial moment in any screenplay, encapsulating the journey they've undergone and the growth they've achieved. This speech should resonate with the audience, providing closure and leaving a lasting impression. Crafting this dialogue requires a deep understanding of the character's arc, the story's themes, and the emotional tone you wish to convey.

The protagonist's final speech often serves as the culmination of their journey. It's a moment of reflection and realization where they articulate the lessons they've learned and the changes they've undergone. In "Rocky," Rocky's final words after his fight, expressing his love for Adrian, encapsulate his personal triumph and the emotional journey he has experienced, regardless of the fight's outcome.

Thematic reinforcement is a key component of the final speech. This is where the protagonist can underline the central themes of the story, offering a clear and resonant message to the audience. In "The Lord of the Rings: The Return of the King," Aragorn's speech to his soldiers, "But it is not this day!" encapsulates themes of hope, courage, and unity, rallying his troops for the final battle.

Emotional honesty is essential in the protagonist's final speech. The character should speak from the heart, expressing their true feelings and vulnerabilities. This authenticity can create a powerful connection with the audience. In "Forrest Gump," Forrest's simple, heartfelt reflections on life and love during his final speech reveal his profound yet uncomplicated understanding of the world, resonating deeply with viewers.

The speech should also provide resolution to the character's arc, tying up loose ends and offering closure. In "Good Will Hunting," Will's letter to Sean, where he says he had to "go see about a girl," beautifully ties up his journey of self-discovery and healing, providing a satisfying conclusion to his story.

Subtext can add depth to the protagonist's final speech. While the character may be speaking plainly, the underlying meanings and emotions can enhance the impact. In "A Beautiful Mind," John Nash's speech upon receiving the Nobel Prize is not just about his academic achievements but also a testament to his personal struggles and the support of his loved ones, adding layers of meaning to his words.

The setting and context of the final speech can greatly influence its impact. The environment in which the protagonist delivers their speech should reflect the culmination of their journey. In "Braveheart," William Wallace's final cry of "Freedom!" as he faces execution underscores the central theme of his fight against oppression and his enduring spirit, even in the face of death.

Pacing and delivery are crucial elements. The speech should be paced to allow the audience to absorb the significance of the words, with pauses for emphasis and reflection. In "The Pursuit of Happyness," Chris Gardner's final narration about achieving his dreams and finding happiness is delivered with a reflective, measured tone that enhances its emotional resonance.

The protagonist's final speech can also serve to inspire or rally other characters and the audience. It can be a call to action or a message of hope. In "Independence Day," President Whitmore's rousing speech before the final battle, "We will not go quietly into the night!" serves to unify and inspire both the characters and the audience, elevating the emotional stakes.

Personal stakes should be highlighted in the final speech. The protagonist's words should reflect their personal journey, struggles, and triumphs, making the speech deeply personal and meaningful. In "The King's Speech," King George VI's final broadcast is a personal victory over his speech impediment and a powerful moment of leadership during a time of crisis.

Memorable language and powerful imagery can make the protagonist's final speech stand out. Using vivid, evocative language can leave a lasting impression on the audience. In "Dead Poets Society," John Keating's final message to his students about the importance of seizing the day and making their lives extraordinary uses poetic language that resonates long after the film ends.

The speech should also reflect the protagonist's unique voice, staying true to their character throughout. Consistency in tone and style ensures that the speech feels authentic and genuine. In "To Kill a Mockingbird," Atticus Finch's closing argument is a reflection of his principled, compassionate nature, staying true to his character's voice and values.

In summary, the protagonist's final speech is a pivotal moment that encapsulates their journey, reinforces the story's themes, and delivers an emotional and memorable conclusion. By focusing on authenticity, thematic resonance, emotional honesty, and powerful delivery, you can craft a final speech that resonates deeply with the audience and provides a fitting end to your screenplay.

Dialogue in the Hero's Moment of Triumph

The hero's moment of triumph is a defining scene in any screenplay, where the protagonist overcomes their greatest challenge and emerges victorious. The dialogue in this scene is critical, as it encapsulates the culmination of the hero's journey, their growth, and the fulfillment of their quest. Crafting effective dialogue for this moment requires a deep understanding of the character's arc, the stakes of the story, and the emotional and thematic goals of the narrative.

The dialogue should reflect the hero's transformation. Throughout the story, the protagonist has faced numerous trials and tribulations, and their words in this moment should highlight the growth they've undergone. In "The Lion King," Simba's triumphant declaration, "I am Simba, son of Mufasa," signifies his acceptance of his destiny and his growth from a fearful exile to a confident leader.

The thematic core of the story should be echoed in the hero's triumphant dialogue. This is an opportunity to reinforce the central message of the narrative. In "Rocky," Rocky Balboa's words, "Yo Adrian, I did it!" capture the theme of perseverance and personal victory, emphasizing that true triumph lies in the effort and determination rather than the outcome of the fight.

Emotional resonance is key. The dialogue should evoke a strong emotional response from the audience, celebrating the hero's victory while also acknowledging the struggles they've endured. In "Harry Potter and the Deathly Hallows Part 2," Harry's final confrontation with Voldemort and his declaration, "Let's finish this the way we started it. Together!" carries immense emotional weight, symbolizing the culmination of his long and arduous journey.

The hero's dialogue in this moment often includes a sense of closure or resolution. This can involve addressing past conflicts, reconciling with other characters, or acknowledging their own internal struggles. In "The Lord of the Rings: The Return of the King," Aragorn's speech, "You bow to no one," to Frodo and the other hobbits provides a powerful resolution to their journey, recognizing their courage and sacrifices.

Subtext can add depth to the triumphant dialogue. While the hero may be expressing victory, underlying meanings or emotions can enhance the impact. In "The Matrix," Neo's final declaration, "I'm going to show them a world where anything is possible," not only signifies his victory over the machines but also hints at the broader implications of his newfound power and the hope he represents.

Pacing is crucial in delivering triumphant dialogue. The timing and rhythm should match the intensity of the moment, allowing for pauses that let the audience absorb the significance of the victory. In "Braveheart," William Wallace's rallying cry, "They may take our lives, but they'll never take our freedom!" is delivered with a deliberate pacing that heightens the emotional and dramatic impact.

The dialogue should also reflect the hero's unique voice and personality. Staying true to the character ensures that the words feel authentic and resonate with the audience. In "Iron Man," Tony Stark's triumphant quip, "I am Iron Man," perfectly encapsulates his confident, charismatic persona, making the moment memorable and true to his character.

Relationships are often highlighted in the hero's moment of triumph. The dialogue can acknowledge the support and contributions of allies, emphasizing themes of friendship, teamwork, or love. In "Star Wars: A New Hope," Luke Skywalker's final words before destroying the Death Star, "The Force will be with you, always," not only signify his triumph but also acknowledge the support and teachings of Obi-Wan Kenobi.

The setting can enhance the dialogue's impact. The environment in which the hero's triumph occurs can reflect the stakes and the journey, adding a layer of symbolism to the words. In "Gladiator," Maximus's final words, "My name is Maximus Decimus Meridius," spoken in the Colosseum, underscore his reclaiming of honor and justice in the place of his greatest trials.

Incorporating callbacks to earlier moments in the story can create a sense of continuity and reinforce character development. Referencing past dialogue or significant events can make the hero's triumph feel even more rewarding. In "The Hunger Games," Katniss's final words in the arena, "I volunteer as tribute," echo her initial sacrifice and underscore her growth and resilience throughout the series.

Finally, the hero's dialogue in the moment of triumph should leave a lasting impression, providing a sense of closure while also inspiring or uplifting the audience. In "The Pursuit of Happyness," Chris Gardner's simple but profound declaration, "This part of my life... this little part... is called happiness," captures the essence of his journey and the hard-won nature of his triumph.

In summary, the dialogue in the hero's moment of triumph should reflect their transformation, reinforce thematic elements, evoke emotional responses, and stay true to the character's voice. By focusing on these elements, you can craft dialogue that powerfully encapsulates the hero's victory and leaves a lasting impact on the audience.

The Denouement: Wrapping Up Loose Ends with Dialogue

The denouement of a screenplay is the final segment where the story's loose ends are tied up, and the characters' fates are clarified. This part is crucial for providing closure and leaving the audience with a sense of completion. Crafting effective dialogue for the denouement requires a focus on resolution, emotional payoff, and thematic reinforcement.

The primary goal of the denouement is to resolve any remaining subplots and character arcs. The dialogue should address these lingering threads, providing answers and tying up loose ends. In "The Lord of the Rings: The Return of the King," the multiple farewells and conversations between the characters, such as Frodo's parting words to Sam, offer closure to their epic journey and individual story arcs.

The dialogue in the denouement should also reflect the characters' growth and transformations throughout the story. This is an opportunity to show how they have changed and what they have learned. In "Toy Story 3," the final dialogue between Andy and his toys as he hands them over to Bonnie highlights his maturation and the bittersweet acceptance of moving on.

Emotional resolution is key. The denouement should provide an emotional payoff, allowing the audience to process the journey they have been on with the characters. In "Forrest Gump," the simple yet profound conversation between Forrest and his son at the bus stop, where Forrest reflects on his life, offers a poignant conclusion that resonates emotionally with the audience.

Thematic reinforcement in the dialogue helps to underscore the central messages of the story. This can provide a sense of coherence and depth to the narrative. In "The Shawshank Redemption," Red's final words about hope and the promise of a new life in Mexico reinforce the film's themes of redemption and the enduring power of hope.

Subtext can add depth to the denouement dialogue. Characters may express their feelings indirectly, allowing for a richer interpretation of their words. In "Lost in Translation," the final whisper between Bob and Charlotte, though inaudible to the audience, carries a weight of unspoken understanding and connection, leaving a lasting impression through subtext.

The pacing of the dialogue in the denouement should be measured and reflective, contrasting with the high intensity of the climax. This allows the audience to absorb the resolution and transition smoothly out of the narrative. In "The Godfather," Michael Corleone's final, understated dialogue and the closing of the door on Kay provide a chilling yet calm resolution to the film's intense conflicts.

Closure for secondary characters is also important. The denouement dialogue should address the fates of supporting characters, ensuring that their arcs are satisfactorily concluded. In "Harry Potter and the Deathly Hallows Part 2," the epilogue's dialogue briefly touches on the lives of the main characters and their children, providing a glimpse into the future and closure for the supporting cast.

The setting of the denouement can enhance the dialogue's impact. The environment in which these final conversations occur can reflect the themes and emotional tone of the resolution. In "Titanic," the final scenes on the ship's deck, where Rose reflects on her life, provide a fittingly tranquil and poignant setting for the film's conclusion.

Callbacks to earlier moments in the story can create a sense of unity and coherence in the denouement. Referencing significant past events or dialogues can highlight character development and bring the story full circle. In "Back to the

Future," Marty's final conversation with Doc about future adventures echoes their earlier interactions and solidifies their enduring friendship.

The protagonist's dialogue in the denouement should encapsulate their journey and the resolution of their internal conflicts. This can be a moment of reflection, acceptance, or new beginnings. In "The Pursuit of Happyness," Chris Gardner's final narration about achieving his dreams and finding happiness provides a deeply satisfying conclusion to his struggle.

Anticipation of the future can also be a theme in denouement dialogue, suggesting new beginnings or continued journeys for the characters. This can leave the audience with a sense of hope and curiosity. In "The Lord of the Rings: The Return of the King," Sam's final words about his future life with Rosie and their children offer a hopeful and forward-looking conclusion.

Finally, the tone of the denouement dialogue should align with the overall mood of the story's resolution. Whether it's joyful, somber, reflective, or hopeful, the tone should enhance the emotional impact of the denouement. In "Casablanca," Rick's final line, "Louis, I think this is the beginning of a beautiful friendship," perfectly captures the film's blend of melancholy and optimism.

In conclusion, the dialogue in the denouement is crucial for wrapping up loose ends, providing emotional and thematic closure, and leaving the audience with a sense of satisfaction. By focusing on resolution, character growth, emotional payoff, thematic reinforcement, and the right tone, you can craft a denouement that effectively concludes your screenplay and resonates with your audience.

Transitioning to the End: Dialogue in the Penultimate Scene

The penultimate scene in a screenplay is a critical moment, setting the stage for the final resolution. Dialogue in this scene must serve multiple purposes: it should heighten tension, provide crucial information, and emotionally prepare the audience for the climax. Crafting effective dialogue for the penultimate scene involves balancing exposition with emotion, foreshadowing the resolution, and deepening character relationships.

The primary function of the penultimate scene is to build anticipation for the climax. The dialogue should heighten the stakes and create a sense of urgency. In "The Dark Knight," the penultimate scene's dialogue between Batman and the Joker heightens the tension by revealing the Joker's plan and forcing Batman into a moral dilemma, setting the stage for the final confrontation.

Exposition is often necessary in the penultimate scene to clarify any remaining plot points or provide crucial information needed for the climax. This should be done seamlessly, integrating exposition into natural dialogue. In "Inception," the penultimate scene's conversation between Cobb and Ariadne provides essential details about the mechanics of the dream world, ensuring the audience understands the stakes as they enter the final layer.

Emotional preparation is key. The dialogue should prepare the characters and the audience emotionally for what is to come. This can involve moments of vulnerability, final confessions, or expressions of hope or fear. In "Harry Potter and the Deathly Hallows Part 2," Harry's conversation with his friends and loved ones before facing Voldemort alone provides emotional depth and prepares the audience for the impending climax.

Foreshadowing in the penultimate scene can create a sense of anticipation and hint at the resolution. Subtle clues or significant lines of dialogue can prepare the audience for the final twist or outcome. In "The Lord of the Rings: The Return of the King," the penultimate dialogue between Frodo and Sam about their journey and the weight of the ring foreshadows the final act of destruction and redemption.

Character relationships often come to the forefront in the penultimate scene. This is a moment to deepen connections, resolve interpersonal conflicts, or highlight the unity or discord among characters. In "Avengers: Endgame," the penultimate scene's dialogue among the Avengers before the final battle emphasizes their camaraderie, resolve, and the personal stakes for each character.

Thematic reinforcement is essential in the penultimate scene's dialogue. This is an opportunity to reiterate the central themes of the story, providing a sense of coherence as the narrative approaches its conclusion. In "Star Wars: The Empire Strikes Back," the dialogue between Luke and Yoda about facing fears and the power of the Dark Side reinforces the film's themes of courage and the struggle between good and evil.

The pacing of the dialogue should reflect the transition from rising action to climax. It should be tight and focused, yet allow for moments of reflection or revelation. In "The Matrix," the penultimate dialogue between Neo and Morpheus is both urgent and contemplative, balancing the need for action with deeper philosophical questions.

The tone of the penultimate scene should align with the impending climax. Whether it's tense, hopeful, somber, or determined, the dialogue should set the emotional tone for the final scene. In "Titanic," the penultimate conversation between Jack and Rose, where they vow to stay together no matter what, sets a tone of tragic determination that carries into the climax.

Subtext can add layers of meaning to the penultimate dialogue, enhancing its impact and setting up the climax. Characters may speak indirectly about their fears or hopes, allowing the audience to infer deeper meanings. In "Blade Runner," the penultimate dialogue between Deckard and Batty, where Batty saves Deckard and reflects on his experiences, is rich with subtext about humanity and mortality.

The penultimate scene is also an opportunity to resolve minor plot points or character arcs, ensuring that the final scene can focus on the main resolution. This can involve tying up subplots or providing closure to secondary characters. In "Back to the Future," the penultimate scene's dialogue resolves the immediate crisis and sets up the final, triumphant return to the present.

Visual and contextual elements can enhance the dialogue in the penultimate scene. The setting, lighting, and overall atmosphere should complement the dialogue and heighten the tension or emotional impact. In "Jurassic Park," the penultimate scene's dialogue amidst the backdrop of the chaotic park underscores the desperation and urgency of the characters' situation.

Lastly, the penultimate scene's dialogue should leave the audience eager for the climax, creating a sense of anticipation and readiness for the final resolution. In "The Hunger Games," the penultimate conversation between Katniss and Peeta about their survival and defiance against the Capitol sets the stage for the final showdown, leaving the audience on the edge of their seats.

In summary, dialogue in the penultimate scene is crucial for transitioning to the end of the story. It should heighten tension, provide necessary exposition, emotionally prepare the audience, foreshadow the resolution, and deepen character relationships. By focusing on these elements, you can craft dialogue that effectively sets the stage for a powerful and satisfying climax.

Foreshadowing the Climax: Strategic Use of Dialogue

Foreshadowing the climax through dialogue is an essential storytelling technique that plants subtle hints and clues about future events, creating anticipation and heightening the impact of the climax. Crafting such dialogue requires a balance of subtlety, thematic resonance, and character consistency. Effective foreshadowing not only enhances the audience's engagement but also provides a deeper, more satisfying resolution when the climax unfolds.

The primary goal of foreshadowing is to create anticipation. Dialogue should hint at the climax without giving away too much, allowing the audience to sense that something significant is coming. In "The Matrix," Morpheus's repeated references to Neo being "The One" and the discussions about fate and choice build anticipation for Neo's ultimate realization of his powers.

Subtlety is key in foreshadowing. The dialogue should not be overt or heavy-handed; instead, it should integrate naturally into the conversations, often disguised as casual remarks or minor details. In "The Sixth Sense," Malcolm's discussions about the nature of perception and Cole's revelation that he "sees dead people" subtly foreshadow the twist that Malcolm himself is dead.

Thematic resonance is crucial. Foreshadowing dialogue should align with the central themes of the story, reinforcing the narrative's core messages. In "The Lion King," Mufasa's dialogue about the Circle of Life and the importance of taking one's place in the world foreshadows Simba's eventual acceptance of his role as king, tying into the film's themes of responsibility and legacy.

Character consistency is important for believable foreshadowing. The hints should come from characters whose knowledge or perspective makes the foreshadowing credible. In "Harry Potter and the Prisoner of Azkaban," Professor Trelawney's prophecies, though often dismissed, provide foreshadowing that is consistent with her role as a seer, adding credibility to the hints she drops.

Foreshadowing can be achieved through recurring motifs or phrases in dialogue. Repeated references or phrases can create a sense of inevitability. In "Romeo and Juliet," the frequent mentions of fate and destiny in the dialogue foreshadow the tragic ending, creating a sense of looming inevitability.

Symbolism in dialogue can also serve as foreshadowing. Characters may use metaphors or symbolic language that hints at future events. In "Jaws," the dialogue about the shark being an unstoppable force of nature and the townspeople's initial dismissals foreshadow the eventual deadly encounters, symbolizing the impending danger.

Conflict and tension in dialogue can hint at future climactic confrontations. The escalation of verbal conflicts can foreshadow physical or emotional battles. In "The Dark Knight," the philosophical clashes between Batman and the Joker in their dialogues foreshadow their ultimate physical and ideological showdown.

Foreshadowing can be layered with multiple hints spread throughout the narrative, creating a richer, more intricate buildup. These layers can interconnect, making the climax feel well-earned and inevitable. In "Inception," the discussions about dream layers, the concept of the "kick," and the totem's importance are layered throughout the dialogue, culminating in the film's complex and thought-provoking climax.

Foreshadowing can also be used to mislead or set up twists. Dialogue that seems to hint at one outcome can later reveal a different truth, adding to the surprise and impact of the climax. In "The Usual Suspects," Verbal Kint's seemingly innocent dialogue about his experiences cleverly misleads the audience, setting up the shocking reveal of his true identity as Keyser Söze.

The emotional tone of foreshadowing dialogue should match the eventual climax. If the climax is tragic, the dialogue should carry an undercurrent of foreboding. If it's triumphant, the dialogue might include hints of hope or determination. In "Titanic," the early conversations about the ship's unsinkable nature and the characters' dreams of the future carry a bittersweet undertone, foreshadowing the impending tragedy.

Characters' reflections on their past or their fears can also serve as foreshadowing. These reflections provide insight into their motivations and hint at future challenges or resolutions. In "The Lord of the Rings: The Two Towers," Sam's reflections on hope and stories during his dialogue with Frodo foreshadow their perseverance and ultimate triumph in the face of overwhelming odds.

The timing of foreshadowing is crucial. Strategic placement of hints throughout the narrative ensures that the audience is continually engaged and looking forward to the resolution. Early foreshadowing plants the seeds, while mid-point and late-stage foreshadowing reinforce and build upon these hints, leading to a satisfying payoff.

In conclusion, foreshadowing the climax through dialogue is a powerful technique that enhances narrative coherence and emotional impact. By focusing on subtlety, thematic resonance, character consistency, and strategic placement, you can craft dialogue that skillfully hints at future events, creating a richer, more engaging storytelling experience.

Creating Suspense with Dialogue Before the Final Scene

Creating suspense with dialogue before the final scene is a crucial storytelling technique that keeps the audience on the edge of their seats, eagerly anticipating the climax. Suspenseful dialogue builds tension, heightens stakes, and maintains a sense of uncertainty, making the eventual resolution more satisfying. Crafting such dialogue involves strategic pacing, subtext, foreshadowing, and emotional intensity.

The primary goal of suspenseful dialogue is to build tension. This can be achieved through careful pacing, where conversations are interspersed with pauses, incomplete sentences, and interruptions. In "No Country for Old Men," the dialogue between Anton Chigurh and the gas station attendant is a masterclass in suspenseful pacing. The seemingly mundane conversation is filled with pregnant pauses and subtle threats, creating an atmosphere of impending danger.

Subtext is a powerful tool for creating suspense. Characters may say one thing while meaning another, allowing the audience to infer hidden threats or deeper implications. In "The Silence of the Lambs," the dialogue between Clarice Starling and Hannibal Lecter is filled with subtext. Hannibal's seemingly polite and intellectual conversations are laced with underlying menace, keeping the audience in a state of tension.

Foreshadowing through dialogue can heighten suspense by hinting at potential dangers or conflicts to come. Subtle references to future events can create a sense of anticipation and unease. In "Jaws," the early dialogue about the shark attacks and the mayor's reluctance to close the beaches foreshadows the impending disaster, building suspense as the audience waits for the inevitable confrontation.

Raising stakes through dialogue is essential. Conversations that reveal the consequences of failure or the high cost of success can increase the audience's investment in the outcome. In "The Dark Knight," the dialogue between Batman and the Joker about Gotham's soul and the stakes of their conflict elevates the tension, making the audience acutely aware of the potential fallout from their final showdown.

Conflict within dialogue can create suspense by showcasing characters' opposing goals and the tension between them. Sharp exchanges and verbal sparring can highlight the stakes and the urgency of the situation. In "Inglourious Basterds," the tense conversation in the tavern between Lt. Hicox and the German officer escalates through sharp dialogue, leading to an explosive climax.

The use of questions and uncertainty in dialogue can maintain suspense. Characters questioning each other's motives, plans, or loyalty can create a sense of unease and anticipation. In "Blade Runner," the conversations between Deckard and Rachael, filled with questions about humanity and identity, keep the audience in suspense about Rachael's true nature and Deckard's intentions.

Revelations and withheld information can also build suspense. Characters may drop hints or partial information, leaving the audience eager to learn more. In "Gone Girl," Amy's cryptic diary entries and the dialogue surrounding her disappearance gradually reveal shocking truths, maintaining suspense until the final scenes.

Emotional intensity in dialogue can heighten suspense. Characters expressing fear, desperation, or determination can evoke a strong emotional response from the audience, increasing their anticipation for the climax. In "The Hunger Games," the dialogue between Katniss and Peeta before the final showdown in the arena is charged with emotion, fear, and determination, keeping the audience on edge.

Contradictory statements and unreliable narrators can add to the suspense. When characters contradict themselves or each other, it creates doubt and uncertainty about what will happen next. In "Fight Club," the conflicting dialogues between the Narrator and Tyler Durden create a sense of unease and suspense as the true nature of their relationship is gradually revealed.

The setting and context of the dialogue can enhance its suspenseful effect. Conversations in confined or dangerous environments can amplify the tension. In "Die Hard," the radio exchanges between John McClane and Hans Gruber, set against the backdrop of a high-stakes hostage situation, create a constant sense of danger and suspense.

Ambiguity and open-ended statements can leave the audience guessing and build suspense. Characters making ambiguous remarks or threats that are not immediately clear can keep the audience in a state of anticipation. In "Se7en," John Doe's cryptic and disturbing dialogue about his crimes and philosophy creates a sense of dread and suspense leading up to the film's shocking climax.

Foreshadowing through dialogue can subtly hint at future conflicts or twists, keeping the audience engaged and on edge. In "The Sixth Sense," Dr. Malcolm Crowe's discussions about perception and reality foreshadow the film's twist, maintaining suspense as the audience pieces together the clues.

Building suspense through dialogue before the final scene involves a combination of pacing, subtext, foreshadowing, emotional intensity, and strategic use of ambiguity and conflict. By carefully crafting conversations that hint at dangers, raise stakes, and maintain a sense of uncertainty, you can create a compelling narrative that keeps the audience eagerly anticipating the climax.

Dialogues that Cement Character Arcs

Dialogues that cement character arcs are pivotal moments in a screenplay where characters express their growth, realizations, and transformations. These dialogues provide clarity and closure, showcasing the journey the characters have undergone. Crafting such dialogues requires an understanding of the characters' development, thematic resonance, and emotional depth.

The primary goal of these dialogues is to encapsulate the character's journey. The dialogue should reflect the changes the character has undergone, highlighting their growth or transformation. In "The Godfather," Michael Corleone's final dialogue, "Don't ask me about my business," marks his complete transformation from a reluctant outsider to a ruthless mafia leader, cementing his character arc.

Thematic reinforcement is crucial in these dialogues. They should echo the central themes of the story, providing a sense of coherence and depth. In "The Shawshank Redemption," Red's final parole hearing speech, where he talks about hope and redemption, encapsulates his transformation and reinforces the film's themes of hope and freedom.

Emotional honesty is essential. Characters should express their true feelings, revealing their inner thoughts and emotions. This authenticity can create powerful, cathartic moments. In "Good Will Hunting," Will's dialogue with Sean where he finally opens up about his abusive past and fears of the future shows his emotional growth and readiness to embrace change.

Subtext can add depth to these dialogues. Characters might say one thing but mean another, allowing the audience to infer deeper meanings and emotions. In "Lost in Translation," Bob and Charlotte's final conversation, filled with unspoken emotions and subtle hints, beautifully captures their connection and personal growth throughout the film.

The setting and context of the dialogue can enhance its impact. The environment should reflect the character's journey and the culmination of their arc. In "Rocky," Rocky's final words to Adrian in the ring, "Yo Adrian, I did it!" capture his personal victory and emotional journey, set against the backdrop of his triumphant moment.

The dialogue should provide resolution to the character's internal conflicts and struggles. This can involve addressing past traumas, reconciling with other characters, or accepting their true selves. In "Silver Linings Playbook," Pat's final conversation with Tiffany, where they confess their feelings and understand each other's struggles, brings closure to their tumultuous relationship and personal journeys.

Callbacks to earlier moments can create a sense of continuity and highlight character development. Referencing past dialogues or events can emphasize how far the character has come. In "The Lion King," Simba's final declaration, "I am Simba, son of Mufasa," echoes his earlier struggles with identity and acceptance, showcasing his growth and readiness to take his place as king.

Conflicts resolved through dialogue can cement character arcs by showing how characters have learned to overcome their differences and grow. In "The Avengers," Tony Stark's final conversation with Captain America, where he acknowledges the value of teamwork and selflessness, marks his growth from a self-centered playboy to a committed hero.

The pacing of the dialogue should allow for reflection and emphasis on key moments. Pauses and silences can give weight to the words and enhance their emotional impact. In "A Beautiful Mind," John Nash's Nobel Prize acceptance speech, where he reflects on his struggles with mental illness and the support of his wife, is delivered with a measured, reflective tone that underscores his journey.

The tone of the dialogue should match the character's state of mind and the overall resolution of their arc. Whether it's triumphant, reflective, or somber, the tone should enhance the emotional resonance. In "The Dark Knight Rises," Bruce Wayne's final conversation with Alfred, where he reveals his survival and new identity, is both reflective and hopeful, marking the end of his journey as Batman and the beginning of a new life.

The dialogue should also showcase the character's unique voice, staying true to their personality and development. Consistency in tone and style ensures that the dialogue feels authentic and resonates with the audience. In "Finding Nemo," Marlin's final words to Nemo, where he expresses trust and pride, reflect his growth from an overprotective father to one who trusts and believes in his son's abilities.

Symbolism in dialogue can add layers of meaning, reflecting the character's journey and transformation. In "The Matrix," Neo's final declaration, "I'm going to show them a world where anything is possible," symbolizes his acceptance of his role and the limitless potential he now embodies.

In summary, dialogues that cement character arcs should encapsulate the character's journey, reinforce thematic elements, provide emotional honesty, and offer resolution. By focusing on these elements and maintaining consistency in voice and tone, you can craft dialogues that effectively showcase character growth and provide a satisfying conclusion to their arcs.

Revealing Hidden Truths through Dialogue

Revealing hidden truths through dialogue is a powerful storytelling technique that can lead to pivotal moments of revelation, transformation, and dramatic tension in a screenplay. Crafting such dialogues requires careful consideration of timing, pacing, subtext, and the impact on character development and plot progression. This technique often leads to significant turning points in the narrative, enhancing the emotional and thematic depth of the story.

Hidden truths can encompass secrets, lies, past events, or unspoken feelings. The revelation of these truths should be strategically placed within the narrative to maximize their impact. In "The Sixth Sense," the dialogue in the climactic scene where Cole reveals, "I see dead people," not only shocks the audience but also recontextualizes the entire story, leading to the profound realization of Dr. Malcolm Crowe's own condition.

Timing and pacing are crucial when revealing hidden truths. The build-up to the revelation should create suspense and anticipation. This can be achieved through dialogue that hints at the truth without fully disclosing it until the right moment. In "A Few Good Men," the courtroom scene where Colonel Jessup exclaims, "You can't handle the truth!" is a culmination of building tension and strategic questioning that leads to a dramatic and impactful revelation.

Subtext plays a vital role in these dialogues. Characters may not explicitly state the truth but instead imply it through their words, body language, and interactions. This allows the audience to infer the hidden meanings, adding layers of complexity to the revelation. In "Gone Girl," Amy's monologue revealing her meticulously planned disappearance and framing of her husband is filled with subtext about her motivations and the dynamics of their toxic relationship.

Emotional intensity is essential when revealing hidden truths. The dialogue should reflect the emotional stakes for the characters involved, whether it's shock, betrayal, relief, or catharsis. In "Star Wars: The Empire Strikes Back," the revelation of Darth Vader's identity to Luke Skywalker, "I am your father," carries immense emotional weight, fundamentally altering Luke's understanding of his heritage and destiny.

Character development is often at the forefront of these revelations. The dialogue should showcase the characters' growth or transformation as they come to terms with the truth. In "The Shawshank Redemption," Andy Dufresne's revelation to Red about his escape plan and the hidden funds is a moment of triumph and transformation, reflecting Andy's resilience and ingenuity.

Thematic reinforcement is another critical aspect. The revelation should tie into the broader themes of the story, providing deeper insights into the narrative's core messages. In "The Usual Suspects," Verbal Kint's final revelation about the true identity of Keyser Söze ties into the themes of deception, perception, and the power of storytelling, leaving a lasting impact on the audience.

Tension and conflict often accompany the revelation of hidden truths. The dialogue should heighten the stakes and create dramatic tension, leading to a confrontation or resolution. In "Breaking Bad," the confrontation between Walter White and Skyler, where he reveals his involvement in the drug trade, is charged with tension and conflict, fundamentally altering their relationship and the direction of the story.

Context and setting can enhance the impact of revealing hidden truths. The environment in which the dialogue takes place can reflect the gravity of the revelation. In "Fight Club," the final confrontation between the Narrator and Tyler

Durden, where the truth about their identities is revealed, takes place in a chaotic and symbolic setting, enhancing the dramatic impact.

The use of irony and contrast can add depth to the revelation. Characters may discover truths that contradict their beliefs or expectations, creating a powerful emotional and narrative impact. In "The Truman Show," Truman's discovery of the artificial nature of his world and the truth about his life is laced with irony, as his seemingly perfect life is revealed to be a controlled illusion.

The revelation should lead to significant consequences for the characters and the plot. The dialogue should propel the narrative forward, leading to new conflicts, resolutions, or transformations. In "The Godfather Part II," Michael Corleone's realization of Fredo's betrayal leads to a dramatic shift in their relationship and the course of the story, highlighting the themes of loyalty and betrayal.

Incorporating foreshadowing can enhance the effectiveness of revealing hidden truths. Earlier dialogues and subtle hints can build up to the revelation, making it feel earned and impactful. In "The Prestige," the final revelation about the nature of the magic tricks and the twin brothers is foreshadowed through earlier dialogues and clues, creating a satisfying and cohesive narrative twist.

In summary, revealing hidden truths through dialogue involves strategic timing, pacing, subtext, emotional intensity, and thematic reinforcement. By focusing on these elements, you can craft dialogues that lead to powerful moments of revelation, enhancing the narrative and emotional depth of your screenplay.

Emotional Highs and Lows: Dialogue in Climactic Moments

Dialogue during climactic moments is pivotal in capturing the emotional highs and lows of a story. These scenes are often the most intense and memorable, requiring dialogue that reflects the characters' emotions, drives the narrative forward, and delivers a powerful impact. Crafting such dialogue involves balancing tension, resolution, character development, and thematic resonance.

Emotional Intensity and Contrast

Climactic moments are characterized by heightened emotional states. The dialogue should reflect this intensity, conveying the characters' deepest fears, hopes, anger, or joy. Contrasting emotional highs and lows within the same scene can amplify the impact. In "Schindler's List," Oskar Schindler's breakdown as he laments not saving more lives contrasts sharply with the gratitude of the people he did save, creating a powerful emotional high and low.

Tension and Release

Creating tension and providing release are essential components of climactic dialogue. The build-up of tension through sharp, confrontational dialogue can lead to a cathartic release when the conflict is resolved. In "Good Will Hunting," the climactic therapy session where Sean tells Will, "It's not your fault," repeatedly builds tension until Will breaks down, providing an emotional release for both the character and the audience.

Character Development and Resolution

Climactic moments often signify a turning point or resolution for characters. The dialogue should reflect their growth or realization. In "The Lord of the Rings: The Return of the King," Frodo's final dialogue with Sam as they stand at the edge of Mount Doom captures their emotional journey and the culmination of their character arcs, with Frodo realizing the burden of the ring and Sam's unwavering loyalty.

Subtext and Layers

Subtext adds depth to climactic dialogue. Characters might express one emotion while hiding another, creating layers of meaning. In "Inception," the final confrontation between Cobb and Mal in the dream world is filled with subtext about guilt, loss, and acceptance, adding complexity to their emotional highs and lows.

Thematic Resonance

The dialogue should reinforce the story's central themes, providing coherence and depth. In "The Dark Knight," the final confrontation between Batman and the Joker underscores the themes of chaos versus order, with the Joker's dialogue about the corruptibility of society and Batman's resolve to protect Gotham creating a thematic climax.

Pacing and Rhythm

The pacing of dialogue in climactic moments is crucial. Quick, sharp exchanges can heighten tension, while slower, more reflective lines can provide emotional depth. In "The Godfather," Michael Corleone's final confrontation with Fredo is marked by deliberate pacing, with pauses that heighten the emotional stakes and underscore the gravity of Michael's decision.

Conflict and Resolution

Dialogue in climactic moments often involves intense conflict, leading to resolution. The conflict can be internal or external, and the dialogue should capture this struggle. In "Harry Potter and the Deathly Hallows Part 2," the final battle between Harry and Voldemort is marked by dialogue that encapsulates their ideological conflict, with Harry's declaration of love and sacrifice ultimately overcoming Voldemort's pursuit of power.

Emotional Honesty

Characters should express their true feelings during climactic moments, providing a sense of authenticity and emotional depth. In "The Pursuit of Happyness," Chris Gardner's emotional outburst upon securing a job, where he can barely contain his tears, is a moment of raw, emotional honesty that delivers a profound emotional high.

Setting and Context

The setting of the climactic moment can enhance the dialogue's impact. The environment can reflect the characters' internal states or the narrative's stakes. In "Titanic," the dialogue between Jack and Rose as they cling to a piece of debris in the freezing water reflects their desperation and love, heightening the scene's emotional intensity.

Memorable Lines

Climactic moments often feature memorable lines that encapsulate the essence of the story or the characters' journeys. In "Braveheart," William Wallace's rallying cry, "They may take our lives, but they'll never take our freedom!" is a powerful declaration that captures the emotional high of the climactic battle.

Contrasting Perspectives

Including contrasting perspectives in the dialogue can enhance the emotional complexity. In "A Few Good Men," the climactic courtroom exchange between Lt. Kaffee and Col. Jessup presents two opposing viewpoints on duty and morality, heightening the emotional stakes and leading to a dramatic resolution.

Foreshadowing and Callbacks

Foreshadowing and callbacks in climactic dialogue can create a sense of unity and payoff. In "The Lion King," Simba's final confrontation with Scar includes callbacks to earlier dialogues about responsibility and bravery, providing a satisfying resolution to Simba's arc.

Emotional Transitions

Climactic dialogue should facilitate emotional transitions, guiding characters and the audience from one emotional state to another. In "Forrest Gump," the dialogue between Forrest and Jenny as she reveals her illness and they discuss their past and future provides a poignant emotional transition from happiness to sorrow and acceptance.

In summary, crafting dialogue for emotional highs and lows in climactic moments involves balancing intensity, conflict, resolution, and thematic depth. By focusing on these elements, you can create powerful, memorable scenes that resonate deeply with the audience and provide a satisfying conclusion to your story.

Delivering the Theme in the Final Dialogue

The final dialogue in a screenplay is a crucial moment where the theme of the story can be powerfully and succinctly conveyed. This dialogue should encapsulate the essence of the narrative, leaving a lasting impression on the audience. Crafting this dialogue requires clarity, emotional resonance, and a deep understanding of the story's core message.

Clarity and Conciseness

The theme should be delivered clearly and concisely in the final dialogue. This doesn't mean the theme needs to be stated outright, but the essence should be easily understood. In "Forrest Gump," Forrest's line, "Life is like a box of chocolates, you never know what you're gonna get," succinctly encapsulates the theme of unpredictability and the unexpected nature of life.

Emotional Resonance

The final dialogue should resonate emotionally with the audience, reflecting the journey they've been on with the characters. In "The Shawshank Redemption," Red's final monologue, "I hope I can make it across the border. I hope to see my friend and shake his hand. I hope the Pacific is as blue as it has been in my dreams. I hope," resonates deeply, capturing the themes of hope and redemption.

Character Consistency

The final dialogue should be true to the character's voice and arc, reflecting their growth and journey. In "The Godfather," Michael Corleone's final line, "Don't ask me about my business," captures his transformation into a ruthless leader, encapsulating the themes of power and corruption.

Thematic Reinforcement

The final dialogue should reinforce the story's central themes, bringing the narrative full circle. In "The Great Gatsby," Nick Carraway's closing line, "So we beat on, boats against the current, borne back ceaselessly into the past," reinforces the themes of the elusive American Dream and the inescapable pull of the past.

Symbolism and Metaphor

Using symbolism and metaphor in the final dialogue can add depth and layers of meaning, enhancing the thematic impact. In "Blade Runner," Roy Batty's final words, "All those moments will be lost in time, like tears in rain," use a powerful metaphor to convey themes of mortality and the fleeting nature of life.

Subtext and Layers

Subtext can add richness to the final dialogue, allowing the theme to be conveyed subtly. In "Lost in Translation," the whispered words between Bob and Charlotte remain unknown to the audience, but the subtext of connection and the impact of their brief encounter are clear, reflecting themes of isolation and human connection.

Resolution and Closure

The final dialogue should provide a sense of resolution and closure, tying up the thematic elements of the story. In "Toy Story 3," Andy's final words to his toys as he gives them to Bonnie, "Thanks, guys," provide closure to his childhood and reflect the themes of letting go and moving on.

Tone and Mood

The tone of the final dialogue should match the overall mood of the story's conclusion, whether it's hopeful, tragic, reflective, or triumphant. In "Casablanca," Rick's final line, "Louis, I think this is the beginning of a beautiful friendship," captures the hopeful, yet bittersweet tone of the film's conclusion.

Impact and Memorability

The final dialogue should leave a lasting impact, being memorable and resonant. In "Dead Poets Society," John Keating's final words to his students, "O Captain! My Captain!" echo throughout the final scene, encapsulating the themes of individuality and the power of inspirational teaching.

Callbacks and Echoes

Referencing earlier moments or dialogues can create a sense of unity and thematic coherence. In "The Lord of the Rings: The Return of the King," Sam's reflection on stories and his final line, "Well, I'm back," echo earlier themes of hope, perseverance, and the cyclical nature of journeys.

Questions and Reflections

Sometimes, ending with a reflective question or thought can leave the audience pondering the theme. In "Inception," the final line, "You're waiting for a train…," brings back a recurring motif and leaves the audience contemplating the nature of reality and dreams, central themes of the film.

Hope and Forward-Looking

Ending with a hopeful note can be powerful, especially if it aligns with the story's theme. In "The Pursuit of Happyness," Chris Gardner's final narration about achieving happiness and the value of perseverance leaves the audience with a sense of hope and inspiration.

Contrasts and Irony

Using contrast or irony in the final dialogue can underscore the theme in a poignant way. In "Fight Club," the Narrator's final line, "You met me at a very strange time in my life," juxtaposes the chaos around him, highlighting themes of identity and self-destruction.

In summary, delivering the theme in the final dialogue involves clarity, emotional resonance, character consistency, and thematic reinforcement. By focusing on these elements and ensuring the dialogue aligns with the tone and mood of the story's conclusion, you can create a powerful and memorable ending that encapsulates the essence of your narrative.

The Hero's Odyssey: Dialogue in the Journey's End

The conclusion of a hero's journey, often referred to as the hero's odyssey, is a moment of profound significance. The dialogue in this scene encapsulates the trials, transformations, and ultimate triumphs or realizations of the hero. Crafting this dialogue requires attention to the character's arc, the overarching themes of the story, and the emotional payoff for the audience.

Reflecting on the Journey

The hero's final dialogue should reflect on their journey, encapsulating the lessons learned and the growth achieved. In "The Lord of the Rings: The Return of the King," Frodo's dialogue with Sam as he prepares to leave Middle-earth reflects on the heavy burden of the ring and the transformative journey they've both undergone, emphasizing themes of sacrifice and friendship.

Emotional Resonance

The dialogue should evoke a strong emotional response, drawing the audience into the hero's experience. In "Gladiator," Maximus's final words, "Now we are free. I will see you again, but not yet... not yet," spoken as he envisions reuniting with his family in the afterlife, deliver a powerful emotional conclusion to his journey of vengeance and redemption.

Closure and Resolution

Providing a sense of closure is crucial. The hero's dialogue should resolve lingering questions and bring their character arc to a satisfying conclusion. In "Harry Potter and the Deathly Hallows Part 2," Harry's final conversation with his friends and family in the epilogue offers closure by showing the peaceful life he's earned after years of conflict, reinforcing themes of love and sacrifice.

Thematic Reinforcement

The dialogue should reinforce the central themes of the story, ensuring that the narrative's core messages resonate clearly. In "The Lion King," Simba's final dialogue as he takes his place as king, "Remember who you are. You are my son, and the one true king," ties back to the themes of identity, responsibility, and the circle of life.

Character Consistency

The dialogue should stay true to the hero's voice and personality, reflecting their growth while maintaining their unique traits. In "Iron Man," Tony Stark's final quip, "I am Iron Man," is consistent with his confident, bold personality and marks his acceptance of his dual identity, highlighting his transformation from a selfish playboy to a responsible hero.

Symbolism and Metaphor

Using symbolism and metaphor in the dialogue can add depth and layers of meaning, enriching the audience's understanding of the hero's journey. In "The Matrix," Neo's final words, "I'm going to show them a world where anything is possible," symbolize his embrace of his role as the savior and his commitment to freeing humanity.

Pacing and Delivery

The pacing of the final dialogue should allow the audience to absorb the significance of the moment. Pauses and reflective moments can give weight to the words and enhance the emotional impact. In "Forrest Gump," the measured, contemplative pace of Forrest's final reflections about life and Jenny provides a poignant conclusion to his journey.

Transformation and Realization

The dialogue should highlight the hero's transformation and the realizations they've made. In "Star Wars: Return of the Jedi," Luke Skywalker's final dialogue with Darth Vader, where he says, "I've got to save you," emphasizes his growth from a young, impulsive fighter to a compassionate, selfless Jedi who believes in redemption.

Acknowledgment of Allies

The hero's dialogue can also acknowledge the support and contributions of allies, underscoring themes of friendship, teamwork, and solidarity. In "The Avengers," Tony Stark's final conversation with his teammates, where he expresses gratitude and trust, highlights the importance of their collective efforts and his personal growth.

Hope and Forward-Looking

Ending on a hopeful note can leave the audience with a sense of optimism and anticipation for the future. In "The Hunger Games: Mockingjay Part 2," Katniss's final words about finding peace and rebuilding her life with Peeta provide a hopeful conclusion to her tumultuous journey, emphasizing themes of healing and resilience.

Ambiguity and Open-Endedness

Sometimes, leaving the dialogue slightly ambiguous can create a sense of mystery and engagement, inviting the audience to ponder the hero's future. In "Inception," Cobb's final line, "You're waiting for a train...," and the subsequent scene leave the audience questioning the nature of reality and dreams, adding depth to his journey's end.

Contrasts and Irony

Using contrasts or irony in the final dialogue can underscore the hero's growth and the journey's significance. In "The Dark Knight Rises," Bruce Wayne's final conversation with Alfred, where he reveals his survival and new identity, contrasts the dark, brooding Batman with the hopeful, rejuvenated Bruce, highlighting his journey towards peace and fulfillment.

Integration with Visuals and Music

The final dialogue should be integrated seamlessly with the visuals and music to enhance its impact. The setting, lighting, and soundtrack can all contribute to the emotional resonance and thematic depth of the hero's concluding words. In "Titanic," Jack's final words to Rose, "You must do me this honor... promise me you'll survive," paired with the haunting music and visuals of the sinking ship, create a powerful, unforgettable moment.

In summary, the hero's final dialogue should reflect their journey, provide emotional resonance, offer closure, reinforce themes, and stay true to the character's voice. By focusing on these elements, you can craft a powerful and memorable conclusion to the hero's odyssey that resonates deeply with the audience and provides a fitting end to the story.

Building Tension: Dialogue in the Rising Action

The rising action in a screenplay is a crucial phase where tension escalates, stakes heighten, and conflicts intensify, leading to the climax. Dialogue during this phase plays a pivotal role in building tension, revealing character motivations, and driving the narrative forward. Effective dialogue in the rising action should create suspense, deepen conflicts, and maintain a sense of urgency.

Establishing Stakes

Dialogue should clearly convey what's at stake for the characters, making the audience aware of the potential consequences of failure. In "Jaws," the conversations about the danger of the shark and the urgency to close the beaches build tension by establishing the high stakes and imminent threat to the community.

Creating Suspense

Suspense is often created through what is left unsaid or hinted at. Characters may withhold information, drop cryptic hints, or engage in ambiguous conversations that keep the audience guessing. In "The Silence of the Lambs," Hannibal Lecter's cryptic and ominous dialogue with Clarice Starling builds suspense by hinting at deeper, more sinister truths.

Heightening Conflicts

Dialogue should escalate conflicts between characters, revealing underlying tensions and disagreements. In "The Avengers," the heated exchanges between Tony Stark and Steve Rogers about leadership and responsibility heighten tension and foreshadow future conflicts, driving the narrative towards its climax.

Pacing and Rhythm

The pacing of dialogue in the rising action should reflect the escalating tension. Quick, sharp exchanges can create a sense of urgency, while longer, more deliberate conversations can build suspense. In "Inception," the rapid-fire dialogue during the planning and execution of the heist builds a sense of urgency and impending danger.

Revealing Character Motivations

Dialogue in the rising action should reveal the characters' motivations and fears, adding depth to their actions and decisions. In "Breaking Bad," Walter White's conversations with Jesse Pinkman reveal his growing ambition and desperation, heightening the tension as he becomes more entangled in the drug trade.

Foreshadowing

Foreshadowing through dialogue can create anticipation and suspense. Subtle hints about future events or dangers can keep the audience engaged. In "The Matrix," Morpheus's discussions about the prophecy and Neo's potential foreshadow the climactic battles, building tension as the story progresses.

Subtext

Subtext adds layers of meaning to dialogue, creating tension through what is implied rather than explicitly stated. Characters may say one thing but mean another, leaving the audience to read between the lines. In "Gone Girl," Amy's seemingly benign conversations are filled with subtext, hinting at her manipulative and sinister plans.

Contradictions and Doubts

Introducing contradictions and doubts through dialogue can create internal and external conflicts. Characters questioning each other's motives or decisions can build tension and suspense. In "The Dark Knight," the dialogue between Batman and the Joker, filled with philosophical contradictions and moral dilemmas, heightens the tension as their conflict deepens.

Building Relationships

Developing relationships through dialogue can also build tension, especially if these relationships are fraught with conflict or hidden agendas. In "Game of Thrones," the intricate dialogues between characters like Tyrion Lannister and various others reveal alliances, betrayals, and underlying tensions that drive the plot forward.

Using Ambiguity

Ambiguous dialogue can create tension by leaving room for multiple interpretations. Characters speaking in riddles, using double meanings, or being intentionally vague can keep the audience on edge. In "Pulp Fiction," the enigmatic conversations between characters often create a sense of unpredictability and tension.

Intensifying Situations

Dialogue should reflect the intensifying situations and the characters' responses to escalating events. In "Jurassic Park," the increasingly frantic dialogue as the dinosaurs begin to escape and wreak havoc builds tension and urgency, propelling the narrative towards its climax.

Emotional Stakes

Highlighting the emotional stakes through dialogue can create personal tension for the characters, making their struggles and conflicts more relatable and intense. In "Titanic," the dialogues between Jack and Rose as they navigate their relationship amidst the looming disaster build emotional tension that complements the physical danger.

Cliffhangers and Revelations

Strategic use of cliffhangers and revelations in dialogue can heighten tension. Ending a scene with a surprising revelation or an unresolved question can keep the audience on the edge of their seats. In "The Empire Strikes Back," the revelation that Darth Vader is Luke's father is a climactic moment of rising action that drastically heightens the tension.

Creating a Sense of Imminence

Dialogue should create a sense of imminence, conveying that something significant is about to happen. In "The Hunger Games," the tributes' dialogues before the games begin build tension and anticipation, making the audience aware of the impending conflict.

Using Silence

Strategic use of silence and pauses in dialogue can also build tension. Allowing moments of silence where characters contemplate, hesitate, or react can heighten the suspense and make the dialogue more impactful. In "No Country for Old Men," the tense, silent exchanges between Anton Chigurh and his victims create an atmosphere of dread.

In summary, building tension through dialogue in the rising action involves establishing stakes, creating suspense, heightening conflicts, and revealing character motivations. By focusing on these elements and maintaining a sense of urgency and anticipation, you can craft dialogue that effectively drives the narrative forward and keeps the audience engaged as the story approaches its climax.

Dialogue that Deepens Conflict

Dialogue that deepens conflict is essential in driving the narrative forward, creating tension, and adding layers of complexity to character relationships. This type of dialogue should reveal underlying tensions, escalate disagreements, and expose hidden motives, making the stakes higher and the storyline more compelling.

Exposing Hidden Motives

Conflict often deepens when characters' hidden motives are revealed through dialogue. This can change the dynamics between characters and escalate tensions. In "The Dark Knight," the Joker's conversations with Batman reveal his chaotic nature and his true motives, intensifying their ideological conflict and deepening the overall tension of the story.

Escalating Disagreements

Dialogues that turn minor disagreements into major confrontations are effective in deepening conflict. Characters might start with a simple argument that evolves into a significant dispute. In "A Few Good Men," the courtroom exchanges between Lt. Kaffee and Col. Jessup escalate from professional disagreements to a dramatic confrontation about ethics and duty.

Revealing Secrets

Revealing secrets through dialogue can drastically deepen conflict. When a character's hidden truth is exposed, it can lead to intense emotional reactions and dramatic shifts in relationships. In "Gone Girl," the revelation of Amy's fake disappearance plan to Nick through her chilling monologue intensifies their conflict and transforms the narrative.

Highlighting Differences

Conflict deepens when dialogue highlights fundamental differences between characters, such as their values, beliefs, or goals. In "Captain America: Civil War," the dialogue between Tony Stark and Steve Rogers during their ideological clash about the Sokovia Accords emphasizes their differing views on freedom and security, deepening the conflict within the Avengers.

Creating Misunderstandings

Misunderstandings can significantly deepen conflict. Dialogue that leads to or stems from misunderstandings can create dramatic irony and tension. In "Romeo and Juliet," the miscommunication about Juliet's fake death results in tragic decisions and escalates the conflict to its heartbreaking climax.

Using Accusations and Blame

Accusations and blame in dialogue can rapidly escalate tensions between characters. When one character blames another for a problem, it can lead to defensiveness, anger, and further conflict. In "Breaking Bad," the intense dialogues between Walter White and Jesse Pinkman, where they accuse each other of betrayal and incompetence, deepen their already strained relationship.

Exploring Emotional Vulnerabilities

Dialogue that exposes characters' emotional vulnerabilities can deepen conflict by making interactions more personal and intense. In "The Godfather," Michael Corleone's dialogue with Fredo, where he confronts him about his betrayal, reveals deep emotional wounds and escalates their conflict.

Building Tension through Subtext

Subtext in dialogue can add layers of conflict by implying more than what is explicitly stated. Characters may express tension through what is unsaid, leaving the audience to read between the lines. In "Pulp Fiction," the seemingly casual conversation between Jules and Vincent about foot massages is laden with subtext about respect and boundaries, deepening their conflict without direct confrontation.

Highlighting Power Dynamics

Dialogue that underscores power imbalances can deepen conflict by emphasizing dominance, control, or submission. In "The Devil Wears Prada," Miranda Priestly's cold, authoritative dialogue with Andy Sachs highlights the power dynamics and deepens the conflict as Andy struggles to assert her own identity.

Contradicting Expectations

Conflict can deepen when characters' expectations are contradicted through dialogue. When a character expects support or agreement and receives opposition instead, it can lead to significant tension. In "La La Land," the dinner scene where Sebastian and Mia argue about their career choices contradicts their earlier mutual support, deepening their relational conflict.

Introducing New Stakes

Dialogue that introduces new stakes can escalate conflict by increasing the pressure on characters. In "The Hunger Games," President Snow's conversations with Katniss about the consequences of her actions introduce new stakes that deepen the conflict and raise the tension.

Exploring Ideological Conflicts

Ideological conflicts are often deeply rooted and can be explored through dialogue to add complexity and depth to the narrative. In "The Matrix," the dialogues between Morpheus and Agent Smith explore their conflicting worldviews, deepening the philosophical and physical conflicts between them.

Using Irony and Sarcasm

Irony and sarcasm in dialogue can deepen conflict by adding a layer of mockery or disdain to the interactions. In "Iron Man," the sarcastic banter between Tony Stark and various characters, like Obadiah Stane, often reveals underlying tensions and escalates conflicts.

Revisiting Past Grievances

Dialogue that brings up past grievances can reignite old conflicts and deepen current tensions. In "The Social Network," the deposition scenes where characters rehash past events and betrayals deepen the conflict and add layers to their relationships.

Provoking Responses

Dialogue that provokes strong emotional responses can deepen conflict by pushing characters to react impulsively or aggressively. In "Whiplash," the intense and provocative dialogue between Andrew and Fletcher often leads to explosive confrontations, deepening the conflict and driving the narrative.

In summary, dialogue that deepens conflict should reveal hidden motives, escalate disagreements, expose secrets, and highlight differences. By focusing on these elements and using techniques like subtext, accusations, and power dynamics, you can create dialogue that intensifies the narrative tension and enriches the character interactions in your screenplay.

Dialogue in the Midpoint: Shifts and Surprises

The midpoint of a screenplay is a pivotal moment that often brings significant shifts and surprises, altering the course of the narrative and deepening the plot. Dialogue at this stage is crucial for highlighting these changes, revealing new information, and redefining character dynamics. Effective midpoint dialogue should reflect these shifts, introduce surprising elements, and propel the story forward with renewed energy and stakes.

Introducing Major Revelations

The midpoint is an ideal place to introduce significant revelations that change the direction of the story. Dialogue should deliver these revelations in a way that shocks the characters and the audience. In "The Sixth Sense," the revelation through dialogue that Cole can see dead people fundamentally shifts the narrative and deepens the connection between Cole and Dr. Malcolm Crowe.

Creating Turning Points

Dialogue at the midpoint can create turning points where characters make crucial decisions that alter their paths. In "The Matrix," Morpheus's dialogue with Neo about the red pill and the blue pill represents a turning point, shifting Neo from a state of ignorance to one of knowledge and action.

Revealing Hidden Motivations

Midpoint dialogue can reveal hidden motivations or secrets that characters have been keeping, leading to shifts in relationships and plot direction. In "The Empire Strikes Back," Darth Vader's revelation to Luke Skywalker, "I am your father," not only surprises the audience but also fundamentally alters Luke's motivations and understanding of his own journey.

Escalating Stakes

Dialogue should reflect the escalation of stakes at the midpoint, making it clear that the characters are now facing greater challenges and higher risks. In "Jaws," the dialogue between Chief Brody and Mayor Vaughn about the dangers of keeping the beaches open escalates the stakes, emphasizing the imminent threat of the shark.

Shifting Dynamics

The midpoint is often where power dynamics shift, and dialogue can highlight these changes. Characters who were once allies may become adversaries, or vice versa. In "The Dark Knight," the Joker's dialogue with Harvey Dent in the hospital shifts Dent's alignment, transforming him from Gotham's white knight into the vengeful Two-Face.

Creating Emotional Surprises

Dialogue at the midpoint can introduce emotional surprises that deepen character development and alter relationships. In "Toy Story 3," the conversation where Woody discovers that Andy intends to put him in the attic instead of taking him to college changes the emotional trajectory for Woody and the other toys.

Foreshadowing Future Events

Midpoint dialogue can foreshadow events that will unfold later in the story, creating anticipation and intrigue. In "Inception," the dialogue about the concept of a "kick" and the deeper levels of the dream state foreshadows the complex heist and the stakes involved in achieving their mission.

Introducing New Characters or Elements

The midpoint can be an opportunity to introduce new characters or elements that add complexity to the plot. Dialogue should effectively integrate these new components into the story. In "Jurassic Park," the dialogue introducing the velociraptors and their intelligence adds a new layer of danger and intrigue to the narrative.

Highlighting Internal Conflicts

Midpoint dialogue can delve into characters' internal conflicts, bringing these struggles to the forefront and setting up their resolutions. In "Silver Linings Playbook," the midpoint conversation between Pat and Tiffany, where they bond over their respective issues, shifts their relationship and sets the stage for their emotional journeys.

Building Suspense

Dialogue at the midpoint should build suspense and create a sense of anticipation for what's to come. In "Pulp Fiction," the dialogue in the diner scene between Jules and Pumpkin builds suspense through its unexpected philosophical turn, leading to a surprising resolution.

Reflecting Character Growth

The midpoint is a chance to show how characters have grown or changed since the beginning of the story. Dialogue should reflect these developments and hint at future growth. In "The Hunger Games," Katniss's dialogue about survival and protecting Peeta during the midpoint of the games reflects her growing determination and resourcefulness.

Pivoting the Plot

The midpoint often pivots the plot in a new direction, and dialogue should clearly convey this shift. In "Titanic," the midpoint conversation between Rose and Jack about her desire to escape her oppressive life marks a turning point, leading to their decision to be together despite the impending disaster.

Creating Tension

Midpoint dialogue should create tension and conflict, setting up the challenges that will be faced in the second half of the story. In "The Godfather," the tense dialogue between Michael Corleone and Sollozzo in the restaurant sets the stage for Michael's transformation and the escalation of the family conflict.

Incorporating Humor or Relief

Sometimes, incorporating humor or moments of relief in midpoint dialogue can provide a contrast to the tension, making the shifts and surprises more impactful. In "Guardians of the Galaxy," the humorous dialogue during the prison escape provides relief while also shifting the dynamics among the team members.

Setting Up the Climax

Finally, midpoint dialogue should set the stage for the climax, hinting at the conflicts and resolutions that will come. In "The Avengers," the dialogue about the team's need to unite against Loki foreshadows the climactic battle and the ultimate coming together of the superheroes.

In summary, dialogue at the midpoint should introduce major revelations, create turning points, escalate stakes, shift dynamics, and build suspense. By focusing on these elements, you can craft dialogue that effectively propels the narrative forward, deepens character development, and prepares the audience for the unfolding climax.

Developing Subplots through Dialogue

Subplots enrich the main narrative by adding depth, complexity, and additional layers of intrigue to a screenplay. Dialogue is a powerful tool for developing subplots, revealing character motivations, and intertwining secondary storylines with the primary plot. Effective subplot dialogue should be seamlessly integrated, enhance character development, and provide thematic resonance.

Revealing Character Backstories

Dialogue can be used to reveal backstories and personal histories that are crucial to subplots. This adds depth to characters and provides context for their actions. In "The Godfather," Michael Corleone's conversations with Kay Adams reveal his reluctance to be part of the family business, a subplot that underscores his eventual transformation.

Introducing Secondary Characters

Subplots often involve secondary characters whose interactions with the main characters add richness to the story. Introducing these characters through dialogue can establish their importance and set the stage for their roles. In "Harry Potter and the Sorcerer's Stone," the introduction of characters like Hagrid through dialogue helps develop subplots related to Harry's past and the wizarding world.

Exploring Relationships

Dialogue is essential for exploring relationships between characters, which are often at the heart of subplots. Conversations can reveal dynamics, conflicts, and growth within these relationships. In "Stranger Things," the dialogues between Eleven and Mike develop their friendship and budding romance, providing a heartfelt subplot that complements the main storyline.

Building Tension and Conflict

Subplots can add tension and conflict to the main narrative. Dialogue that highlights disagreements, secrets, or competing goals between characters can deepen these conflicts. In "Breaking Bad," the tension between Walter White and his wife Skyler is developed through their dialogues, adding a domestic conflict subplot that runs parallel to Walter's criminal activities.

Providing Exposition

Dialogue can provide exposition for subplots, explaining the context and stakes without resorting to lengthy explanations. In "Inception," the conversations between Cobb and his team about the rules and dangers of dream-sharing serve to develop the heist subplot and set up future conflicts.

Highlighting Thematic Elements

Subplots often mirror or contrast the main themes of the story. Dialogue that highlights these thematic connections can enrich the narrative. In "To Kill a Mockingbird," the subplot involving Boo Radley and the children's curiosity about him is developed through their dialogues and ties into the main themes of prejudice and moral integrity.

Advancing Plot Points

Subplot dialogue should advance the plot by introducing new developments, challenges, or revelations. In "The Lord of the Rings: The Fellowship of the Ring," the dialogues about the lore of the ring and the history of Middle-earth provide critical background for subplots involving various characters and their motivations.

Creating Foreshadowing

Dialogue in subplots can foreshadow future events in the main plot, creating anticipation and suspense. In "The Dark Knight," Harvey Dent's dialogues about justice and fairness foreshadow his transformation into Two-Face and the ensuing subplot about his fall from grace.

Enhancing Character Development

Subplot dialogues often provide opportunities for character development that might not be possible in the main plot. These interactions can reveal different facets of characters and their growth. In "Friends," the subplot involving Chandler's struggles with commitment is explored through his dialogues with Monica and his friends, adding depth to his character arc.

Balancing Humor and Drama

Subplots can introduce elements of humor or drama that balance the tone of the main narrative. Dialogue can effectively convey these shifts in tone. In "Pulp Fiction," the humorous subplot involving Vincent and Mia's night out is developed through witty and engaging dialogues, providing a counterbalance to the film's darker moments.

Resolving Subplot Arcs

Dialogue is crucial in resolving subplots, providing closure and tying up loose ends. The resolution should feel natural and satisfying. In "The Shawshank Redemption," the subplot involving Red's parole hearings is resolved through his final speech, which encapsulates his transformation and provides a poignant conclusion to his arc.

Creating Interconnectedness

Effective subplot dialogue can create a sense of interconnectedness within the story. Characters from different subplots can interact, revealing how their stories intersect with the main plot. In "Game of Thrones," the dialogues between characters from different regions and backgrounds weave together numerous subplots, creating a rich, interconnected narrative tapestry.

Evolving Relationships

Subplots often involve evolving relationships, and dialogue is key to showcasing this evolution. Conversations that reflect changing dynamics, such as growing trust or increasing tension, are essential. In "The Office," the evolving relationship between Jim and Pam is developed through their dialogues, adding a romantic subplot that enriches the main narrative.

Highlighting Personal Stakes

Subplot dialogues can highlight personal stakes for characters, making their actions and decisions more relatable and compelling. In "The Hunger Games," the dialogues between Katniss and her family and friends underscore the personal stakes involved in her participation in the games, adding emotional depth to the subplot.

Using Dialogue for World-Building

In genres like fantasy and science fiction, subplot dialogues can contribute to world-building, providing details about the setting, culture, and history. In "Star Wars," the dialogues about the Force, the Jedi, and the Sith develop subplots that enhance the richness of the universe.

In summary, developing subplots through dialogue involves revealing character backstories, exploring relationships, building tension, providing exposition, and highlighting thematic elements. By integrating these elements seamlessly, you can create engaging and enriching subplots that complement and enhance the main narrative.

Voice and Subtext: Mastering Indirect Dialogue

Mastering indirect dialogue, where characters communicate using subtext rather than explicit statements, is a powerful tool for adding depth and complexity to a screenplay. This technique involves conveying underlying meanings, emotions, and conflicts through what is implied rather than directly stated. Effective use of voice and subtext can reveal character intentions, create tension, and enrich the narrative.

Understanding Subtext

Subtext is the underlying meaning or message that is not explicitly stated in the dialogue but is understood by the audience through context, tone, and delivery. It adds layers to the conversation, allowing characters to communicate more than what is said on the surface. In "The Godfather," when Michael Corleone says, "I'll make him an offer he can't refuse," the subtext is a clear threat of violence, adding a menacing undertone to the dialogue.

Establishing Character Voice

Each character's voice should be distinct and consistent, reflecting their personality, background, and emotional state. Mastering this helps convey subtext more effectively. In "The Big Lebowski," The Dude's laid-back, rambling speech pattern contrasts sharply with Walter's aggressive, confrontational style, adding depth to their interactions and revealing their underlying dynamics.

Using Tone and Delivery

The tone and delivery of dialogue can significantly influence its subtext. How a line is spoken—whether it's calm, sarcastic, anxious, or angry—can change its meaning entirely. In "Gone Girl," Amy's seemingly polite and calm tone when discussing her relationship with Nick hides her manipulative and vengeful intentions, creating a chilling subtext.

Reading between the Lines

Characters often say one thing but mean another, allowing the audience to read between the lines. This indirect communication can reveal true feelings, intentions, or conflicts without stating them outright. In "Pulp Fiction," the conversation between Jules and Vincent about foot massages is ostensibly casual but loaded with subtext about respect and boundaries.

Contextual Clues

The context in which dialogue occurs can provide important subtextual clues. The setting, situation, and previous interactions between characters inform the audience about the underlying meanings. In "Casablanca," when Rick says to Ilsa, "Here's looking at you, kid," in the context of their shared past and current tensions, the line carries a deep, bittersweet subtext about love and loss.

Body Language and Actions

Non-verbal cues such as body language, facial expressions, and actions can enhance the subtext of dialogue. These physical elements can contradict or reinforce what is being said, adding complexity. In "There Will Be Blood," Daniel Plainview's calm demeanor and steady voice contrast with his violent actions, creating a subtext of suppressed rage and ambition.

Irony and Contradictions

Using irony and contradictions in dialogue can create rich subtext. Characters may say the opposite of what they mean, or their words may clash with their actions, creating tension and revealing deeper truths. In "American Beauty," Lester Burnham's polite dinner table conversations with his family are laden with irony and masked contempt, reflecting the dysfunctional family dynamics.

Layering Information

Subtext can be layered by providing bits of information gradually, allowing the audience to piece together the full meaning over time. This technique keeps the audience engaged and adds depth to the dialogue. In "Inception," the dialogues about dreams and reality are layered with philosophical questions and personal stakes, creating a complex subtext that unfolds throughout the film.

Power Dynamics

Dialogue that subtly highlights power dynamics between characters can add significant subtext. Who holds power, who seeks it, and how it shifts can be communicated through indirect dialogue. In "The Silence of the Lambs," the power play between Clarice and Hannibal is evident in their dialogues, with Hannibal's calm, controlled language contrasting with Clarice's more direct, probing questions.

Implying Backstory

Indirect dialogue can imply a rich backstory without explicitly stating it. Characters can refer to past events, shared experiences, or unspoken histories that hint at deeper connections. In "Silver Linings Playbook," the conversations between Pat and Tiffany reveal their troubled pasts and emotional scars through indirect references and implications, adding depth to their characters.

Creating Ambiguity

Subtext can create intentional ambiguity, leaving room for multiple interpretations and adding a layer of mystery. This can be particularly effective in thrillers or dramas. In "Blade Runner," the ambiguous dialogue between Deckard and Rachael about memories and identity leaves the audience questioning the nature of reality and humanity.

Emotional Subtext

Emotions often lie beneath the surface of what is being said. Characters might hide their true feelings, and the subtext can reveal their internal struggles. In "Eternal Sunshine of the Spotless Mind," Joel and Clementine's seemingly casual conversations are filled with emotional subtext about their failed relationship and deep feelings for each other.

Foreshadowing

Indirect dialogue can foreshadow future events, creating anticipation and suspense. Subtle hints and implications in the dialogue can prepare the audience for what's to come. In "The Sixth Sense," the dialogues between Dr. Crowe and Cole subtly foreshadow the film's twist, with layered subtext about life, death, and unresolved issues.

Contrasting Dialogue Styles

Using contrasting dialogue styles between characters can highlight differences and create subtext. In "Pulp Fiction," the contrast between Jules's philosophical musings and Vincent's straightforward pragmatism adds depth to their relationship and the situations they face.

In summary, mastering indirect dialogue involves understanding subtext, establishing character voice, using tone and delivery effectively, and layering information. By focusing on these elements, you can create dialogue that communicates more than what is said, adding depth, complexity, and intrigue to your screenplay.

Deception and Revelation: Hidden Meanings in Dialogue

Dialogue that incorporates deception and revelation, with hidden meanings, can add layers of intrigue and complexity to a screenplay. Characters may use deceit to achieve their goals, conceal their true intentions, or manipulate others, while revelations can turn the story on its head, providing shocking twists and deepening the narrative. Crafting such dialogue requires skill in subtext, timing, and understanding character motivations.

Establishing Deception

Deceptive dialogue involves characters saying one thing but meaning another, or deliberately misleading other characters. This can create dramatic irony, where the audience knows more than the characters, heightening tension and engagement. In "The Usual Suspects," Verbal Kint's seemingly innocent dialogue with the police is filled with deception, as he constructs a false narrative that cleverly misleads both the characters and the audience.

Layering Subtext

Subtext is crucial for deceptive dialogue. The true meaning of the conversation lies beneath the surface, hinted at through word choice, tone, and context. In "Gone Girl," Amy's interactions with Nick are layered with subtext about her true intentions and feelings, which only become clear as the story unfolds.

Using Tone and Delivery

The way dialogue is delivered can reveal hidden meanings. A calm tone might mask anger, while a friendly demeanor might conceal hostility. In "House of Cards," Frank Underwood's polite and charming dialogue often hides his ruthless ambition and manipulative schemes, with his true intentions revealed only through his asides to the audience.

Creating Ambiguity

Ambiguity in dialogue can leave room for multiple interpretations, allowing for later revelations to change the audience's understanding of earlier scenes. In "Inception," the ambiguous nature of the dialogues about reality and dreams keeps the audience guessing and sets up for the film's surprising revelations.

Foreshadowing Through Deception

Deceptive dialogue can foreshadow future events, hinting at revelations to come. Subtle hints planted in early conversations can lead to significant payoffs later. In "The Sixth Sense," Dr. Malcolm Crowe's dialogues with Cole contain foreshadowing elements that only make sense after the twist is revealed.

Revelations through Dialogue

Revelations in dialogue can be dramatic and transformative, altering the course of the narrative. These moments should be carefully timed for maximum impact. In "Star Wars: The Empire Strikes Back," Darth Vader's revelation to Luke, "I am your father," is a pivotal moment that changes everything for the characters and the audience.

Contrasting Deception and Honesty

Dialogue that contrasts deceptive and honest characters can highlight the hidden meanings and create dramatic tension. In "The Departed," the conversations between Billy Costigan and Colin Sullivan are filled with deception and double meanings, reflecting their undercover roles and conflicting loyalties.

Gradual Unveiling

Gradual unveiling through dialogue can create suspense and maintain interest. Characters might drop hints and partial truths before the full revelation. In "Shutter Island," the dialogue gradually unveils the true nature of the island and Teddy Daniels' identity, keeping the audience engaged and guessing.

Dramatic Irony

Dramatic irony occurs when the audience knows more about the true nature of the situation than the characters do. This can be used effectively in dialogue to create tension. In "Romeo and Juliet," the audience is aware of Juliet's fake death, while Romeo is not, making his dialogues filled with dramatic irony and impending tragedy.

Re-contextualizing Previous Dialogue

A revelation can recontextualize previous dialogue, providing new meanings to earlier conversations. In "Fight Club," the revelation that Tyler Durden is a figment of the Narrator's imagination recontextualizes all their previous interactions, adding depth and complexity to the narrative.

Power Dynamics

Deceptive dialogue can highlight power dynamics between characters. Those in power often use deception to maintain control or manipulate others. In "The Godfather," Don Vito Corleone's calm and measured dialogues often mask his strategic thinking and manipulative tactics.

Emotional Impact

Revelatory dialogue can have a profound emotional impact on both the characters and the audience. The timing and delivery of such revelations should be crafted to maximize their effect. In "The Pursuit of Happyness," the revelation of Chris Gardner's job offer, delivered through a simple, understated dialogue, has a powerful emotional impact due to the buildup and context.

Subtle Clues

Planting subtle clues in deceptive dialogue can make the eventual revelation more satisfying. These clues should be noticeable upon a second viewing, rewarding attentive audience members. In "The Prestige," the dialogues about sacrifice and dedication subtly hint at the final revelation of the twin brothers.

Maintaining Consistency

For deceptive dialogue to be effective, characters must remain consistent with their portrayed intentions until the revelation. Sudden, uncharacteristic changes can undermine the credibility of the deception. In "The Silence of the Lambs," Hannibal Lecter's consistently calm and articulate speech masks his true nature, making the moments of revelation more shocking.

Exploring Themes

Deception and revelation in dialogue can explore deeper themes such as truth, identity, and morality. In "Blade Runner," the dialogues about memories and humanity explore themes of identity and reality, with revelations that challenge the characters' and audience's perceptions.

In summary, crafting dialogue with hidden meanings involves using subtext, tone, ambiguity, and careful timing to create deception and revelation. By focusing on these elements, you can add depth and complexity to your screenplay, keeping the audience engaged and enhancing the narrative impact.

Semantic Nuances: Playing with Language

Playing with language and leveraging semantic nuances in dialogue can add layers of meaning, create richer character interactions, and enhance the thematic depth of a screenplay. This technique involves the deliberate use of wordplay, ambiguity, idioms, cultural references, and multiple meanings to convey complex ideas and emotions. Mastering semantic nuances can make dialogue more engaging and thought-provoking.

Wordplay and Double Meanings

Wordplay and double meanings can make dialogue more engaging and add a layer of complexity. Characters might use puns, metaphors, or phrases that have multiple interpretations. In "Pulp Fiction," the famous "Royale with Cheese" dialogue between Vincent and Jules uses cultural differences in language to reveal character traits and provide humor, while also subtly commenting on globalization.

Ambiguity and Open-Ended Statements

Ambiguous dialogue allows for multiple interpretations, creating depth and inviting the audience to read between the lines. This can be particularly effective in creating tension or mystery. In "Inception," Cobb's final line, "You're waiting for a train...," is left open-ended, allowing for different interpretations about the nature of reality and dreams.

Idioms and Cultural References

Using idioms and cultural references can enrich dialogue by grounding it in a specific context or cultural background. These nuances can reveal character backgrounds and enhance realism. In "The Big Lebowski," The Dude's frequent use of laid-back, Californian idioms like "The Dude abides" captures his character's ethos and adds authenticity to the dialogue.

Euphemisms and Understatements

Euphemisms and understatements can be used to soften the impact of harsh truths or to add a layer of irony. In "The Godfather," the phrase "sleeping with the fishes" is a euphemism for murder, adding a darkly humorous and cultural nuance to the dialogue.

Irony and Sarcasm

Irony and sarcasm can reveal a character's true feelings or highlight contradictions between what is said and what is meant. This can add humor or tension to the dialogue. In "Dr. Strangelove," the ironic dialogue about the "doomsday device" highlights the absurdity of nuclear war, adding a satirical edge to the film's commentary.

Playing with Syntax and Grammar

Altering syntax and grammar can reflect a character's unique way of speaking and thinking, adding depth to their portrayal. In "Yoda's dialogue in Star Wars," his unusual sentence structure, "Do or do not, there is no try," emphasizes his wisdom and distinctiveness, making his speech memorable and character-defining.

Historical and Literary References

Incorporating historical and literary references can add layers of meaning and connect the narrative to broader themes. In "The Lion King," Scar's line, "I'm surrounded by idiots," echoes similar sentiments expressed by Shakespearean villains, adding a layer of classical villainy to his character.

Dialect and Regional Speech Patterns

Using dialect and regional speech patterns can add authenticity and depth to characters, reflecting their background and social context. In "True Grit," the distinct Old West dialect and formal speech patterns of characters like Rooster Cogburn and Mattie Ross add to the film's period authenticity and character depth.

Symbolic Language

Symbolic language uses metaphors and similes to convey deeper meanings and themes. In "Blade Runner," Roy Batty's line, "All those moments will be lost in time, like tears in rain," uses a poignant metaphor to reflect on the ephemeral nature of life and memory.

Contrasts and Juxtapositions

Contrasting different styles of speech within the same scene can highlight differences between characters or underscore thematic contrasts. In "The Great Gatsby," the contrasting dialogue styles of the opulent Gatsby and the more grounded Nick Carraway highlight their differing perspectives on wealth and morality.

Playing with Expectations

Subverting expectations in dialogue can create surprise and engage the audience. In "The Princess Bride," the repeated line, "As you wish," shifts in meaning as it is revealed to be a declaration of love, transforming a simple phrase into a significant emotional touchstone.

Layering Dialogue

Layering dialogue with multiple levels of meaning can create rich, complex interactions. Characters may speak on one level while implying something entirely different. In "The Graduate," the repeated question, "Are you here for an affair, sir?" plays on multiple levels of misunderstanding and subtext, creating humor and tension.

Rhetorical Questions and Philosophical Musings

Using rhetorical questions and philosophical musings can add depth and invite the audience to ponder larger themes. In "The Matrix," Morpheus's question, "What is real? How do you define real?" encourages both Neo and the audience to question their perceptions and reality.

Creating Rhythms and Patterns

Creating distinct rhythms and patterns in dialogue can enhance its impact and memorability. In "Pulp Fiction," the rhythmic, almost musical quality of Jules's biblical monologue, "Ezekiel 25:17," adds gravitas and makes the speech more memorable.

Highlighting Contradictions

Highlighting contradictions within a character's speech can reveal internal conflicts and add depth. In "Fight Club," Tyler Durden's dialogue often contains contradictions that reflect his complex, dual nature and the film's exploration of identity and consumerism.

Using Silence and Pauses

Strategic use of silence and pauses can be as powerful as the dialogue itself, adding weight and meaning to what is unsaid. In "No Country for Old Men," the tense silences in the dialogue between Anton Chigurh and the gas station attendant add layers of menace and uncertainty.

In summary, playing with semantic nuances in dialogue involves using wordplay, ambiguity, cultural references, irony, and other techniques to add layers of meaning and depth. By focusing on these elements, you can create rich, engaging dialogue that enhances character development, deepens themes, and keeps the audience engaged.

Perspectives and Rhetoric: Dialogue from Different Viewpoints

Writing dialogue that presents different perspectives and utilizes rhetoric effectively can enrich a screenplay by adding depth to characters, highlighting conflicts, and exploring complex themes. This technique involves crafting conversations where characters express distinct viewpoints, engage in persuasive rhetoric, and challenge each other's beliefs. Such dialogue not only advances the plot but also deepens the audience's understanding of the characters and the story's central issues.

Establishing Distinct Voices

Each character should have a unique voice that reflects their background, beliefs, and personality. This distinction is crucial for effectively presenting different perspectives. In "To Kill a Mockingbird," Atticus Finch's measured, principled dialogue contrasts sharply with the prejudiced, emotionally charged speech of Bob Ewell, highlighting their differing worldviews.

Engaging in Rhetorical Techniques

Characters can use rhetorical techniques such as ethos (credibility), pathos (emotion), and logos (logic) to persuade others or assert their viewpoints. In "The Dark Knight," Harvey Dent's dialogues employ logos and pathos to argue for justice and order, while the Joker uses chaos and unpredictability, embodying pathos and disrupting logical structures.

Creating Tension through Ideological Conflict

Dialogue that presents conflicting ideologies can create tension and drive the narrative. Characters debating or clashing over fundamental beliefs can lead to compelling drama. In "The Avengers," Tony Stark and Steve Rogers frequently engage in ideological conflicts, with Tony's pragmatic approach clashing with Steve's idealism, adding depth to their relationship and the story.

Exploring Themes through Different Viewpoints

Using dialogue to present different perspectives allows for the exploration of complex themes. Characters can articulate various facets of an issue, providing a more nuanced understanding. In "12 Angry Men," the jurors' dialogues present multiple perspectives on justice, prejudice, and reasonable doubt, enriching the thematic depth of the film.

Highlighting Character Development

Dialogue that showcases changing viewpoints can highlight character development. As characters grow and evolve, their perspectives should reflect this transformation. In "A Beautiful Mind," John Nash's dialogues transition from paranoid and isolated to insightful and collaborative, reflecting his journey through mental illness and recovery.

Using Subtext and Implication

Subtext can reveal differing perspectives subtly, allowing the audience to infer underlying beliefs and tensions. Characters may imply their true feelings without stating them outright. In "The Godfather," the dialogues between Michael Corleone and his family members are filled with subtext about power, loyalty, and betrayal, revealing their complex relationships and differing perspectives on family and business.

Contrasting Formal and Informal Speech

Contrasting formal and informal speech can highlight differences in status, education, or personality. This contrast can underscore differing viewpoints and add depth to character interactions. In "Pygmalion," the contrast between Eliza Doolittle's initial informal speech and Professor Higgins's formal language highlights their differing social backgrounds and perspectives.

Employing Irony and Satire

Irony and satire can be used to present differing viewpoints humorously or critically. Characters might use ironic statements to critique or undermine opposing views. In "Dr. Strangelove," the satirical dialogue about nuclear war and deterrence highlights the absurdity of the Cold War mindset, using irony to critique prevailing attitudes.

Balancing Dialogue and Action

While dialogue is crucial for presenting perspectives, it should be balanced with action to maintain narrative momentum. Characters' actions can reinforce or contradict their spoken beliefs, adding layers to their portrayal. In "Mad Max: Fury Road," Furiosa's terse, action-driven dialogue contrasts with Immortan Joe's grandiose speeches, reflecting their differing approaches to power and survival.

Creating Sympathetic Antagonists

Giving antagonists well-developed viewpoints can create more complex and engaging conflicts. Their perspectives should be understandable, even if not agreeable. In "Black Panther," Killmonger's dialogue articulates his perspective on oppression and justice, making him a more sympathetic and multidimensional antagonist.

Developing Relationships through Dialogue

Dialogue that explores different perspectives can deepen relationships between characters. Conversations where characters challenge, support, or influence each other's views can reveal the dynamics of their relationships. In "Before Sunrise," the dialogues between Jesse and Celine explore their differing perspectives on life, love, and destiny, deepening their connection.

Foreshadowing Through Perspectives

Different viewpoints in dialogue can foreshadow future conflicts or resolutions. Characters' expressed beliefs or predictions can hint at events to come. In "The Matrix," Morpheus's dialogues about fate and choice foreshadow Neo's journey to accepting his role as "The One."

Reflecting Real-World Issues

Dialogue presenting different perspectives can reflect real-world issues, making the narrative more relatable and thought-provoking. Characters discussing topical themes like ethics, politics, or social justice can ground the story in reality. In "The Social Network," the dialogues about ambition, friendship, and betrayal reflect broader themes of technology and entrepreneurship.

Creating Dramatic Irony

Dramatic irony, where the audience knows more than the characters, can be used to enhance dialogues with differing perspectives. Characters might express beliefs or make decisions based on incomplete information, creating tension and engagement. In "Romeo and Juliet," the audience's awareness of the characters' true identities and fates adds poignancy to their dialogues.

Integrating Exposition Smoothly

Exposition can be integrated into dialogue that presents different viewpoints, making necessary information engaging and relevant. Characters can explain their perspectives while providing background information. In "Inception," the dialogues about dream-sharing and the mechanics of the heist provide exposition through engaging discussions on morality and reality.

In summary, dialogue that presents different perspectives and utilizes rhetoric can add depth, tension, and thematic richness to a screenplay. By focusing on distinct voices, rhetorical techniques, subtext, and balanced action, you can create compelling interactions that drive the narrative and deepen character development.

Witty Banter: Adding Humor to Dialogue

Witty banter is an effective way to add humor to dialogue, making characters more relatable and scenes more engaging. It involves clever, quick exchanges that reveal character traits, build relationships, and entertain the audience. Crafting witty banter requires a good sense of timing, an ear for rhythm, and an understanding of character dynamics.

Character Voice and Timing

Witty banter should reflect the unique voices of the characters involved. Each character's personality and speech patterns should inform their contributions to the exchange. Timing is crucial, as the humor often relies on quick, back-and-forth exchanges. In "Iron Man," Tony Stark's rapid-fire, sarcastic dialogue showcases his sharp wit and confidence, making his interactions entertaining and character-defining.

Play on Words

Wordplay, including puns, double entendres, and clever use of language, is a staple of witty banter. It adds a layer of intellectual humor to the dialogue. In "The Princess Bride," the exchanges between Westley and Inigo Montoya are filled with clever wordplay, making their dialogues memorable and amusing.

Contrasting Characters

Witty banter often works best between characters with contrasting personalities or viewpoints. The clash of different perspectives can create humorous tension and highlight character differences. In "Sherlock," the dynamic between Sherlock Holmes and Dr. John Watson provides plenty of opportunities for witty banter, with Sherlock's eccentric brilliance contrasting with Watson's grounded pragmatism.

Situational Humor

Banter that arises naturally from the situation can feel more organic and less forced. Characters reacting to their circumstances with humor can make the dialogue more relatable and engaging. In "Guardians of the Galaxy," the situational humor during action sequences, such as Star-Lord's sarcastic comments amidst chaos, adds levity and makes the characters more endearing.

Cultural References and In-Jokes

Using cultural references and in-jokes can make witty banter more specific and resonant, especially for audiences familiar with the references. However, it's important to ensure that these references enhance the humor without alienating those who might not get them. In "Gilmore Girls," the rapid-fire dialogue between Lorelai and Rory is peppered with pop culture references, adding a layer of humor for those in the know.

Subtext and Double Meanings

Witty banter can carry subtext and double meanings, adding depth to the humor. Characters might say one thing but mean another, creating layers of meaning that enhance the comedy. In "Pulp Fiction," the banter between Jules and Vincent about trivial topics like fast food serves as a humorous distraction while also revealing their personalities and building tension.

Rhythm and Pacing

The rhythm and pacing of witty banter are crucial. The exchanges should feel like a natural, fast-paced conversation, with each line building on the previous one. In "His Girl Friday," the rapid-fire exchanges between Hildy and Walter are a masterclass in timing and pacing, creating a lively, humorous dynamic.

Sarcasm and Irony

Sarcasm and irony are effective tools for witty banter, adding a layer of cynicism or playful mockery to the dialogue. Characters using sarcasm can highlight absurdities or express disdain humorously. In "The Office," Jim Halpert's sarcastic remarks and ironic observations often serve as humorous commentary on the office's mundane and absurd situations.

Callbacks and Running Gags

Using callbacks and running gags can create a sense of continuity and deepen the humor over time. Repeating a witty line or situation in different contexts can make it funnier with each iteration. In "Arrested Development," the running gags and callbacks, such as Gob's "I've made a huge mistake," build humor through repetition and familiarity.

Teasing and Playful Insults

Teasing and playful insults, when done in a lighthearted and affectionate manner, can create humorous and endearing interactions. This type of banter can reveal the closeness between characters. In "Parks and Recreation," the playful insults between Leslie Knope and Ron Swanson highlight their mutual respect and affection, despite their differing views.

Breaking Tension

Witty banter can be an effective way to break tension in more serious scenes, providing a moment of relief for the characters and the audience. In "Star Wars," Han Solo's quips during tense moments, like his casual "I know" in response to Leia's "I love you," add humor and break the tension.

Juxtaposing Formality and Informality

Juxtaposing formal and informal language can create humorous contrasts. Characters who switch between formal and informal speech, especially in unexpected contexts, can add a layer of humor. In "Monty Python and the Holy Grail," the contrast between the formal quest language and the absurd, informal banter creates a comedic effect.

Building Relationships

Witty banter can be used to build and develop relationships between characters. Through humorous exchanges, characters can express their personalities and grow closer or establish rivalries. In "When Harry Met Sally," the witty banter between Harry and Sally throughout the film develops their relationship and showcases their chemistry.

Emotional Underpinnings

Witty banter can have emotional underpinnings, revealing characters' vulnerabilities or deeper feelings beneath the humor. This adds depth to the dialogue and makes the characters more relatable. In "Juno," the witty exchanges between Juno and her father blend humor with underlying emotional truths, making their relationship feel genuine and heartfelt.

In summary, adding humor to dialogue through witty banter involves using wordplay, contrasting characters, situational humor, cultural references, subtext, rhythm, sarcasm, and other techniques to create engaging and memorable interactions. By focusing on these elements, you can craft dialogue that not only entertains but also deepens character relationships and enriches the narrative.

Colloquialisms and Realism: Authentic Dialogue

Creating authentic dialogue that captures the nuances of real speech and the distinctive voices of characters is crucial for making a screenplay believable and engaging. Colloquialisms, regional dialects, and realistic speech patterns can add depth to characters and enhance the story's setting. Here are strategies for achieving authenticity in dialogue.

Understanding Character Backgrounds

Characters' speech should reflect their backgrounds, including their regional origins, social status, education, and personal experiences. Understanding these factors helps create realistic and distinct voices. In "Good Will Hunting," Will's use of colloquial language and Boston accent reflect his working-class background and add authenticity to his character.

Using Colloquialisms and Slang

Incorporating colloquialisms and slang can make dialogue sound more natural and relatable. These elements should be used appropriately to reflect the character's background and the story's setting. In "The Wire," the authentic use of Baltimore street slang and colloquial speech patterns adds depth and realism to the characters and setting.

Capturing Regional Dialects

Regional dialects can add authenticity and specificity to characters, making their voices distinct and reflective of their origins. It's important to research and accurately represent these dialects. In "Fargo," the use of Minnesotan accents and regional phrases like "You betcha" enhances the film's setting and character authenticity.

Reflecting Natural Speech Patterns

Realistic dialogue often includes interruptions, overlapping speech, and incomplete sentences. Capturing these natural speech patterns can make conversations feel more genuine. In "Pulp Fiction," the casual, meandering dialogues between characters like Vincent and Jules reflect natural speech patterns, adding to the film's realism.

Avoiding Overly Polished Dialogue

Real speech is rarely perfect. Overly polished dialogue can feel artificial. Characters should occasionally use filler words, hesitate, and make mistakes. In "Moonlight," the characters' dialogues include pauses, stutters, and informal grammar, making their interactions feel authentic and emotionally raw.

Using Contractions and Informal Grammar

Contractions and informal grammar are common in everyday speech and should be reflected in dialogue. This can make conversations feel more natural. In "Silver Linings Playbook," the casual, often grammatically imperfect dialogues between Pat and Tiffany enhance the realism of their interactions.

Incorporating Non-Verbal Communication

Non-verbal communication, such as gestures, facial expressions, and body language, plays a significant role in real conversations. Including these elements in the script can add depth and realism to dialogue. In "Lost in Translation," the nuanced, often silent interactions between Bob and Charlotte convey deep emotions and unspoken thoughts, enhancing the authenticity of their relationship.

Capturing Different Speech Styles

Different characters should have distinct speech styles that reflect their personalities and backgrounds. This differentiation adds depth and makes interactions more dynamic. In "The Big Lebowski," the distinct speech styles of The Dude, Walter, and Donny create a rich tapestry of dialogue that enhances each character's individuality.

Balancing Realism and Clarity

While authenticity is important, dialogue should also be clear and understandable. Striking a balance between realism and clarity ensures that the audience can follow the conversation without getting lost. In "Juno," the dialogue captures the quirky, rapid-fire speech patterns of the characters while remaining clear and engaging.

Using Specific and Concrete Language

Specific and concrete language can make dialogue more vivid and realistic. Characters should use specific terms and references that reflect their knowledge and experiences. In "Goodfellas," the use of specific mafia terminology and detailed descriptions of activities adds realism and immerses the audience in the world of organized crime.

Reflecting Emotional States

Characters' emotional states should influence their speech patterns. Excitement, fear, anger, and other emotions can lead to faster speech, interruptions, or changes in tone. In "Marriage Story," the emotionally charged arguments between Charlie and Nicole reflect their heightened states, with overlapping speech and intense, raw dialogue.

Using Humor and Sarcasm

Humor and sarcasm are common in real conversations and can add authenticity to dialogue. These elements should fit the character's personality and the context of the conversation. In "The Office," the use of humor and sarcasm in the dialogue captures the dynamics of a typical workplace, making the characters and interactions feel real and relatable.

Avoiding Exposition Dumps

Exposition should be integrated naturally into dialogue, avoiding lengthy, unnatural speeches that explain background information. Characters should convey information through realistic conversations. In "The Social Network," the background and motivations of characters are revealed through sharp, realistic dialogues rather than expository monologues.

Adapting to Context and Setting

Dialogue should adapt to the context and setting of the scene. Characters might speak differently in formal settings compared to casual environments. In "Pride and Prejudice," the dialogue reflects the formal, polite speech of the Regency era, enhancing the authenticity of the setting and characters.

Using Silence and Pauses

Silence and pauses can be powerful in dialogue, reflecting natural speech rhythms and adding tension or emphasis. These moments can convey as much as spoken words. In "No Country for Old Men," the use of silence and sparse dialogue creates a tense, realistic atmosphere that enhances the film's impact.

In summary, creating authentic dialogue involves capturing the nuances of real speech, reflecting characters' backgrounds, using colloquialisms and slang, and incorporating natural speech patterns. By focusing on these elements, you can create dialogue that feels genuine, engaging, and true to life, enhancing the realism and depth of your screenplay.

Language and Cultural Contexts in Dialogue

Incorporating language and cultural contexts into dialogue can enrich a screenplay by adding depth, authenticity, and relatability to characters and their interactions. This approach involves understanding the cultural backgrounds of the characters, using language that reflects their heritage, and integrating cultural references and nuances that make the dialogue more immersive and believable.

Reflecting Cultural Backgrounds

Characters' dialogues should reflect their cultural backgrounds, incorporating idioms, phrases, and speech patterns unique to their heritage. This adds authenticity and helps the audience connect with the characters on a deeper level. In "Crazy Rich Asians," the dialogue incorporates Chinese and Singaporean cultural references, enhancing the authenticity of the characters and setting.

Using Multilingual Dialogue

Incorporating multiple languages in dialogue can reflect the multilingual realities of many cultures and add layers of authenticity. It's important to balance this with accessibility for the audience, possibly using subtitles or context to convey meaning. In "Inglourious Basterds," the use of German, French, and Italian dialogue with subtitles adds to the film's authenticity and immersion.

Integrating Cultural References

Cultural references, such as mentioning traditional foods, festivals, historical events, or popular cultural icons, can make dialogue more relatable and specific. These references should be accurate and respectful, enhancing the characters' cultural identities. In "The Big Sick," the references to Pakistani culture and customs add depth to the characters and their backgrounds.

Capturing Accents and Dialects

Accents and regional dialects can add realism to dialogue, reflecting characters' geographical origins and social backgrounds. However, it's important to use them accurately and sensitively to avoid stereotypes. In "Brooklyn," the Irish accents and colloquialisms of the characters contribute to the authenticity of the period and setting.

Highlighting Cultural Tensions and Conflicts

Dialogue can reflect cultural tensions and conflicts, providing insight into characters' struggles and adding dramatic tension. In "My Big Fat Greek Wedding," the humorous dialogues between Toula and her family highlight cultural differences and the challenges of balancing traditional values with modern life.

Exploring Identity and Belonging

Dialogue can explore themes of identity and belonging, particularly for characters navigating multiple cultural contexts. This can add depth to character development and thematic richness. In "The Joy Luck Club," the dialogues between the Chinese-American daughters and their immigrant mothers explore issues of identity, generational conflict, and cultural heritage.

Respecting Cultural Sensitivities

It's crucial to approach cultural contexts with sensitivity and respect. Stereotypes and clichés should be avoided, and cultural nuances should be represented accurately. Research and consultation with cultural experts can help ensure respectful and authentic representation. In "Black Panther," the dialogues reflect African cultural elements thoughtfully, enhancing the film's cultural significance.

Using Formal and Informal Speech

Different cultures have varying norms for formal and informal speech, and incorporating these can add authenticity to dialogue. Characters may switch between formal and informal language depending on the context and their relationship with other characters. In "Parasite," the contrast in speech between the wealthy Park family and the struggling Kim family highlights their different social standings and cultural attitudes.

Incorporating Cultural Humor

Humor rooted in cultural context can add relatability and depth to dialogue. Cultural humor often relies on shared knowledge and experiences, which can make it resonate more deeply with audiences familiar with the culture. In "Bend It Like Beckham," the cultural humor around British-Indian family dynamics adds a layer of authenticity and warmth to the film.

Contextualizing Non-Verbal Communication

Non-verbal communication can vary significantly across cultures, and incorporating these differences can add depth to dialogue. Gestures, body language, and facial expressions should reflect cultural norms and enhance the authenticity of interactions. In "Slumdog Millionaire," the non-verbal cues and physical interactions among characters reflect Indian cultural norms and add to the film's realism.

Adapting Dialogue for Historical Contexts

When writing period pieces, dialogue should reflect the historical context, incorporating the language, idioms, and cultural references of the time. This can transport the audience to the period and enhance the story's authenticity. In "Pride and Prejudice," the formal, polite speech reflects the social norms and cultural context of Regency-era England.

Balancing Authenticity and Accessibility

While it's important to reflect cultural authenticity, dialogue should also be accessible to a broad audience. Using context, visual cues, or subtitled translations can help convey meaning without alienating viewers unfamiliar with the cultural nuances. In "Roma," the use of Spanish and Mixtec languages with subtitles ensures authenticity while keeping the story accessible.

Exploring Multicultural Interactions

Dialogue can highlight the dynamics of multicultural interactions, showcasing how characters from different cultural backgrounds communicate and relate to each other. This can add depth to character relationships and reflect real-world diversity. In "Crash," the dialogues explore the complexities of racial and cultural interactions in Los Angeles, adding depth to the film's exploration of prejudice and identity.

Representing Cultural Rituals and Traditions

Incorporating cultural rituals and traditions into dialogue can provide insight into characters' lives and add richness to the narrative. Characters discussing or participating in these traditions can make the story more immersive and authentic. In "Coco," the dialogues about Día de los Muertos (Day of the Dead) traditions are integral to the story, reflecting Mexican cultural practices and beliefs.

Developing Cultural Identity through Dialogue

Characters' dialogues can reflect their journey of cultural identity, exploring how they relate to their heritage and navigate different cultural environments. This can add depth to character arcs and thematic complexity. In "The Farewell," Billi's dialogues reflect her struggle to reconcile her Chinese heritage with her American upbringing, adding emotional depth to her character.

In summary, incorporating language and cultural contexts in dialogue involves understanding and reflecting characters' backgrounds, using regional dialects and colloquialisms, integrating cultural references, and exploring themes of identity and belonging. By focusing on these elements, you can create authentic, relatable dialogue that enhances the depth and realism of your screenplay.

Establishing Setting through Dialogue

Dialogue can be an effective tool for establishing the setting of a screenplay, providing context, and immersing the audience in the world of the story. This technique involves using characters' conversations to reveal details about the time, place, and social environment in which the story takes place. Here are strategies for using dialogue to establish setting effectively.

Referencing Specific Locations

Characters can mention specific locations to ground the story in a particular place. This can include street names, landmarks, and local businesses, which help to paint a vivid picture of the setting. In "Midnight in Paris," characters frequently reference famous Parisian landmarks and neighborhoods, immersing the audience in the city's atmosphere.

Incorporating Local Culture and Customs

Dialogue that reflects local customs, traditions, and cultural practices can provide depth and authenticity to the setting. This helps the audience understand the social environment and cultural context of the story. In "The Godfather," the dialogues about Sicilian customs and the emphasis on family honor help establish the cultural backdrop of the Italian-American mafia world.

Using Dialects and Accents

Characters' use of regional dialects and accents can immediately signal where the story is set. Accurate and respectful representation of these speech patterns can add realism and specificity to the setting. In "Fargo," the distinctive Minnesotan accents and colloquialisms enhance the authenticity of the Midwestern setting.

Discussing Historical Events

References to historical events or periods can establish the time setting of the story. Characters might discuss recent or ongoing events, providing context and grounding the narrative in a specific era. In "Forrest Gump," the dialogues referencing historical events like the Vietnam War and Watergate scandal help to place the story within its historical context.

Mentioning Weather and Environment

Dialogue about the weather and environmental conditions can help establish the physical setting and atmosphere. This can create a sense of place and influence the mood of the scene. In "Blade Runner," the frequent references to the constant rain and darkness contribute to the dystopian, noir atmosphere of the setting.

Highlighting Social and Economic Conditions

Characters' discussions about their daily lives, jobs, and economic situations can reveal the social and economic conditions of the setting. This can add depth to the story and provide insight into the characters' motivations and challenges. In "The Pursuit of Happyness," the dialogues about financial struggles and job hunting highlight the economic conditions and societal pressures of the time.

Using Local Slang and Expressions

Incorporating local slang and expressions can make the dialogue more authentic and reflective of the setting. This helps to establish the characters' connection to their environment and adds specificity to their interactions. In "Trainspotting," the use of Scottish slang and idiomatic expressions grounds the story in its Edinburgh setting.

Describing Physical Surroundings

Characters can describe their physical surroundings in their dialogue, helping to paint a picture of the setting for the audience. This can be particularly useful in establishing new locations or transitions between scenes. In "The Shining," the dialogues describing the isolation and vastness of the Overlook Hotel enhance the eerie and unsettling atmosphere.

Discussing Local Events and Traditions

References to local events, festivals, or traditions can provide a sense of community and place. These elements help to create a lived-in world and establish the setting's unique character. In "The Sound of Music," the references to Austrian traditions and the upcoming music festival help to ground the story in its cultural and geographical setting.

Reflecting the Setting in Character Behavior

Characters' behavior and interactions can reflect the norms and values of their environment, helping to establish the setting indirectly through dialogue. In "Mad Max: Fury Road," the harsh, survival-driven dialogue and actions of the characters reflect the post-apocalyptic world they inhabit.

Using Contextual Clues

Subtle contextual clues in dialogue can hint at the setting without directly stating it. These clues can be woven into conversations to gradually build a sense of place. In "Lost in Translation," the characters' dialogues about cultural misunderstandings and experiences in Tokyo gradually immerse the audience in the setting.

Exploring Themes Related to the Setting

Dialogue can explore themes that are closely tied to the setting, providing deeper insight into the environment and its impact on the characters. In "Dead Poets Society," the discussions about tradition and conformity at a conservative boarding school help to establish the restrictive and hierarchical setting.

Employing Seasonal References

References to the seasons or time of year can help to establish the temporal setting and influence the mood of the story. In "The Great Gatsby," the dialogues about summer parties and the heat of New York contribute to the decadent and restless atmosphere of the story.

Integrating Soundscapes

While not strictly dialogue, characters' references to sounds in their environment can enhance the setting. This can include mentions of city noises, wildlife, or ambient sounds that help to paint a more vivid picture of the location. In "No Country for Old Men," the sparse dialogue and references to the silent, desolate landscape of West Texas enhance the film's tension and isolation.

Reflecting Technological and Societal Contexts

Dialogue that reflects the technological and societal context of the setting can add realism and specificity. Characters might discuss contemporary issues, technologies, or societal norms, grounding the story in its particular time and place. In "Her," the dialogues about artificial intelligence and human relationships reflect the futuristic setting and its societal implications.

In summary, establishing setting through dialogue involves using specific locations, cultural references, dialects, historical events, environmental conditions, social and economic contexts, and other elements to create a vivid and immersive world. By focusing on these strategies, you can craft dialogue that effectively grounds the story in its setting, enhancing the narrative's authenticity and depth.

Thematic Dialogue: Weaving in the Message

Thematic dialogue is a powerful tool for weaving the central message or theme of a screenplay into the narrative. This technique involves subtly embedding the theme in the characters' conversations, making it a natural part of the story rather than an overt declaration. Effective thematic dialogue can deepen the audience's understanding of the narrative's core ideas and add layers of meaning to the characters' interactions.

Subtlety and Nuance

Thematic dialogue should be woven subtly into conversations, avoiding heavy-handedness or overt statements of the theme. The goal is to make the theme a natural part of the dialogue, enhancing the narrative without being preachy. In "The Shawshank Redemption," the theme of hope is subtly woven into Red's dialogue about getting busy living or getting busy dying, making the message impactful without being explicit.

Character-Driven Themes

Themes should emerge organically from the characters' experiences, beliefs, and conflicts. This makes the dialogue feel authentic and grounded in the story. In "Forrest Gump," the theme of destiny versus choice is explored through Forrest's dialogues about his life being like a box of chocolates, reflecting his unique perspective and experiences.

Reflecting Internal Conflicts

Dialogue that reflects a character's internal conflicts can effectively convey the theme. This allows the audience to understand the character's struggles and growth while reinforcing the central message. In "The Dark Knight," Harvey Dent's dialogue about dying a hero or living long enough to see oneself become the villain encapsulates his internal struggle and the film's exploration of morality and corruption.

Contrasting Perspectives

Presenting contrasting perspectives through dialogue can highlight the theme and add depth to the narrative. Characters with differing viewpoints can engage in conversations that illuminate the theme from multiple angles. In "12 Angry Men," the jurors' dialogues present various perspectives on justice, prejudice, and reasonable doubt, deepening the film's exploration of these themes.

Using Symbolism and Metaphors

Symbolic language and metaphors in dialogue can convey the theme in a more nuanced and layered way. These elements can add depth and richness to the characters' conversations. In "The Great Gatsby," the repeated references to the green light symbolize Gatsby's unattainable dreams and the broader theme of the American Dream.

Repetition and Echoes

Repetition of key phrases or ideas in dialogue can reinforce the theme and make it more memorable. Echoing thematic elements throughout the screenplay can create a cohesive narrative. In "Dead Poets Society," the repeated invocation of "Carpe Diem" reinforces the theme of seizing the day and living life fully.

Situational Context

Dialogue that arises naturally from the situation and context can effectively convey the theme. Characters' responses to their circumstances can reflect the central message without feeling forced. In "The Pursuit of Happyness," the dialogues about struggling for a better life and the importance of perseverance naturally convey the film's theme.

Interpersonal Dynamics

Dialogue that explores the dynamics between characters can reveal the theme through their relationships and interactions. This can add emotional depth and resonance to the theme. In "A Beautiful Mind," the dialogues between John Nash and his wife Alicia explore themes of love, commitment, and the struggle for mental stability through their relationship.

Juxtaposition and Irony

Juxtaposing different ideas and using irony in dialogue can highlight the theme in a thought-provoking way. This technique can make the theme more engaging and impactful. In "Fight Club," the ironic dialogue about consumerism and identity crisis underscores the film's critique of modern society.

Character Arcs and Development

Thematic dialogue should align with the characters' arcs and development. As characters grow and change, their dialogues should reflect their evolving understanding of the theme. In "The Lion King," Simba's journey from doubt to acceptance of his destiny is reflected in his dialogues about responsibility and courage.

Historical and Social Context

Embedding the theme in dialogue that reflects the historical and social context can add relevance and depth to the narrative. Characters' discussions about their world can highlight broader thematic concerns. In "Selma," the dialogues about civil rights and justice reflect the historical context and reinforce the film's themes.

Philosophical and Reflective Conversations

Philosophical and reflective dialogues can directly engage with the theme, allowing characters to explore and articulate the central message. These conversations can be deeply impactful when well-integrated into the story. In "The Matrix," Morpheus's philosophical dialogues about reality and choice engage directly with the film's themes.

Using Subtext

Subtext in dialogue can convey the theme subtly, allowing the audience to infer the deeper meaning beneath the surface conversation. This adds complexity and depth to the narrative. In "Lost in Translation," the understated dialogues between Bob and Charlotte reveal themes of loneliness and connection through subtext rather than explicit statements.

Building to a Thematic Climax

Thematic dialogue can build towards a climax where the theme is fully realized or articulated. This can provide a satisfying and impactful resolution to the narrative. In "Schindler's List," Schindler's final dialogue about wishing he had saved more lives encapsulates the film's themes of humanity and moral responsibility.

Integrating with Visuals and Actions

Dialogue should be integrated with visuals and actions to reinforce the theme holistically. Characters' words should align with what is shown on screen and their actions, creating a cohesive thematic presentation. In "WALL-E," the dialogues about environmental preservation and human connection are reinforced by the visual storytelling and the characters' actions.

In summary, weaving thematic dialogue into a screenplay involves subtly embedding the theme in characters' conversations, using symbolism, repetition, situational context, and subtext. By focusing on these strategies, you can create dialogue that naturally and effectively conveys the central message, adding depth and resonance to your story.

Action Scenes: Balancing Dialogue with Movement

Balancing dialogue with movement in action scenes is crucial for maintaining pace, intensity, and clarity. While action sequences primarily rely on visual storytelling, well-crafted dialogue can enhance these scenes by adding context, revealing character, and heightening tension. Here are strategies for effectively integrating dialogue into action scenes.

Keep Dialogue Concise and Relevant

In action scenes, dialogue should be concise and to the point. Long-winded speeches can disrupt the flow and urgency of the action. Characters should speak only when necessary, conveying crucial information or adding to the emotional intensity. In "Die Hard," John McClane's terse, witty lines during action sequences add humor and build his character without slowing down the pace.

Use Dialogue to Clarify Action

Dialogue can clarify complex actions or plot points, ensuring the audience understands what is happening. Characters might shout commands, give instructions, or react to unfolding events. In "The Matrix," the dialogue between Morpheus and Neo during the training simulations helps explain the rules of the Matrix, making the action clearer and more engaging.

Integrate Dialogue with Movement

Seamlessly integrating dialogue with movement ensures that the pace remains brisk. Characters should talk while they move, fight, or navigate obstacles, making the conversation feel natural and dynamic. In "Mad Max: Fury Road," Furiosa and Max exchange crucial dialogue while driving and battling enemies, maintaining the scene's relentless momentum.

Reveal Character through Dialogue

Action scenes can reveal character traits and relationships through dialogue. How characters speak and interact under pressure can provide insight into their personalities and dynamics. In "Lethal Weapon," the banter between Riggs and Murtaugh during action scenes highlights their contrasting personalities and deepening partnership.

Heighten Tension with Dialogue

Well-timed dialogue can heighten tension and suspense in action scenes. Characters might express fear, determination, or desperation, adding an emotional layer to the physical conflict. In "Jurassic Park," the dialogue between characters as they evade the velociraptors increases the sense of danger and urgency.

Use Dialogue for Exposition

Action scenes can be an effective place to deliver exposition, especially if it's integrated seamlessly with the action. Characters might explain critical plot points or provide background information amidst the chaos. In "Inception," the dialogue during the various dream levels helps the audience understand the complex rules of the heist, even as the action unfolds.

Reflect the Setting and Stakes

Dialogue in action scenes should reflect the setting and stakes, adding to the immersion and intensity. Characters might comment on their environment or the severity of the situation, reinforcing the scene's atmosphere. In "Star Wars: A New Hope," the dialogue during the Death Star trench run highlights the high stakes and the pilots' emotions, enhancing the scene's impact.

Balance Silence and Sound

Sometimes, the absence of dialogue can be as powerful as spoken words. Silence can heighten tension and focus the audience's attention on the visuals and sounds of the action. In "No Country for Old Men," the sparse dialogue during the hotel shootout intensifies the suspense and realism, making the action more gripping.

Provide Comic Relief

Strategic use of humor and witty dialogue can provide comic relief in intense action scenes, offering a momentary break from the tension. This can make the characters more relatable and the action more enjoyable. In "Guardians of the Galaxy," Star-Lord's humorous remarks during battles add levity and charm, balancing the high-stakes action.

Maintain Realism

Dialogue in action scenes should maintain a sense of realism. Characters should react naturally to the situation, avoiding overly stylized or unrealistic conversations. In "Black Hawk Down," the realistic military dialogue during combat scenes adds authenticity and immerses the audience in the chaos of battle.

Use Dialogue to Foreshadow

Dialogue in action scenes can foreshadow future events or conflicts, adding depth and continuity to the narrative. Characters might drop hints or make cryptic comments that pay off later in the story. In "The Dark Knight," the Joker's taunting dialogue during his confrontations with Batman foreshadows his larger plans and adds to the psychological tension.

Highlight Team Dynamics

In ensemble action scenes, dialogue can highlight team dynamics and relationships. Characters might coordinate strategies, express concern for each other, or showcase their camaraderie. In "Avengers: Endgame," the dialogue during the final battle emphasizes the teamwork and unity of the Avengers, enhancing the emotional weight of the action.

Capture the Moment's Emotion

Dialogue can capture the emotion of the moment, whether it's fear, anger, hope, or despair. Characters expressing their emotions amidst the action can make the scene more compelling and relatable. In "Gladiator," Maximus's speeches during battle scenes convey his determination and leadership, adding emotional depth to the action.

Provide Clear Objectives

Dialogue can clarify the characters' objectives during action scenes, making the stakes and goals clear to the audience. This helps maintain narrative coherence and keeps the audience engaged. In "Mission: Impossible – Fallout," the dialogue during the helicopter chase clearly outlines Ethan Hunt's objectives, enhancing the clarity and excitement of the scene.

Avoid Overuse

While dialogue can enhance action scenes, it's important not to overuse it. Too much talking can detract from the visual impact and intensity of the action. Finding the right balance between dialogue and movement ensures that the scene remains dynamic and engaging. In "John Wick," the minimal dialogue during fight scenes keeps the focus on the choreography and intensity of the action.

In summary, balancing dialogue with movement in action scenes involves keeping dialogue concise and relevant, integrating it seamlessly with the action, revealing character, heightening tension, and maintaining realism. By focusing on these strategies, you can create action scenes that are dynamic, engaging, and enriched by well-crafted dialogue.

Dialogue in Moments of Crisis

Dialogue during moments of crisis is crucial for conveying urgency, tension, and emotional intensity. It can reveal character under pressure, advance the plot, and heighten the stakes. Crafting effective dialogue for these high-stress situations requires a keen understanding of pacing, emotional nuance, and clarity. Here are strategies for writing impactful dialogue in moments of crisis.

Reflecting Urgency and Tension

Dialogue should reflect the urgency and tension of the crisis. Short, clipped sentences and rapid exchanges can convey the immediacy of the situation. In "Apollo 13," the urgent, technical exchanges between the astronauts and mission control during the spacecraft's malfunction heighten the tension and realism.

Revealing Character under Pressure

Crisis situations reveal true character. Dialogue can show how different characters respond to stress, fear, and uncertainty. In "Saving Private Ryan," the varied responses of the soldiers under fire, from fear to leadership, are revealed through their dialogue, adding depth to their characters.

Balancing Clarity and Emotion

In moments of crisis, characters may need to convey critical information quickly and clearly, while also expressing intense emotions. Striking a balance between clarity and emotion ensures that the dialogue is both effective and impactful. In "Gravity," the dialogue between Ryan Stone and Matt Kowalski during the space disaster balances technical instructions with emotional exchanges, enhancing the scene's intensity.

Using Interruptions and Overlapping Speech

Interruptions and overlapping speech can add realism and urgency to crisis dialogue. Characters may talk over each other, shout, or cut each other off as they react to the unfolding events. In "The Hurt Locker," the chaotic dialogue during bomb defusal scenes reflects the high-stress environment and the characters' heightened states.

Expressing Desperation and Determination

Dialogue can convey characters' desperation and determination in crisis moments. Their words can reveal their will to survive, protect others, or accomplish a mission despite overwhelming odds. In "The Martian," Mark Watney's dialogue, filled with determination and problem-solving, conveys his will to survive on Mars.

Highlighting Conflicts and Alliances

Crisis situations can intensify existing conflicts or forge new alliances. Dialogue can reflect these dynamics, revealing tensions or cooperation among characters. In "Jurassic Park," the dialogue between Dr. Grant, Dr. Sattler, and the other characters during the dinosaur attacks highlights their differing approaches to survival and reveals shifting alliances.

Incorporating Subtext and Hidden Meanings

Subtext can add depth to crisis dialogue, revealing underlying fears, motivations, or conflicts without being explicitly stated. In "The Dark Knight," the dialogue between Batman and the Joker during their confrontations is laden with subtext about morality, chaos, and order, adding layers to the crisis.

Using Silence and Pauses

Strategic use of silence and pauses can heighten the tension and impact of crisis dialogue. Moments of silence can underscore the gravity of the situation or the weight of decisions being made. In "A Quiet Place," the lack of dialogue and the characters' use of sign language during crises heightens the suspense and emotional intensity.

Infusing Humor

Occasional humor can provide relief in tense situations, making characters more relatable and adding layers to the scene. Well-timed humorous dialogue can break the tension without undermining the seriousness of the crisis. In "Guardians of the Galaxy," Star-Lord's quips during dangerous situations add humor while maintaining the stakes.

Revealing Stakes and Consequences

Dialogue should make clear the stakes and potential consequences of the crisis. Characters can discuss what's at risk, what they stand to lose, or what their goals are. In "Armageddon," the dialogue between the astronauts about the consequences of failure (global destruction) underscores the high stakes of their mission.

Capturing the Moment's Emotion

Dialogue in moments of crisis should capture the raw emotion of the characters, whether it's fear, anger, sadness, or hope. Genuine emotional expressions make the scene more impactful and relatable. In "Titanic," the dialogues between Jack and Rose during the sinking ship crisis convey their fear, love, and desperation.

Facilitating Plot Progression

Crisis dialogue should also serve to advance the plot, providing necessary information or driving the action forward. Characters might outline plans, react to new developments, or make critical decisions. In "The Hunger Games," Katniss's dialogues during the games, including her strategic decisions and alliances, drive the plot and heighten the tension.

Conveying Resilience and Hope

In the midst of crisis, dialogue can convey themes of resilience and hope, showing characters' determination to overcome the odds. Inspirational or reassuring words can be powerful, providing a contrast to the chaos. In "Lord of the Rings: The Two Towers," Sam's speech about hope and perseverance during the battle of Helm's Deep adds emotional weight to the crisis.

Reflecting Realistic Reactions

Characters' dialogue should reflect realistic reactions to crisis, including fear, confusion, anger, and resolve. Authentic reactions make the scene more believable and engaging. In "28 Days Later," the characters' dialogues during zombie attacks reflect their panic, fear, and survival instincts, enhancing the realism.

Using Physical Actions to Complement Dialogue

Physical actions can complement dialogue, adding a dynamic layer to the scene. Characters might perform crucial actions while speaking, making the dialogue and movement feel integrated and natural. In "Mission: Impossible – Ghost Protocol," the dialogue during the high-stakes action scenes is interwoven with physical actions, maintaining a high level of intensity.

In summary, dialogue in moments of crisis should reflect urgency, reveal character, balance clarity and emotion, and drive the plot forward. By focusing on these elements, you can create impactful and engaging dialogue that enhances the intensity and emotional depth of crisis scenes in your screenplay.

The Hero's Journey: Dialogue in Key Steps

The Hero's Journey is a narrative structure that outlines the typical adventure of the archetype known as The Hero. This journey involves various stages, each with its own specific needs for dialogue to advance the plot, develop characters, and convey themes. Here's how to craft effective dialogue for each key step of the Hero's Journey:

1. The Ordinary World

In the Ordinary World, the hero's normal life is established. Dialogue should highlight the hero's current state, setting, and relationships, and hint at their dissatisfaction or longing for something more.

Example: In "The Lord of the Rings: The Fellowship of the Ring," Frodo's conversations in the Shire establish his peaceful, content life, while his dialogues with Gandalf hint at a world beyond and a sense of unease.

2. The Call to Adventure

The Call to Adventure disrupts the hero's ordinary world, presenting a challenge or quest. Dialogue here should convey the urgency and importance of the call.

Example: In "Star Wars: A New Hope," Obi-Wan Kenobi's dialogue with Luke Skywalker about joining him to learn the ways of the Force and fight the Empire presents the call to adventure.

3. Refusal of the Call

Often, the hero initially refuses the call due to fear or reluctance. Dialogue should express their hesitation and the reasons behind it.

Example: In "The Matrix," Neo's initial skepticism and refusal to believe Morpheus about the true nature of reality reflect his reluctance to embrace his destiny.

4. Meeting the Mentor

The hero meets a mentor who provides guidance, wisdom, or magical aid. Dialogue here should be inspirational and informative, setting the stage for the journey ahead.

Example: In "Harry Potter and the Sorcerer's Stone," Hagrid's dialogues with Harry introduce him to the wizarding world and his true identity, providing the necessary push to accept his adventure.

5. Crossing the Threshold

The hero commits to the journey and leaves the ordinary world. Dialogue should emphasize this commitment and the transition into the unknown.

Example: In "The Hunger Games," Katniss's dialogue with her family and friends before departing for the Capitol highlights her commitment and the gravity of her journey.

6. Tests, Allies, and Enemies

The hero encounters tests, allies, and enemies in the new world. Dialogue during this stage should reveal character traits, build relationships, and advance subplots.

Example: In "The Fellowship of the Ring," the dialogues among the members of the Fellowship reveal their personalities, forge bonds, and set up future conflicts and alliances.

7. Approach to the Inmost Cave

The hero prepares for the major challenge in the inmost cave. Dialogue should build tension, reveal the hero's doubts and fears, and set the stakes for the upcoming ordeal.

Example: In "The Lion King," Simba's dialogues with Nala and Rafiki before returning to Pride Rock reveal his internal conflict and fear of facing Scar.

8. The Ordeal

The hero faces their greatest challenge, experiencing a symbolic death and rebirth. Dialogue should heighten the drama, reveal critical character insights, and emphasize the stakes.

Example: In "The Dark Knight," the intense dialogues between Batman and the Joker during their final confrontation reveal deep philosophical conflicts and drive the climactic action.

9. The Reward

After surviving the ordeal, the hero receives a reward. Dialogue here can convey relief, celebration, and newfound insights.

Example: In "Indiana Jones and the Last Crusade," the dialogue between Indiana Jones and his father after finding the Holy Grail reflects their reconciliation and the personal growth of the hero.

10. The Road Back

The hero begins the journey back to the ordinary world, but new challenges may arise. Dialogue should reflect the hero's transformation and foreshadow the final test.

Example: In "The Lord of the Rings: The Return of the King," the dialogues among the characters as they prepare for the final battle against Sauron show their resolve and readiness for the ultimate test.

11. The Resurrection

The hero faces a final test where everything is at stake. Dialogue should be intense, conveying the urgency and high stakes of the situation.

Example: In "Harry Potter and the Deathly Hallows Part 2," Harry's dialogue with Voldemort during their final battle encapsulates the culmination of their long-standing conflict and Harry's growth.

12. Return with the Elixir

The hero returns to the ordinary world with the elixir, bringing change or enlightenment. Dialogue should reflect the hero's transformation and the impact on their world.

Example: In "The Wizard of Oz," Dorothy's dialogues with her family upon returning to Kansas reflect her growth and the lessons learned during her journey.

General Tips for Crafting Hero's Journey Dialogue

- **Maintain Consistency**: Ensure that the dialogue remains true to the characters' voices and the overall tone of the story throughout the journey.
- **Show Growth**: Use dialogue to show the hero's growth and transformation at each stage of the journey.
- **Build Relationships**: Dialogue should deepen relationships between the hero and other characters, reflecting alliances, conflicts, and personal bonds.
- **Advance the Plot**: Ensure that dialogue serves to advance the plot, providing necessary information and driving the story forward.
- **Emphasize Themes**: Use dialogue to subtly weave in the story's central themes, reinforcing the overarching message of the hero's journey.

By focusing on these strategies, you can craft compelling and meaningful dialogue that enhances each key step of the Hero's Journey, adding depth and resonance to your screenplay.

Dialogue in the First Act: Setting the Scene

The first act of a screenplay is crucial for establishing the setting, introducing characters, and laying the groundwork for the plot. Dialogue in this act should be carefully crafted to convey essential information, build intrigue, and set the tone for the story. Here are strategies for using dialogue effectively in the first act.

Introducing Characters

Dialogue should introduce characters in a way that reveals their personalities, backgrounds, and relationships. This can be done through their interactions with others and their unique speech patterns.

Example: In "The Social Network," Mark Zuckerberg's rapid, sarcastic dialogue in the opening scene establishes his character's intellect and social awkwardness, setting the tone for his interactions throughout the film.

Establishing the Setting

Dialogue can provide context about the time, place, and environment in which the story takes place. Characters' conversations about their surroundings, daily routines, and local customs can help establish the setting organically.

Example: In "Brooklyn," the dialogues between Eilis and her family and friends in Ireland convey the small-town setting and her sense of confinement, setting up her desire to move to America.

Revealing Backstory

Subtly woven dialogue can reveal backstory without resorting to heavy exposition. Characters might refer to past events, relationships, or experiences that inform their current situation.

Example: In "Inception," the early dialogues between Cobb and his team members provide glimpses into their past heists and Cobb's unresolved issues, setting the stage for the story.

Setting the Tone

Dialogue in the first act should establish the tone of the film, whether it's comedic, dramatic, suspenseful, or romantic. Characters' speech patterns, humor, and interactions should reflect the overall mood.

Example: In "Juno," the witty, quirky dialogues between Juno and her friends set a lighthearted, irreverent tone that permeates the film.

Building Relationships

Early dialogues should establish the relationships between characters, showing how they interact and relate to one another. This helps the audience understand the dynamics at play.

Example: In "The Breakfast Club," the initial dialogues among the students reveal their stereotypes and preconceptions, setting up the exploration of their relationships throughout the film.

Introducing Conflict

Dialogue in the first act should hint at or introduce the central conflict or challenges the characters will face. This creates intrigue and sets up the narrative drive.

Example: In "The Hunger Games," the early dialogues about the Reaping and the Capitol's oppression establish the stakes and hint at the impending conflict.

Conveying Themes

Dialogue can subtly introduce the themes of the story. Characters' conversations might touch on key ideas or motifs that will be explored more deeply as the narrative unfolds.

Example: In "The Truman Show," the early dialogues about Truman's life and his sense of unease hint at the themes of reality and free will that will be central to the film.

Providing Exposition

While exposition is necessary, it should be delivered naturally through dialogue. Characters might discuss their world, the rules governing it, or recent events in a way that feels organic.

Example: In "Blade Runner," the early dialogues between Deckard and Bryant provide exposition about replicants and the societal context without feeling forced.

Creating Intrigue

Dialogue in the first act should create intrigue and draw the audience in. Hints, unanswered questions, and mysterious references can pique interest and build anticipation.

Example: In "The Matrix," Morpheus's cryptic dialogues with Neo about the nature of reality create intrigue and set up the central mystery of the film.

Establishing Protagonist's Goals and Motivations

Dialogue should clearly establish the protagonist's goals and motivations, giving the audience a reason to root for them and invest in their journey.

Example: In "Rocky," the early dialogues between Rocky and his friends and trainers reveal his dream of becoming a successful boxer and his struggles, setting up his motivation.

Setting Up the Inciting Incident

The first act should build up to the inciting incident that propels the protagonist into the main conflict. Dialogue can foreshadow this event and prepare the audience for its impact.

Example: In "The Lion King," the dialogues between Simba, Mufasa, and Scar set up the dynamics and tensions that lead to the inciting incident of Mufasa's death.

Balancing Show and Tell

While dialogue is important, it should be balanced with visual storytelling. Characters' actions, expressions, and interactions should complement their words, creating a richer narrative.

Example: In "Up," the early dialogues between Carl and Ellie, combined with the visual montage of their life together, beautifully set the scene and establish the emotional core of the story.

Reflecting the Protagonist's Ordinary World

Dialogue should reflect the protagonist's ordinary world before the adventure begins, highlighting what's at stake and what might be lost or gained.

Example: In "Harry Potter and the Sorcerer's Stone," the early dialogues between Harry and the Dursleys show his unhappy life, setting the stage for his transformation upon entering the wizarding world.

Foreshadowing Future Events

Subtle foreshadowing through dialogue can hint at future events or conflicts, adding layers of meaning and building anticipation.

Example: In "The Sixth Sense," Dr. Malcolm Crowe's early dialogues with his wife about their relationship subtly foreshadow the film's twist, adding depth to the story.

In summary, dialogue in the first act should introduce characters, establish the setting, reveal backstory, set the tone, build relationships, introduce conflict, convey themes, provide exposition, create intrigue, establish the protagonist's goals and motivations, set up the inciting incident, balance show and tell, reflect the protagonist's ordinary world, and foreshadow future events. By focusing on these elements, you can craft effective and engaging dialogue that sets the scene and draws the audience into your story.

Introducing Characters through Dialogue

Introducing characters effectively through dialogue is essential for establishing their personalities, backgrounds, motivations, and relationships right from the start. Well-crafted dialogue can provide a clear, engaging introduction to characters, making them memorable and setting the stage for their development throughout the story. Here are strategies for introducing characters through dialogue.

Establishing Voice and Personality

Characters' speech patterns, vocabulary, and tone should reflect their unique personalities. This makes them immediately recognizable and gives the audience insight into who they are.

Example: In "Pulp Fiction," Jules Winnfield's distinctive, philosophical way of speaking immediately sets him apart and provides insight into his complex personality.

Revealing Background and Context

Dialogue can provide hints about a character's background, such as their upbringing, education, or cultural context. This helps the audience understand where they come from.

Example: In "Good Will Hunting," Will's casual, colloquial speech reveals his working-class background, contrasting with the more formal speech of the academic characters.

Showing Relationships

Characters' interactions with others can reveal a lot about their relationships. Dialogue can indicate friendships, rivalries, family ties, and professional dynamics.

Example: In "The Godfather," the respectful, formal dialogue between Michael Corleone and his father, Vito, establishes their close family bond and the respect within the family hierarchy.

Conveying Motivations and Goals

Early dialogue should hint at or explicitly state a character's goals and motivations, giving the audience a sense of their driving forces and what they seek to achieve.

Example: In "The Hunger Games," Katniss's early conversations with Gale about hunting and survival reveal her motivation to protect her family and her skills as a hunter.

Highlighting Strengths and Flaws

Dialogue can showcase a character's strengths and weaknesses, making them more well-rounded and relatable. This helps the audience understand their potential for growth and conflict.

Example: In "Iron Man," Tony Stark's witty, confident dialogue highlights his intelligence and arrogance, setting up his character arc and the challenges he will face.

Using Subtext and Implication

Subtext can add depth to character introductions, allowing the audience to infer more about the characters than what is explicitly stated. This can make the dialogue more engaging and layered.

Example: In "The Social Network," Mark Zuckerberg's dialogue in the opening scene is filled with subtext, revealing his ambition and social insecurities through a conversation about trivial matters.

Employing Humor and Wit

Introducing characters through humorous or witty dialogue can make them immediately likable and memorable. It also sets the tone for their personality and role in the story.

Example: In "Deadpool," Wade Wilson's irreverent, humorous dialogue establishes his character's personality and tone, making him instantly engaging.

Creating Tension and Conflict

Dialogue that introduces characters through conflict or tension can be highly effective. It immediately engages the audience and reveals key aspects of the characters' personalities.

Example: In "Inglourious Basterds," the tense dialogue between Colonel Hans Landa and the French farmer during their first meeting establishes Landa's menacing intelligence and the power dynamics at play.

Reflecting the Setting and Context

Characters' dialogue can reflect the setting and context, providing insight into their environment and how it shapes them. This helps ground the characters in the world of the story.

Example: In "Mad Men," the dialogues between the advertising executives in the 1960s office setting reflect the cultural and social norms of the time, establishing the characters within their historical context.

Introducing Unique Traits and Quirks

Highlighting a character's unique traits or quirks through dialogue can make them stand out and be more memorable. This can include distinctive speech patterns, habits, or interests.

Example: In "Sherlock," Sherlock Holmes's rapid, deductive monologues immediately establish his unique intellect and observational skills, setting him apart as a character.

Setting Up Future Development

Dialogue can foreshadow a character's development or hint at future changes in their arc. This creates anticipation and adds depth to their introduction.

Example: In "The Lion King," Simba's early dialogues about wanting to be king set up his future journey and growth from a carefree cub to a responsible leader.

Balancing Show and Tell

While dialogue is crucial, it should be balanced with actions and visuals to provide a complete picture of the character. Characters' words should be complemented by their behavior and surroundings.

Example: In "Indiana Jones and the Last Crusade," Indiana Jones's dialogue with his students about archaeology, combined with his adventurous actions, establishes his dual identity as a professor and adventurer.

Using Dialogue to Reflect Inner Thoughts

Inner thoughts and monologues can also introduce characters, providing direct insight into their minds and personalities. This technique should be used judiciously to avoid over-exposition.

Example: In "Fight Club," the Narrator's inner monologue provides a direct window into his psyche, revealing his discontent and internal conflicts.

Creating Immediate Connections

Dialogue that fosters immediate connections between characters and the audience can make introductions more impactful. This can be achieved through relatable experiences, emotions, or universal themes.

Example: In "E.T. the Extra-Terrestrial," Elliott's dialogues with E.T. quickly establish a bond between the boy and the alien, making both characters endearing and relatable.

Integrating with the Plot

Character introductions should seamlessly integrate with the plot, advancing the story while revealing key aspects of the characters. This ensures that the introduction feels organic and purposeful.

Example: In "The Matrix," Neo's introduction through his search for answers about the Matrix serves both to reveal his character's curiosity and set up the central plot.

In summary, introducing characters through dialogue involves establishing their voice and personality, revealing background and context, showing relationships, conveying motivations and goals, highlighting strengths and flaws, using subtext, employing humor, creating tension, reflecting the setting, introducing unique traits, setting up future development, balancing show and tell, using inner thoughts, creating immediate connections, and integrating with the plot. By focusing on these strategies, you can create compelling and memorable character introductions that engage the audience and set the stage for their development.

Building Relationships with Dialogue

Dialogue is a powerful tool for building and revealing relationships between characters in a screenplay. Through conversations, characters can express emotions, reveal histories, and develop connections that drive the narrative forward. Here are strategies for using dialogue to build and deepen relationships.

Establishing Initial Dynamics

Dialogue can set the stage for the initial dynamics between characters, whether they are friends, rivals, lovers, or strangers. The way characters speak to each other can reveal their relationship status and set up future developments.

Example: In "The Shawshank Redemption," the initial dialogues between Andy and Red establish their relationship as one of cautious curiosity, setting the stage for their eventual deep friendship.

Expressing Emotions

Characters can express a wide range of emotions through dialogue, from love and affection to anger and jealousy. These emotional exchanges help to build and define relationships.

Example: In "La La Land," the dialogues between Mia and Sebastian convey their growing romantic connection, as well as the tensions that arise from their individual dreams and aspirations.

Revealing Shared History

Dialogue can reveal shared history and past experiences between characters, providing context and depth to their relationship. These references help the audience understand the bonds and conflicts that exist.

Example: In "Good Will Hunting," the conversations between Will and his therapist, Sean, reveal their shared experiences and struggles, deepening their relationship.

Creating Conflict and Resolution

Dialogue can be used to create conflict between characters and subsequently resolve it, showing the evolution of their relationship. These interactions add drama and complexity.

Example: In "Marriage Story," the intense, emotional dialogues between Charlie and Nicole during their divorce negotiations reveal the depth of their relationship and the pain of their separation.

Building Trust and Loyalty

Characters can build trust and loyalty through their dialogues, expressing their reliance on and commitment to each other. These moments strengthen the relationship and make it more meaningful.

Example: In "The Lord of the Rings: The Fellowship of the Ring," the dialogues between Frodo and Sam highlight their growing trust and loyalty, crucial for their journey.

Showing Support and Encouragement

Supportive and encouraging dialogue can reveal the positive aspects of a relationship, showing how characters uplift and motivate each other.

Example: In "The Pursuit of Happyness," the supportive dialogues between Chris Gardner and his son Christopher highlight their strong bond and mutual encouragement despite facing hardships.

Highlighting Differences and Similarities

Dialogue can highlight the differences and similarities between characters, showcasing the unique dynamics of their relationship. These contrasts and commonalities add richness to their interactions.

Example: In "The Odd Couple," the dialogues between Felix and Oscar humorously highlight their contrasting personalities, which forms the basis of their relationship.

Evolving Relationships Over Time

Dialogue should reflect the evolution of relationships over the course of the narrative. Characters' conversations can show how their connections deepen, change, or deteriorate.

Example: In "Toy Story," the evolving dialogues between Woody and Buzz Lightyear reflect their transition from rivals to friends, marking significant development in their relationship.

Creating Subtext

Subtext in dialogue can reveal underlying tensions, unspoken feelings, and hidden motivations in a relationship. This adds depth and complexity to the characters' interactions.

Example: In "Lost in Translation," the subtle, understated dialogues between Bob and Charlotte reveal their growing connection and mutual understanding, often through what is left unsaid.

Using Humor and Banter

Humorous and playful dialogues can establish a sense of camaraderie and ease between characters, making their relationship feel more authentic and enjoyable.

Example: In "Guardians of the Galaxy," the banter between the team members, particularly Rocket and Star-Lord, builds a sense of camaraderie and mutual affection.

Creating Tension and Suspense

Tense and suspenseful dialogues can highlight the conflicts and stakes within a relationship, adding drama and urgency to their interactions.

Example: In "The Silence of the Lambs," the dialogues between Clarice Starling and Hannibal Lecter are charged with tension and psychological intrigue, defining their complex relationship.

Exploring Power Dynamics

Dialogue can explore the power dynamics within a relationship, showing how characters exert influence over each other and navigate their roles.

Example: In "House of Cards," the dialogues between Frank and Claire Underwood reveal the shifting power dynamics in their partnership, characterized by manipulation and strategic alliances.

Revealing Vulnerabilities

Characters can reveal their vulnerabilities through dialogue, creating moments of intimacy and connection. These disclosures help build deeper, more genuine relationships.

Example: In "Eternal Sunshine of the Spotless Mind," the intimate dialogues between Joel and Clementine reveal their vulnerabilities and insecurities, deepening their emotional connection.

Creating Relatable Interactions

Realistic, relatable interactions through dialogue make relationships more believable and engaging. Characters should speak and react in ways that reflect real-life conversations.

Example: In "Before Sunrise," the naturalistic dialogues between Jesse and Celine as they wander through Vienna capture the spontaneity and depth of their developing connection.

Foreshadowing Relationship Arcs

Dialogue can foreshadow the future of a relationship, hinting at potential developments, conflicts, or resolutions. This adds a layer of anticipation and depth to the narrative.

Example: In "Romeo and Juliet," the initial dialogues between the titular characters foreshadow the intensity and tragedy of their relationship, adding dramatic weight to their interactions.

Balancing Dialogue with Action

While dialogue is essential, it should be balanced with actions that also convey the relationship dynamics. Characters' behaviors, gestures, and expressions should complement their words.

Example: In "Titanic," the dialogues between Jack and Rose are complemented by their actions, such as the iconic scene on the ship's bow, which together build their romantic relationship.

In summary, building relationships through dialogue involves establishing initial dynamics, expressing emotions, revealing shared history, creating conflict and resolution, building trust and loyalty, showing support and encouragement, highlighting differences and similarities, evolving relationships over time, creating subtext, using humor and banter, creating tension and suspense, exploring power dynamics, revealing vulnerabilities, creating relatable interactions, foreshadowing relationship arcs, and balancing dialogue with action.

Establishing Conflict through Dialogue

Conflict is a driving force in storytelling, creating tension and propelling the narrative forward. Dialogue is an effective tool for establishing and escalating conflict between characters. Here are strategies for using dialogue to introduce and develop conflict in your screenplay.

Revealing Contrasting Goals and Desires

Conflict often arises from characters having opposing goals or desires. Dialogue can highlight these differences, setting the stage for tension and clashes.

Example: In "The Dark Knight," the dialogue between Batman and the Joker reveals their opposing philosophies—order versus chaos—establishing a fundamental conflict that drives the narrative.

Expressing Tension and Hostility

Characters can express tension and hostility through their words, using confrontational language, sarcasm, or veiled threats. This creates an immediate sense of conflict.

Example: In "The Social Network," the sharp, biting dialogues between Mark Zuckerberg and Eduardo Saverin showcase their growing hostility and the conflict over Facebook's direction and ownership.

Highlighting Misunderstandings

Misunderstandings and miscommunications are common sources of conflict. Dialogue can reveal these misunderstandings, creating tension and potential for resolution or escalation.

Example: In "Much Ado About Nothing," the misunderstandings and deceptions revealed through dialogue create comedic and dramatic conflicts between the characters.

Using Subtext and Implication

Subtext and implication can add depth to conflict, allowing characters to express underlying tensions and unspoken issues. This can make the conflict more layered and nuanced.

Example: In "American Beauty," the seemingly polite but tense dialogues between Lester Burnham and his wife Carolyn are filled with subtext, revealing deeper marital conflicts.

Creating Power Struggles

Power struggles often drive conflict. Dialogue can highlight characters' attempts to assert dominance or control over each other, creating dramatic tension.

Example: In "House of Cards," the power-laden dialogues between Frank Underwood and his political adversaries reveal constant jockeying for power and influence.

Introducing Ethical or Moral Dilemmas

Conflicts can stem from ethical or moral dilemmas. Dialogue can bring these dilemmas to the forefront, forcing characters to confront difficult choices and question their values.

Example: In "A Few Good Men," the courtroom dialogues between Lt. Kaffee and Col. Jessup revolve around ethical questions of duty, honor, and the rule of law, driving the central conflict.

Escalating Stakes

Conflict often escalates as the stakes increase. Dialogue can be used to raise the stakes, making the consequences of the conflict more significant and urgent.

Example: In "Gladiator," the escalating dialogues between Maximus and Commodus reveal the increasing stakes of their conflict, from personal revenge to the fate of the Roman Empire.

Exposing Secrets and Lies

Secrets and lies are fertile ground for conflict. Dialogue can reveal or hint at hidden truths, creating tension and leading to dramatic confrontations.

Example: In "Gone Girl," the dialogues between Nick and Amy Dunne reveal layers of deception and manipulation, driving the psychological conflict of the story.

Reflecting Internal Conflict

Characters can express their internal conflicts through dialogue, revealing their doubts, fears, and inner struggles. This can add depth to their external conflicts.

Example: In "The King's Speech," the dialogues between King George VI and his speech therapist Lionel Logue reflect the king's internal battle with his speech impediment and his external conflict with public speaking.

Using Wit and Sarcasm

Wit and sarcasm can create conflict by highlighting differences and challenging characters. This can make the exchanges more engaging and dynamic.

Example: In "Pride and Prejudice," the witty, sarcastic dialogues between Elizabeth Bennet and Mr. Darcy reveal their initial misunderstandings and prejudices, setting up their romantic conflict.

Highlighting Cultural or Ideological Differences

Cultural or ideological differences can be a source of conflict. Dialogue can highlight these differences, creating tension and challenging characters to navigate their contrasting views.

Example: In "Guess Who's Coming to Dinner," the dialogues between the characters reveal cultural and generational conflicts regarding interracial marriage.

Creating Ambiguity and Doubt

Ambiguous or cryptic dialogues can create conflict by introducing doubt and uncertainty. Characters might question each other's motives or trustworthiness, leading to tension.

Example: In "Inception," the ambiguous dialogues about dreams and reality create conflict and doubt among the characters, heightening the narrative tension.

Building Rivalries

Rivalries are a natural source of conflict. Dialogue can establish and develop rivalries, whether in professional, personal, or romantic contexts.

Example: In "Amadeus," the dialogues between Salieri and Mozart reveal their professional rivalry, driven by jealousy and admiration, fueling the story's central conflict.

Challenging Authority

Characters challenging authority figures can create significant conflict. Dialogue can highlight these challenges, revealing the characters' motivations and the stakes involved.

Example: In "Dead Poets Society," the dialogues between Mr. Keating and the school's administration, as well as his interactions with the students, highlight the conflict between individualism and conformity.

Confronting Past Grievances

Conflicts often arise from unresolved past grievances. Dialogue can bring these grievances to the surface, forcing characters to confront their histories and unresolved issues.

Example: In "The Godfather Part II," the dialogues between Michael Corleone and his brother Fredo reveal deep-seated resentments and betrayals, driving their familial conflict.

Foreshadowing Future Conflicts

Dialogue can foreshadow future conflicts, planting seeds of tension that will develop later in the story. This builds anticipation and keeps the audience engaged.

Example: In "Harry Potter and the Sorcerer's Stone," the early dialogues about Voldemort and the dangers at Hogwarts foreshadow the conflicts Harry will face throughout the series.

Expressing Conflicting Emotions

Characters experiencing conflicting emotions can create internal and external conflicts. Dialogue that captures these emotions can add complexity and depth to the story.

Example: In "Eternal Sunshine of the Spotless Mind," the dialogues between Joel and Clementine during their tumultuous relationship reveal their conflicting emotions and the resulting tension.

Dialogue in the Inciting Incident

The inciting incident is a pivotal moment in a screenplay that propels the protagonist into the main conflict of the story. Dialogue during this moment should effectively convey the significance of the event, the stakes involved, and the emotional impact on the characters. Here are strategies for crafting compelling dialogue in the inciting incident.

Conveying Urgency and Importance

Dialogue should immediately convey the urgency and importance of the inciting incident, making it clear that this event will change the protagonist's life.

Example: In "The Hunger Games," the dialogue during the Reaping ceremony, when Prim's name is called and Katniss volunteers to take her place, conveys the life-or-death stakes and the urgency of the situation.

Expressing Emotional Impact

Characters' emotional reactions to the inciting incident should be clearly expressed through dialogue, highlighting their fears, hopes, or shock.

Example: In "Up," the dialogue between Carl and the developers who want to buy his house reflects his emotional attachment to his home and his resistance to change, setting up the journey ahead.

Introducing Conflict

The dialogue should introduce the central conflict of the story, making it clear what the protagonist will be up against.

Example: In "The Matrix," the dialogue between Neo and Morpheus during their first meeting introduces the conflict between the humans and the machines, and the need for Neo to make a choice about his reality.

Foreshadowing Future Events

Dialogue during the inciting incident can foreshadow future events and conflicts, hinting at what's to come and creating anticipation.

Example: In "Harry Potter and the Philosopher's Stone," Hagrid's dialogue when he tells Harry he is a wizard foreshadows the magical adventures and conflicts Harry will face at Hogwarts.

Establishing Stakes

Characters should discuss or react to the stakes involved, making it clear what they stand to lose or gain as a result of the inciting incident.

Example: In "Jurassic Park," the dialogue between the park's staff and the visiting scientists during the initial dinosaur tour reveals the stakes of the park's success and the potential dangers involved.

Creating Intrigue

Dialogue can create intrigue and curiosity about the inciting incident, drawing the audience in and making them want to know more.

Example: In "Inception," the dialogue between Cobb and Saito about the concept of inception and planting an idea creates intrigue and sets up the complex heist that will drive the story.

Reflecting Internal Conflict

Characters' dialogues can reflect their internal conflicts and doubts about the inciting incident, adding depth to their reactions and setting up their personal journeys.

Example: In "Frozen," Anna's dialogue with Elsa during the coronation day reveals Anna's desire for a closer relationship and Elsa's internal struggle with her powers, foreshadowing the conflict to come.

Building Relationships

Dialogue during the inciting incident can reveal or establish key relationships between characters, highlighting how these dynamics will influence the story.

Example: In "Toy Story," the dialogue between Woody and Buzz when Buzz first arrives introduces their rivalry and sets up the central relationship conflict of the film.

Setting the Tone

The dialogue should help set the tone for the story, whether it's dramatic, comedic, suspenseful, or romantic, providing a glimpse of what to expect.

Example: In "Guardians of the Galaxy," the humorous and irreverent dialogue during Star-Lord's escape from the planet Morag sets the tone for the film's blend of action and comedy.

Revealing Motivations

Characters' dialogues should reveal their motivations and desires, helping the audience understand why the inciting incident is significant to them.

Example: In "The Lion King," the dialogue between Mufasa and Simba about the Circle of Life and Simba's future as king establishes Simba's motivations and the significance of his journey.

Highlighting the Disruption

The dialogue should highlight how the inciting incident disrupts the protagonist's ordinary world, creating a clear before-and-after scenario.

Example: In "Finding Nemo," Marlin's dialogue with Nemo about the dangers of the ocean and the subsequent kidnapping of Nemo highlight the dramatic disruption to their lives.

Using Subtext

Subtext can add depth to the dialogue during the inciting incident, hinting at underlying tensions or hidden truths that will be explored later.

Example: In "Fight Club," the initial conversations between the Narrator and Tyler Durden are filled with subtext about consumerism and personal identity, foreshadowing the film's deeper themes.

Creating Tension

Dialogue should create tension and suspense, making the audience feel the weight of the inciting incident and its potential consequences.

Example: In "Jaws," the dialogue between Chief Brody, the mayor, and the townspeople about the shark attacks creates tension and sets up the central conflict of man versus nature.

Highlighting Character Traits

The way characters react and what they say during the inciting incident can highlight key traits and attributes, providing insight into their personalities.

Example: In "Iron Man," Tony Stark's witty, confident dialogue during the weapons demonstration and subsequent capture highlights his arrogance and sets up his transformation journey.

Setting Up the Plot

The dialogue should set up the main plot, providing enough information to propel the story forward and engage the audience.

Example: In "The Incredibles," the dialogue during the family dinner scene and the call to action for Mr. Incredible sets up the return to superheroics and the central plot of the film.

In summary, dialogue during the inciting incident should convey urgency and importance, express emotional impact, introduce conflict, foreshadow future events, establish stakes, create intrigue, reflect internal conflict, build relationships, set the tone, reveal motivations, highlight the disruption, use subtext, create tension, highlight character traits, and set up the plot. By focusing on these elements, you can craft compelling and effective dialogue that enhances the impact of the inciting incident and propels the narrative forward.

Raising Stakes with Dialogue

Raising the stakes in a screenplay is essential for maintaining audience engagement and driving the narrative forward. Dialogue plays a crucial role in heightening the stakes by revealing the increasing consequences of the characters' actions, deepening conflicts, and intensifying emotional investment. Here are strategies for using dialogue to raise the stakes effectively.

Highlighting Consequences

Dialogue can reveal the potential consequences of the characters' actions, making the stakes clear and pressing. This adds urgency and tension to the narrative.

Example: In "The Dark Knight," the dialogue between Batman and the Joker, where the Joker threatens to unleash chaos and destroy Gotham, raises the stakes by emphasizing the dire consequences of their conflict.

Expressing Fear and Anxiety

Characters expressing their fears and anxieties can heighten the stakes by showing the emotional toll and the risks involved. This makes the audience feel the weight of the situation.

Example: In "Gravity," the dialogue between Ryan Stone and Matt Kowalski, as they discuss their limited oxygen and the vast emptiness of space, heightens the stakes by conveying their fear and desperation.

Introducing New Threats

Dialogue can introduce new threats or complications that raise the stakes, making the characters' challenges more difficult and the outcome more uncertain.

Example: In "Jurassic Park," the dialogue between Dr. Sattler and John Hammond about the impending storm and the park's failing systems introduces new threats that escalate the stakes.

Revealing Hidden Agendas

Characters uncovering hidden agendas or secrets through dialogue can raise the stakes by adding layers of complexity and increasing the potential for conflict.

Example: In "The Departed," the dialogues where characters reveal their true identities and hidden motives intensify the stakes by exposing the web of deception and betrayal.

Escalating Conflict

Dialogue can escalate existing conflicts, making the stakes higher by intensifying the characters' struggles and the potential for loss or failure.

Example: In "A Few Good Men," the heated courtroom dialogue between Lt. Kaffee and Col. Jessup escalates the conflict and raises the stakes as Kaffee seeks to expose the truth.

Highlighting Personal Stakes

Characters discussing their personal stakes, such as their loved ones, reputations, or dreams, can make the stakes feel more immediate and relatable.

Example: In "Rocky," the dialogues between Rocky and Adrian about his fears and motivations highlight the personal stakes of the fight, making his journey more compelling.

Building Tension through Subtext

Subtext in dialogue can raise the stakes by hinting at underlying tensions and unresolved issues, creating a sense of impending conflict.

Example: In "No Country for Old Men," the terse, subtext-laden dialogue between Anton Chigurh and his victims raises the stakes by creating an atmosphere of dread and inevitability.

Revealing Limited Time

Characters discussing a ticking clock or a deadline can raise the stakes by adding time pressure, making the need for action more urgent.

Example: In "Inception," the dialogues about the limited time within the dream layers and the impending "kick" create urgency and heighten the stakes of the mission.

Discussing Higher Powers or Authorities

Dialogue that introduces higher powers or authorities can raise the stakes by showing that the characters are up against formidable opponents or systems.

Example: In "The Hunger Games," the dialogues about the Capitol's control and President Snow's power emphasize the high stakes of Katniss's rebellion.

Illustrating Growing Risks

Dialogue can illustrate the growing risks the characters face, making it clear that the situation is becoming more dangerous and the potential for loss is increasing.

Example: In "The Revenant," the dialogues about the harsh environment and the hostile natives raise the stakes by highlighting the increasing dangers faced by Hugh Glass.

Highlighting Moral or Ethical Dilemmas

Characters discussing moral or ethical dilemmas can raise the stakes by adding layers of complexity and forcing difficult decisions.

Example: In "Schindler's List," the dialogues between Oskar Schindler and Itzhak Stern about saving Jews from the Holocaust raise the stakes by highlighting the moral imperative and the personal risks involved.

Creating Emotional Stakes

Dialogue that reveals characters' emotional investments can raise the stakes by making their struggles more personal and impactful.

Example: In "Toy Story 3," the dialogues about Andy growing up and the toys facing an uncertain future raise the emotional stakes, making their journey more poignant.

Increasing Scarcity of Resources

Characters discussing dwindling resources or limited options can raise the stakes by emphasizing the urgency and desperation of the situation.

Example: In "Apollo 13," the dialogues about the limited oxygen supply and the damaged spacecraft raise the stakes by highlighting the dire situation faced by the astronauts.

Reflecting Character Growth

Dialogue that shows characters' growth and increasing resolve can raise the stakes by highlighting their determination and the higher expectations placed upon them.

Example: In "The Lion King," the dialogues between Simba and Rafiki about his destiny and responsibility raise the stakes by reflecting Simba's growth and the weight of his decision to return.

Foreshadowing Potential Catastrophes

Dialogue that foreshadows potential catastrophes can raise the stakes by hinting at dire consequences and building anticipation.

Example: In "Titanic," the early dialogues about the ship's unsinkability and the icebergs in the North Atlantic foreshadow the impending disaster, raising the stakes for the characters' journey.

In summary, raising stakes through dialogue involves highlighting consequences, expressing fear and anxiety, introducing new threats, revealing hidden agendas, escalating conflict, highlighting personal stakes, building tension through subtext, revealing limited time, discussing higher powers or authorities, illustrating growing risks, highlighting moral or ethical dilemmas, creating emotional stakes, increasing scarcity of resources, reflecting character growth, and foreshadowing potential catastrophes. By focusing on these strategies, you can craft dialogue that effectively raises the stakes and keeps the audience engaged and invested in your screenplay.

Character Voices: Crafting Unique Speech Patterns

Creating distinct and unique speech patterns for your characters is essential for making them memorable and believable. Each character should have their own voice that reflects their background, personality, and role in the story. Here are strategies for crafting unique speech patterns for your characters.

Understanding Background and Culture

A character's background and culture significantly influence their speech patterns. Consider their geographical origin, ethnicity, education, and social class when crafting dialogue.

Example: In "The Wire," the dialogue reflects the diverse backgrounds of the characters, with street slang for the drug dealers and formal, bureaucratic language for the police officers.

Reflecting Personality Traits

A character's personality should be evident in their speech. Confident characters might use assertive, direct language, while shy characters might speak more hesitantly or use filler words.

Example: In "Sherlock," Sherlock Holmes's rapid, precise, and often condescending speech reflects his intelligence and arrogance, contrasting with Dr. Watson's more grounded and conversational tone.

Using Unique Vocabulary and Idioms

Characters can have distinctive vocabularies, including unique words, phrases, or idioms they frequently use. This helps differentiate them from others.

Example: In "Parks and Recreation," Ron Swanson's use of terse, no-nonsense language and libertarian catchphrases sets him apart from other characters.

Incorporating Accents and Dialects

Accents and dialects can add authenticity and uniqueness to a character's voice. However, they should be used thoughtfully and accurately to avoid stereotypes.

Example: In "Brave," Merida's Scottish accent and use of Scottish idioms reflect her heritage and distinguish her speech from other Disney princesses.

Varying Sentence Structure

Characters can have different sentence structures based on their thought processes and communication styles. Some might speak in long, complex sentences, while others prefer short, simple statements.

Example: In "Deadwood," Al Swearengen's eloquent, verbose speech contrasts with the more straightforward, blunt dialogue of other characters, reflecting his manipulative and calculating nature.

Utilizing Repetition and Catchphrases

Repetition of certain words or phrases can become a character's signature, making their speech more recognizable and unique.

Example: In "The Simpsons," Homer Simpson's repeated use of "D'oh!" and other catchphrases make his dialogue instantly identifiable.

Adapting to Context and Audience

Characters might adjust their speech depending on who they're talking to and the context of the conversation. This can reveal different facets of their personality.

Example: In "Breaking Bad," Walter White's speech changes from mild-mannered chemistry teacher to the more authoritative and menacing Heisenberg, depending on the situation and who he's addressing.

Reflecting Occupation and Expertise

Characters' professions and areas of expertise can influence their speech. They might use jargon or technical language relevant to their field.

Example: In "The Big Bang Theory," Sheldon Cooper's dialogue is filled with scientific terminology and pedantic corrections, reflecting his background as a physicist.

Creating Speech Idiosyncrasies

Unique speech idiosyncrasies, such as stuttering, frequent use of filler words, or a specific rhythm, can make a character's voice distinct.

Example: In "A Fish Called Wanda," Ken's stutter and Otto's use of misquoted philosophy create memorable and distinct speech patterns.

Developing Consistency

A character's speech patterns should be consistent throughout the story. Inconsistencies can confuse the audience and weaken character development.

Example: In "The Great Gatsby," Jay Gatsby's formal, almost archaic manner of speaking remains consistent, reflecting his constructed persona and aspirations.

Using Silence and Pauses

How a character uses silence and pauses can also define their speech. Strategic pauses can indicate thoughtfulness, hesitation, or emotional weight.

Example: In "No Country for Old Men," Anton Chigurh's deliberate pauses and sparse dialogue create a chilling, methodical presence.

Incorporating Emotional States

A character's emotional state can affect their speech patterns. Anger, fear, excitement, or sadness can change how they communicate, adding depth and realism.

Example: In "Marriage Story," the emotionally charged arguments between Charlie and Nicole reflect their distress and frustration, with rapid, overlapping speech.

Mirroring Psychological Traits

A character's psychological traits can be mirrored in their dialogue. An anxious character might speak quickly and nervously, while a confident character might have a relaxed, assured manner of speaking.

Example: In "Fight Club," Tyler Durden's confident, provocative speech contrasts with the Narrator's more hesitant and confused dialogue, reflecting their psychological states.

Employing Humor and Sarcasm

Characters who frequently use humor, sarcasm, or irony can have distinctive voices that stand out. Their wit can reveal their intelligence, worldview, and coping mechanisms.

Example: In "Iron Man," Tony Stark's sarcastic, quick-witted dialogue is a hallmark of his character, showcasing his intelligence and playful arrogance.

Balancing Show and Tell

While dialogue is important, it should be balanced with actions and body language to fully convey a character's voice. How they speak should be complemented by how they act and react.

Example: In "The Godfather," Michael Corleone's calm, measured speech is often contrasted with his decisive and sometimes violent actions, adding depth to his character.

Allowing Evolution

Characters' speech patterns can evolve over the course of the story, reflecting their growth and changing circumstances. This evolution should feel natural and align with their development.

Example: In "Harry Potter," Hermione Granger's initially formal and bookish speech becomes more relaxed and emotionally expressive as she grows and faces various challenges.

In summary, crafting unique speech patterns involves understanding characters' backgrounds and personalities, reflecting their traits and emotions, using distinctive vocabulary and idioms, incorporating accents and dialects thoughtfully, varying sentence structures, and developing consistent and evolving speech patterns. By focusing on these strategies, you can create memorable and distinct voices that enhance your characters and enrich your screenplay.

The Protagonist's Voice: Defining the Hero

The protagonist's voice is crucial for defining their character and making them relatable and memorable. The way the protagonist speaks reflects their personality, background, motivations, and growth throughout the story. Here are strategies for defining the hero's voice in your screenplay.

Reflecting Personality and Traits

The protagonist's dialogue should reflect their core personality traits, such as confidence, humor, intelligence, or vulnerability. This helps the audience connect with them on a deeper level.

Example: In "Iron Man," Tony Stark's witty, sarcastic dialogue showcases his confidence and playfulness, making his character both charismatic and relatable.

Conveying Background and Experience

The protagonist's speech should hint at their background and life experiences, providing context for their actions and motivations.

Example: In "Good Will Hunting," Will's use of casual, street-smart language reflects his working-class upbringing and contrasts with the more formal speech of the academic characters.

Expressing Motivations and Goals

Dialogue can reveal the protagonist's motivations and goals, making their journey clear to the audience and providing a sense of purpose.

Example: In "Rocky," Rocky Balboa's dialogues about wanting to prove himself as a boxer reveal his deep-seated need for respect and self-worth.

Showing Growth and Development

The protagonist's voice should evolve throughout the story, reflecting their personal growth and the challenges they face. This evolution should be natural and align with their character arc.

Example: In "The Lord of the Rings," Frodo's dialogues change from naive and carefree to more somber and determined as he undertakes the perilous journey to destroy the One Ring.

Balancing Strengths and Flaws

A well-rounded protagonist has both strengths and flaws, which should be evident in their speech. This balance makes them more relatable and believable.

Example: In "Harry Potter," Harry's dialogues often reflect his bravery and loyalty, but also his insecurities and moments of doubt, making him a complex and relatable hero.

Using Consistent Speech Patterns

The protagonist's speech patterns should be consistent, creating a distinct and recognizable voice. This includes their vocabulary, sentence structure, and use of idioms or catchphrases.

Example: In "Sherlock," Sherlock Holmes's rapid, precise, and often condescending speech remains consistent throughout, reflecting his intellect and arrogance.

Incorporating Humor and Wit

If the protagonist has a humorous or witty side, their dialogue should reflect this, adding charm and relatability. This can also provide comic relief in tense moments.

Example: In "Deadpool," Wade Wilson's irreverent, humorous dialogues are a key aspect of his character, providing a unique and entertaining hero voice.

Creating Emotional Depth

The protagonist's voice should convey a range of emotions, from joy and love to fear and anger. This emotional depth makes them more human and relatable.

Example: In "La La Land," Mia's dialogues with Sebastian range from playful and hopeful to frustrated and heartbroken, reflecting the emotional highs and lows of their relationship and her career aspirations.

Highlighting Inner Conflict

The protagonist's inner conflicts and dilemmas can be expressed through dialogue, revealing their struggles and making their journey more compelling.

Example: In "The Dark Knight," Bruce Wayne's dialogues reflect his internal struggle between his desire for a normal life and his duty as Batman, adding depth to his character.

Aligning with Themes

The protagonist's voice should align with the themes of the story, reinforcing the central messages and adding coherence to the narrative.

Example: In "The Pursuit of Happyness," Chris Gardner's dialogues often reflect themes of perseverance and hope, reinforcing the film's message about overcoming adversity.

Using Subtext and Nuance

Subtext in the protagonist's dialogue can add layers of meaning and reveal hidden motivations or feelings, making their voice more complex and engaging.

Example: In "Lost in Translation," Bob Harris's understated dialogues with Charlotte often contain subtext about his dissatisfaction with life and search for connection, adding depth to his character.

Responding to Conflict

The way the protagonist responds to conflict through dialogue can reveal their resilience, resourcefulness, and growth. Their reactions to challenges are crucial for defining their heroism.

Example: In "Die Hard," John McClane's dialogues during crises, filled with wit and determination, showcase his resourcefulness and bravery, defining him as a quintessential action hero.

Reflecting Relationships

The protagonist's voice should change subtly depending on who they are speaking to, reflecting their relationships and dynamics with other characters.

Example: In "The Hunger Games," Katniss Everdeen's dialogues with Peeta are more tender and vulnerable, while her interactions with President Snow are more guarded and defiant, highlighting different facets of her character.

Maintaining Authenticity

Above all, the protagonist's voice should feel authentic and true to their character. This authenticity helps the audience invest in their journey and root for their success.

Example: In "Forrest Gump," Forrest's simple, honest dialogue remains authentic throughout the film, endearing him to the audience and making his journey impactful.

Evolving with the Plot

As the plot progresses, the protagonist's voice should evolve to reflect the changing circumstances and their responses to these events. This evolution keeps their character dynamic and engaging.

Example: In "The Matrix," Neo's dialogue evolves from uncertain and questioning to confident and assertive as he embraces his role as "The One," reflecting his character's transformation.

In summary, defining the protagonist's voice involves reflecting their personality and traits, conveying their background and experiences, expressing their motivations and goals, showing growth and development, balancing strengths and flaws, maintaining consistent speech patterns, incorporating humor and wit, creating emotional depth, highlighting inner conflict, aligning with themes, using subtext and nuance, responding to conflict, reflecting relationships, maintaining authenticity, and evolving with the plot. By focusing on these strategies, you can craft a compelling and memorable hero whose voice resonates with the audience and drives the narrative forward.

The Antagonist's Voice: Crafting the Villain

Crafting the antagonist's voice is crucial for creating a compelling and memorable villain. The way the antagonist speaks can reveal their motivations, personality, and role in the story, making them more nuanced and engaging. Here are strategies for defining the villain's voice in your screenplay.

Reflecting Personality and Traits

The antagonist's dialogue should reflect their core personality traits, such as cunning, arrogance, cruelty, or charisma. This helps the audience understand who they are and why they pose a threat.

Example: In "The Silence of the Lambs," Hannibal Lecter's calm, articulate, and psychologically probing dialogue reflects his intelligence and sinister nature, making him a chilling antagonist.

Conveying Motivations and Goals

Dialogue can reveal the antagonist's motivations and goals, providing insight into why they are in conflict with the protagonist.

Example: In "Black Panther," Erik Killmonger's dialogues about reclaiming his heritage and empowering oppressed people reveal his motivations, making his villainy more complex and relatable.

Expressing Power and Dominance

The antagonist's voice should often convey a sense of power and dominance, reflecting their control over the situation and their threat to the protagonist.

Example: In "The Lion King," Scar's manipulative and condescending dialogue demonstrates his desire for power and control over the Pride Lands.

Using Unique Vocabulary and Speech Patterns

The antagonist's unique vocabulary and speech patterns can set them apart and make their voice distinct. This might include specific jargon, formal or archaic language, or idiosyncratic phrases.

Example: In "The Dark Knight," the Joker's unpredictable, chaotic speech patterns and dark humor make his dialogue instantly recognizable and unsettling.

Creating Contrasts with the Protagonist

The antagonist's dialogue should contrast with the protagonist's, highlighting their opposing viewpoints and approaches. This contrast can emphasize the central conflict.

Example: In "Harry Potter," Voldemort's cold, imperious dialogue contrasts with Harry's more compassionate and determined speech, highlighting their opposing values.

Revealing Ethical or Moral Dilemmas

Antagonists can present ethical or moral dilemmas through their dialogue, challenging the protagonist and adding depth to their character.

Example: In "Avengers: Infinity War," Thanos's dialogues about his belief in balance and the necessity of his actions create a complex moral dilemma, making him a more compelling villain.

Using Subtext and Nuance

Subtext in the antagonist's dialogue can add layers of meaning and reveal hidden motivations or feelings, making their character more complex.

Example: In "No Country for Old Men," Anton Chigurh's cryptic dialogues often contain subtext about fate and morality, adding depth to his character.

Expressing Sadism or Cruelty

If the antagonist has a sadistic or cruel streak, their dialogue should reflect this, showcasing their enjoyment of others' suffering or their lack of empathy.

Example: In "Gladiator," Commodus's dialogues often reveal his cruelty and desire to manipulate and dominate those around him, emphasizing his villainous nature.

Displaying Intelligence and Wit

An intelligent and witty antagonist can be particularly compelling. Their sharp dialogue can make them formidable opponents and add a layer of sophistication to their villainy.

Example: In "Sherlock Holmes," Moriarty's clever, sophisticated dialogue reflects his intelligence and makes him a worthy adversary for Sherlock Holmes.

Highlighting Obsession or Insanity

If the antagonist is driven by obsession or insanity, their dialogue should reflect their unhinged nature, making them unpredictable and dangerous.

Example: In "Se7en," John Doe's methodical, obsession-driven dialogue reveals his twisted logic and moral righteousness, making him a disturbing antagonist.

Creating Psychological Tension

The antagonist's dialogue can create psychological tension, manipulating or intimidating the protagonist and the audience.

Example: In "Inglourious Basterds," Hans Landa's polite yet menacing dialogue during the opening scene creates intense psychological tension, showcasing his manipulative nature.

Expressing Desperation or Fear

In moments of vulnerability, the antagonist's dialogue can reveal their desperation or fear, adding depth and complexity to their character.

Example: In "Star Wars: Return of the Jedi," Emperor Palpatine's dialogue reveals his fear and desperation as Luke Skywalker resists the dark side, adding layers to his character.

Reflecting Themes

The antagonist's voice should align with the themes of the story, reinforcing the central messages and adding coherence to the narrative.

Example: In "The Matrix," Agent Smith's dialogues about the flaws of humanity and the inevitability of the machines' victory reflect the film's themes of control and freedom.

Creating Memorable Quotes

Crafting memorable quotes for the antagonist can make them more impactful and enduring in the audience's mind. These lines should encapsulate their essence and leave a lasting impression.

Example: In "The Dark Knight," the Joker's line, "Why so serious?" becomes iconic, encapsulating his chaotic and menacing nature.

Evolving with the Plot

As the plot progresses, the antagonist's voice may evolve to reflect their changing circumstances and strategies. This evolution keeps their character dynamic and engaging.

Example: In "Breaking Bad," Walter White's transformation into Heisenberg is reflected in his increasingly assertive and menacing dialogue, showcasing his evolution into the antagonist.

Balancing Show and Tell

While dialogue is important, it should be balanced with actions and body language to fully convey the antagonist's character. Their words should be complemented by their behavior and expressions.

Example: In "The Silence of the Lambs," Hannibal Lecter's calm, articulate speech is complemented by his unsettling gaze and precise movements, creating a chilling presence.

In summary, crafting the antagonist's voice involves reflecting their personality and traits, conveying their motivations and goals, expressing power and dominance, using unique vocabulary and speech patterns, creating contrasts with the protagonist, revealing ethical or moral dilemmas, using subtext and nuance, expressing sadism or cruelty, displaying intelligence and wit, highlighting obsession or insanity, creating psychological tension, expressing desperation or fear, reflecting themes, creating memorable quotes, evolving with the plot, and balancing show and tell. By focusing on these strategies, you can create a compelling and memorable villain whose voice adds depth and intensity to your screenplay.

Supporting Characters: Giving Them a Voice

Supporting characters play crucial roles in enriching the narrative, providing depth, and complementing the protagonist's journey. Giving them distinct and authentic voices makes the story more engaging and realistic. Here are strategies for crafting unique voices for supporting characters.

Reflecting Their Roles and Personalities

Supporting characters' voices should reflect their roles in the story and their unique personalities. This differentiation helps the audience understand their contributions to the narrative.

Example: In "The Lord of the Rings," Samwise Gamgee's earnest, loyal dialogue reflects his role as Frodo's steadfast companion, contrasting with Gandalf's wise and authoritative speech.

Using Distinct Speech Patterns

Distinct speech patterns, such as specific vocabulary, sentence structures, and idiomatic expressions, can set supporting characters apart and make them memorable.

Example: In "Forrest Gump," Bubba's dialogue about shrimping is repetitive and focused, reflecting his singular passion and making him stand out.

Highlighting Background and Culture

A character's background and culture can significantly influence their speech. Incorporating regional dialects, cultural references, and unique idioms can add authenticity and depth.

Example: In "Black Panther," Shuri's dialogue includes modern, playful slang that contrasts with the more formal speech of other Wakandan characters, reflecting her youth and technological expertise.

Expressing Relationships with the Protagonist

Dialogue should reflect the nature of the relationship between supporting characters and the protagonist, whether it's supportive, antagonistic, or complex.

Example: In "Good Will Hunting," Chuckie's casual, supportive dialogues with Will highlight their deep friendship, while Sean's more probing and insightful conversations reveal his mentor role.

Balancing Humor and Seriousness

Supporting characters often provide comic relief or moments of seriousness. Their dialogue should balance these elements according to their role in the story.

Example: In "The Avengers," Tony Stark's witty banter contrasts with Natasha Romanoff's more serious and professional dialogue, reflecting their different roles within the team.

Revealing Motivations and Goals

Supporting characters should have their own motivations and goals, which can be revealed through dialogue, adding complexity to their interactions with the protagonist.

Example: In "Harry Potter," Hermione Granger's dialogues about studying and preparing for the future reveal her motivations and add depth to her character.

Using Subtext

Subtext in the dialogue of supporting characters can add layers of meaning and hint at deeper emotions or hidden agendas, making their interactions more intriguing.

Example: In "The Godfather," Tom Hagen's calm, measured dialogues often contain subtext about loyalty and the complexities of his position as the family consigliere.

Creating Consistency

Maintaining consistent speech patterns and vocabulary for supporting characters ensures they remain believable and distinct throughout the story.

Example: In "The Princess Bride," Inigo Montoya's repeated line, "Hello, my name is Inigo Montoya. You killed my father. Prepare to die," reinforces his singular focus on revenge and makes him memorable.

Reflecting Emotional States

Supporting characters' dialogue should reflect their emotional states, whether they are stressed, happy, fearful, or angry, adding depth to their character portrayal.

Example: In "Finding Nemo," Dory's cheerful and forgetful dialogue contrasts with Marlin's anxious and determined speech, highlighting their different emotional states and personalities.

Providing Exposition

Supporting characters often provide necessary exposition in a natural way. Their dialogue can convey important information without feeling forced.

Example: In "Inception," Ariadne's dialogues with Cobb help explain the complex rules of dream-building, providing exposition in an engaging and informative manner.

Showing Character Development

Supporting characters should also experience growth and change. Their evolving dialogue can reflect their development over the course of the story.

Example: In "The Lord of the Rings," Aragorn's dialogue evolves from uncertain and reluctant to confident and kingly, reflecting his growth as a leader.

Balancing Dialogue with Action

While dialogue is important, it should be balanced with actions that reinforce the character's voice and role. What supporting characters do is as important as what they say.

Example: In "The Matrix," Morpheus's philosophical dialogues are complemented by his decisive actions, reinforcing his role as a mentor and leader.

Highlighting Conflicts and Alliances

Supporting characters' dialogues can highlight conflicts and alliances, providing insight into the dynamics of the story's world and the relationships between characters.

Example: In "Game of Thrones," Tyrion Lannister's sharp, insightful dialogues often reveal political conflicts and alliances, adding depth to the story's complex power dynamics.

Creating Memorable Moments

Crafting memorable lines or catchphrases for supporting characters can make them stand out and enhance their impact on the story.

Example: In "Star Wars," Yoda's unique syntax and memorable lines, such as "Do, or do not. There is no try," make him an iconic and enduring character.

Reflecting Their Function in the Plot

Supporting characters often serve specific functions in the plot, such as mentors, comic relief, or antagonists. Their dialogue should reflect their role and contribute to the story's progression.

Example: In "Back to the Future," Doc Brown's enthusiastic, scientific jargon and exclamations like "Great Scott!" highlight his role as the eccentric inventor and mentor to Marty.

Incorporating Humor and Banter

Supporting characters can add humor and lightness to the story. Their dialogues can provide comic relief and balance more serious moments.

Example: In "Guardians of the Galaxy," Rocket Raccoon's sarcastic and irreverent dialogues provide humor and contrast with the more serious characters, adding balance to the team dynamics.

In summary, giving supporting characters a voice involves reflecting their roles and personalities, using distinct speech patterns, highlighting their background and culture, expressing their relationships with the protagonist, balancing humor and seriousness, revealing their motivations and goals, using subtext, maintaining consistency, reflecting emotional states, providing exposition, showing character development, balancing dialogue with action, highlighting conflicts and alliances, creating memorable moments, reflecting their function in the plot, and incorporating humor and banter.

Dialogue in Group Dynamics

Writing dialogue for group dynamics can be challenging but rewarding, as it allows for rich interactions and the development of multiple characters simultaneously. Effective dialogue in group settings should reveal individual personalities, establish relationships, and advance the plot while maintaining clarity and coherence. Here are strategies for crafting compelling group dialogue.

Distinguishing Individual Voices

Ensure that each character in the group has a distinct voice. Their speech patterns, vocabulary, and tone should reflect their unique personalities and backgrounds.

Example: In "The Breakfast Club," each character's dialogue reflects their distinct backgrounds and personalities—Bender's rebellious attitude, Claire's privileged tone, and Brian's academic focus—making the group dynamic rich and varied.

Balancing Dialogue Participation

Distribute dialogue evenly among characters to give each one a presence in the scene. Avoid having one character dominate unless it serves a specific purpose.

Example: In "Ocean's Eleven," the dialogue is balanced among the group members, with each character contributing to the planning and execution of the heist, highlighting their unique skills and personalities.

Reflecting Relationships and Hierarchies

Use dialogue to reflect the relationships and hierarchies within the group. Show respect, rivalry, friendship, or tension through their interactions.

Example: In "The Lord of the Rings: The Fellowship of the Ring," the dialogues among the Fellowship members reveal the hierarchy (with Gandalf and Aragorn often taking leadership roles) and the evolving camaraderie and trust among them.

Managing Interruptions and Overlapping Speech

Group dialogue often includes interruptions and overlapping speech. This can add realism but must be managed carefully to avoid confusion.

Example: In "The Avengers," the group's planning sessions often feature characters talking over each other, especially during heated moments, which reflects their strong personalities and the tension in high-stakes situations.

Highlighting Conflicts and Alliances

Group dynamics are rich with potential for conflict and alliances. Use dialogue to showcase these shifting dynamics, revealing who supports or opposes whom.

Example: In "12 Angry Men," the dialogues among the jurors highlight their conflicts and alliances, with characters like Juror 8 challenging the majority, leading to shifting opinions and alliances.

Using Subtext

Group interactions can be layered with subtext, where characters say one thing but mean another. This adds depth and complexity to the dialogue.

Example: In "Reservoir Dogs," the group's dialogue is filled with subtext about trust and suspicion, particularly as they discuss the botched heist and the potential presence of a traitor among them.

Creating Tension and Resolution

Build tension through group dialogue by escalating conflicts and then resolving them, which can drive the narrative forward and deepen character development.

Example: In "Glengarry Glen Ross," the dialogues among the salesmen escalate tension as they compete for leads, revealing their desperation and ethical boundaries, leading to dramatic resolutions.

Balancing Humor and Seriousness

Mix humor and seriousness in group dialogue to keep the interactions dynamic and engaging. This balance can also highlight different character traits and relationships.

Example: In "Guardians of the Galaxy," the group's dialogue often shifts between humorous banter and serious discussions about their mission, reflecting their diverse personalities and the high stakes of their adventures.

Showing Character Development

Group dialogues should reflect the development of characters over time. As relationships evolve, so should the way characters interact with each other.

Example: In "Stranger Things," the dialogues among the group of kids show their growing maturity and the deepening of their friendships as they face increasingly dangerous situations together.

Maintaining Clarity

Ensure clarity in group dialogues by avoiding too many simultaneous conversations. Use techniques like breaking characters into smaller subgroups or focusing on key exchanges.

Example: In "The Big Bang Theory," group dialogues often involve multiple conversations, but the focus shifts between pairs or small groups to maintain clarity while showcasing the dynamics.

Incorporating Body Language and Actions

Dialogue in group settings should be complemented by body language and actions. Characters' physical interactions can add layers to their spoken words.

Example: In "The Godfather," the group meetings often feature subtle body language and actions—like passing drinks, lighting cigarettes, or shifting glances—that add depth to the dialogue and reveal underlying tensions.

Foreshadowing and Plot Advancement

Use group dialogue to foreshadow future events and advance the plot. Characters can discuss plans, express concerns, or reveal critical information that propels the narrative.

Example: In "The Goonies," the group's dialogue about their treasure hunt plans and the challenges they anticipate serves to foreshadow upcoming adventures and plot twists.

Managing Different Perspectives

Group dialogues are an opportunity to showcase different perspectives on a situation. Allow each character to voice their opinion, reflecting their unique viewpoint and adding to the narrative's complexity.

Example: In "Jurassic Park," the dialogue among the experts and park staff about the ethics and safety of cloning dinosaurs presents multiple perspectives, enriching the story's moral and scientific debates.

Using Silence and Pauses

Strategic use of silence and pauses in group dialogues can emphasize key moments, create tension, or highlight the weight of a situation.

Example: In "12 Angry Men," the use of silence and pauses after key arguments heightens the tension and allows the impact of the words to sink in, emphasizing the gravity of their decision.

Creating Memorable Group Interactions

Crafting memorable lines or exchanges within the group can make scenes stand out and leave a lasting impression on the audience.

Example: In "The Breakfast Club," the group's dialogue during their circle confessions creates a memorable and poignant moment, revealing their vulnerabilities and forming a deeper connection.

In summary, writing effective group dialogue involves distinguishing individual voices, balancing participation, reflecting relationships and hierarchies, managing interruptions, highlighting conflicts and alliances, using subtext, creating tension and resolution, balancing humor and seriousness, showing character development, maintaining clarity, incorporating body language and actions, foreshadowing and advancing the plot, managing different perspectives, using silence and pauses, and creating memorable interactions. By focusing on these strategies, you can craft dynamic and engaging group dialogues that enrich your screenplay and deepen character interactions.

Interpersonal Conflict: Dialogue in Arguments

Crafting dialogue for arguments and interpersonal conflicts is an essential skill for screenwriters, as it adds tension, drives character development, and propels the narrative forward. Effective dialogue in arguments should be emotionally charged, reveal character traits, and reflect the stakes of the conflict. Here are strategies for writing compelling dialogue in arguments.

Reflecting Emotional Intensity

Dialogue in arguments should capture the emotional intensity of the conflict. Characters might speak faster, raise their voices, or use more emphatic language.

Example: In "Marriage Story," the intense argument between Charlie and Nicole is raw and emotionally charged, with raised voices and rapid exchanges reflecting their deep-seated frustrations.

Using Interruptions and Overlapping Speech

Arguments often involve interruptions and overlapping speech, which can add realism and urgency to the dialogue.

Example: In "The Social Network," the heated exchanges between Mark Zuckerberg and Eduardo Saverin include frequent interruptions and overlapping speech, heightening the tension and chaos of their falling out.

Revealing Character Traits and Motivations

Dialogue during arguments can reveal key character traits, motivations, and vulnerabilities, making the characters more complex and relatable.

Example: In "A Few Good Men," the courtroom argument between Lt. Kaffee and Col. Jessup reveals Kaffee's determination and Jessup's arrogance and sense of superiority.

Escalating Conflict

Start the argument with a smaller disagreement that escalates into a more significant conflict. This escalation can make the dialogue more dynamic and engaging.

Example: In "La La Land," the argument between Mia and Sebastian starts with a discussion about their careers but escalates into a deeper conflict about their relationship and priorities.

Using Subtext and Hidden Meanings

Subtext can add depth to arguments, with characters saying one thing but implying another, reflecting deeper issues and tensions.

Example: In "The Godfather," Michael Corleone's argument with his brother Fredo is laden with subtext about loyalty and betrayal, revealing the underlying tensions in their relationship.

Highlighting Power Dynamics

Arguments can highlight power dynamics between characters, showing who has control, who feels marginalized, and how they navigate these dynamics.

Example: In "Whiplash," the arguments between Andrew and Fletcher reveal the power struggle between the student and the tyrannical teacher, with Fletcher often dominating the exchanges.

Using Repetition for Emphasis

Repetition of certain words or phrases can emphasize key points and heighten the emotional impact of the argument.

Example: In "Revolutionary Road," the repeated accusations and phrases in the arguments between Frank and April Wheeler highlight their frustrations and the repetitive nature of their conflicts.

Balancing Dialogue with Action

Arguments should be balanced with actions and body language. Characters might pace, gesture, or physically react, adding a layer of realism and intensity.

Example: In "Inglourious Basterds," the argument between Lt. Aldo Raine and Sgt. Wilhelm is intensified by their physical movements and actions, such as Aldo's aggressive stance and gestures.

Exploring Ethical and Moral Dilemmas

Arguments often arise from ethical or moral dilemmas. Characters can debate these issues, revealing their values and deepening the conflict.

Example: In "The Dark Knight," the argument between Batman and Joker about the nature of humanity and morality adds depth to their conflict and reveals their opposing worldviews.

Using Pauses and Silence

Strategic pauses and moments of silence can add tension and emphasize the weight of the argument. Silence can be as powerful as spoken words.

Example: In "Manchester by the Sea," the pauses and silences during arguments between Lee and Randi Chandler add emotional weight and tension to their exchanges.

Incorporating Flashbacks or References

Characters might reference past events or bring up old grievances during arguments, adding layers to the conflict and revealing backstory.

Example: In "Silver Linings Playbook," the argument between Pat and his parents frequently references past incidents, adding context and depth to their ongoing conflicts.

Reflecting Internal Conflict

Dialogue in arguments can also reflect a character's internal conflict, showing their doubts, fears, and struggles.

Example: In "Good Will Hunting," the argument between Will and Sean reveals Will's internal conflicts and fears about intimacy and vulnerability.

Using Metaphors and Analogies

Characters might use metaphors or analogies to articulate their points during arguments, making their dialogue more vivid and impactful.

Example: In "Erin Brockovich," Erin's argument with Ed Masry includes powerful analogies and metaphors to convey her passion and frustration about the case and her personal struggles.

Creating Dramatic Irony

Arguments can be enriched by dramatic irony, where the audience knows more than the characters, adding layers of tension and anticipation.

Example: In "Breaking Bad," the argument between Walter White and Skyler about his drug activities is charged with dramatic irony, as the audience knows more about Walter's true nature and activities than Skyler does.

Resolving or Deepening the Conflict

The conclusion of the argument should either resolve the conflict or deepen it, driving the narrative forward and affecting the characters' relationships.

Example: In "Frozen," the argument between Elsa and Anna about Elsa's powers initially deepens the conflict and sets off a chain of events that drive the plot forward.

In summary, writing effective dialogue for arguments involves reflecting emotional intensity, using interruptions and overlapping speech, revealing character traits and motivations, escalating conflict, using subtext, highlighting power dynamics, using repetition for emphasis, balancing dialogue with action, exploring ethical and moral dilemmas, using pauses and silence, incorporating flashbacks or references, reflecting internal conflict, using metaphors and analogies, creating dramatic irony, and resolving or deepening the conflict. By focusing on these strategies, you can craft compelling and realistic arguments that enhance your screenplay and develop your characters.

Dialogue that Reveals Character Flaws

Revealing character flaws through dialogue is an effective way to add depth and complexity to your characters. Flaws make characters relatable and human, driving their personal growth and the overall narrative. Here are strategies for using dialogue to reveal character flaws in your screenplay.

Self-Deprecation and Insecurity

Characters can reveal their flaws through self-deprecating remarks or expressions of insecurity. This makes them relatable and vulnerable.

Example: In "Bridget Jones's Diary," Bridget often speaks about her weight, lack of relationship success, and general clumsiness, revealing her insecurities and flaws.

Defensiveness and Blame

A character who becomes defensive or shifts blame onto others during conversations can reveal flaws such as insecurity, guilt, or an unwillingness to take responsibility.

Example: In "Breaking Bad," Walter White's defensiveness and tendency to blame others, like his partner Jesse, reveal his pride and moral corruption.

Exaggeration and Boasting

Characters who exaggerate their achievements or boast about their abilities can reveal flaws such as arrogance, insecurity, or a need for validation.

Example: In "The Great Gatsby," Gatsby's grandiose stories about his wealth and accomplishments highlight his insecurity and desire to impress others.

Hypocrisy and Contradiction

Characters can reveal flaws by saying one thing but doing another, or by holding contradictory beliefs and behaviors, showcasing their hypocrisy.

Example: In "Mad Men," Don Draper's dialogues about the importance of family and integrity starkly contrast with his actions, such as infidelity and deceit, revealing his hypocrisy.

Judgment and Prejudice

Dialogue that includes judgmental or prejudiced remarks can reveal flaws such as narrow-mindedness, intolerance, or superiority complexes.

Example: In "To Kill a Mockingbird," various characters' dialogues reveal their racial prejudices and societal flaws, such as Bob Ewell's blatant racism.

Overconfidence and Recklessness

Characters who display overconfidence or take reckless risks in their dialogue can reveal flaws such as arrogance, lack of foresight, or impulsiveness.

Example: In "Top Gun," Maverick's cocky dialogue about his flying skills reveals his overconfidence and recklessness, which are central to his character arc.

Manipulation and Deceit

Characters who use manipulative or deceitful language reveal flaws such as dishonesty, selfishness, or a lack of empathy.

Example: In "House of Cards," Frank Underwood's manipulative dialogues and deceitful strategies showcase his ruthless ambition and moral corruption.

Avoidance and Procrastination

Characters who frequently make excuses or avoid addressing issues in their dialogue reveal flaws such as laziness, fear, or lack of responsibility.

Example: In "The Big Lebowski," The Dude's laid-back, avoidant dialogues reflect his tendency to procrastinate and avoid responsibility.

Short Temper and Impatience

A short temper or impatience in dialogue can reveal flaws such as anger issues, lack of self-control, or frustration.

Example: In "The Wolf of Wall Street," Jordan Belfort's impatient and often explosive dialogues with his colleagues reveal his volatile nature and underlying insecurity.

Jealousy and Envy

Dialogue that expresses jealousy or envy can reveal flaws such as insecurity, inferiority complexes, or resentment.

Example: In "Amadeus," Salieri's envious dialogues about Mozart's talent highlight his deep-seated jealousy and sense of inadequacy.

Overly Critical and Judgmental

Characters who frequently criticize or judge others in their dialogue reveal flaws such as perfectionism, insecurity, or a superiority complex.

Example: In "Whiplash," Fletcher's harsh, critical dialogues with his students reveal his perfectionism and abusive tendencies.

Naivety and Gullibility

Dialogue that shows a character's naivety or gullibility can reveal flaws such as inexperience, lack of judgment, or overly trusting nature.

Example: In "Forrest Gump," Forrest's simple, trusting dialogues reveal his naivety and innocence, which are central to his character.

Fear and Paranoia

Characters who express excessive fear or paranoia in their dialogue reveal flaws such as anxiety, lack of trust, or past trauma.

Example: In "A Beautiful Mind," John Nash's paranoid dialogues reflect his struggle with schizophrenia and his deep-seated fears.

Stubbornness and Rigidity

Dialogue that shows stubbornness or rigidity can reveal flaws such as inflexibility, unwillingness to compromise, or arrogance.

Example: In "Up," Carl's stubborn dialogues about his house and the past reveal his rigidity and reluctance to move on, which he eventually overcomes.

Self-Righteousness and Moral Superiority

Characters who speak with a tone of self-righteousness or moral superiority reveal flaws such as arrogance, lack of empathy, or hypocrisy.

Example: In "Les Misérables," Inspector Javert's self-righteous dialogues about law and order reveal his moral rigidity and inability to see shades of gray.

Lack of Confidence and Self-Doubt

Dialogue that expresses lack of confidence or self-doubt can reveal flaws such as insecurity, fear of failure, or low self-esteem.

Example: In "The King's Speech," King George VI's dialogues filled with hesitation and stammering reveal his lack of confidence and self-doubt, which he strives to overcome.

In summary, revealing character flaws through dialogue involves using self-deprecation, defensiveness, exaggeration, hypocrisy, judgment, overconfidence, manipulation, avoidance, short temper, jealousy, criticism, naivety, fear, stubbornness, self-righteousness, and lack of confidence. By focusing on these strategies, you can create rich, multidimensional characters whose flaws make them more relatable and drive their development throughout your screenplay.

Expository Dialogue: Balancing Information and Flow

Expository dialogue is essential for providing necessary information to the audience, but it must be balanced with natural flow to avoid feeling forced or clunky. The goal is to deliver exposition seamlessly within the narrative while maintaining engaging and believable dialogue. Here are strategies for balancing information and flow in expository dialogue.

Integrate Exposition Naturally

Incorporate exposition into conversations that feel natural and relevant to the characters' current situation, making the information part of their normal interactions.

Example: In "Inception," the character of Ariadne learns about the rules of the dream world through natural conversations with Cobb, who acts as a mentor explaining the concepts as they walk through a city.

Show, Don't Tell

Whenever possible, show the information visually or through actions, and use dialogue to complement or clarify what is being shown, rather than relying solely on words.

Example: In "Jurassic Park," the tour of the park and the interactive DNA presentation provide visual exposition about how the dinosaurs were created, while characters' dialogues add context and details.

Use Subtext

Deliver exposition through subtext, where characters imply information without stating it directly. This makes the dialogue more engaging and less obvious.

Example: In "The Matrix," Morpheus's cryptic dialogue about reality and the Matrix hints at deeper truths, encouraging Neo (and the audience) to seek out more information.

Incorporate Conflict

Embed exposition within conflicts or arguments between characters, making the exchange more dynamic and engaging while revealing necessary information.

Example: In "The Social Network," the legal depositions reveal the backstory of Facebook's creation through conflicting testimonies, making the exposition dramatic and engaging.

Utilize Character Relationships

Deliver exposition through relationships, where characters naturally share information based on their roles and connections, such as a mentor explaining to a student or a parent to a child.

Example: In "Harry Potter and the Sorcerer's Stone," Hagrid explains the wizarding world to Harry, who is new to it, making the exposition feel natural and necessary.

Break It Up

Avoid long, uninterrupted expository monologues. Break up the information into smaller pieces, interspersed with actions, reactions, and other dialogue to maintain the flow.

Example: In "Blade Runner," the exposition about replicants and their lifespan is broken up through various scenes and dialogues, making it more digestible and less overwhelming.

Use Questions and Curiosity

Have a character who is new to the world or situation ask questions, prompting others to provide the needed exposition. This technique helps to keep the dialogue natural and interactive.

Example: In "The Hunger Games," Katniss's questions about the Capitol and the games allow other characters to explain these elements naturally within the conversation.

Make It Character-Driven

Ensure that the exposition reflects the character's voice and personality. Characters should explain things in ways that align with their traits and experiences, making the dialogue feel authentic.

Example: In "Guardians of the Galaxy," Rocket Raccoon's sarcastic and cynical explanations about the galaxy's underworld fit his character perfectly, making the exposition entertaining.

Utilize Urgency

Deliver exposition in moments of urgency or high stakes, where characters must explain quickly to move the plot forward, making the information feel necessary and immediate.

Example: In "Edge of Tomorrow," the rapid explanations about the time loop by Sergeant Rita Vrataski to Major Cage are urgent and critical, fitting the high-stakes context of the story.

Add Humor

Incorporate humor into expository dialogue to make the information more engaging and less dry. Characters can use jokes, sarcasm, or witty remarks to convey necessary details.

Example: In "The Big Short," the film uses humorous and unconventional methods, such as celebrity cameos explaining financial concepts, to make complex exposition more entertaining.

Anchor to Visuals

Pair expository dialogue with relevant visuals that reinforce the information being provided, creating a more immersive and understandable experience.

Example: In "Interstellar," the explanations about black holes and time dilation are paired with visual simulations and diagrams, helping to clarify complex scientific concepts.

Reflect Emotional Stakes

Tie exposition to the characters' emotional stakes and motivations, making the information feel more relevant and impactful to the audience.

Example: In "Titanic," the exposition about the ship's design and potential risks is tied to the characters' concerns and fears, adding emotional weight to the technical details.

Use Flashbacks or Memories

Deliver exposition through flashbacks or characters' memories, providing context and backstory in a visually engaging way that complements the dialogue.

Example: In "The Godfather Part II," the flashbacks to Vito Corleone's past provide rich exposition about the family's history, intertwined with dialogues that reveal more about his character.

Employ Indirect Dialogue

Characters can reveal information indirectly, through hints, implications, or partial explanations, encouraging the audience to piece together the details.

Example: In "Tinker Tailor Soldier Spy," the dialogue often provides cryptic clues and partial information, reflecting the complexity and secrecy of the espionage world.

Create Tension and Mystery

Introduce exposition gradually and create a sense of mystery or tension around the information, making the audience eager to learn more as the story unfolds.

Example: In "Lost," the gradual revelation of the island's mysteries through character dialogues and discoveries keeps the audience engaged and curious.

In summary, balancing information and flow in expository dialogue involves integrating exposition naturally, showing rather than telling, using subtext, incorporating conflict, utilizing character relationships, breaking up information, using questions and curiosity, making it character-driven, utilizing urgency, adding humor, anchoring to visuals, reflecting emotional stakes, using flashbacks or memories, employing indirect dialogue, and creating tension and mystery. By focusing on these strategies, you can deliver essential information seamlessly while maintaining engaging and natural dialogue.

Internal Dialogue: Revealing Thoughts

Internal dialogue is a powerful tool for revealing a character's inner thoughts, emotions, and conflicts. It provides insight into their motivations and fears, adding depth to their character. Here are strategies for effectively incorporating internal dialogue in your screenplay.

Using Voiceover

Voiceover is a common technique for internal dialogue, allowing the audience to hear the character's thoughts directly. This can be especially effective in revealing motivations and emotional states.

Example: In "Fight Club," the Narrator's voiceover provides a window into his thoughts, revealing his dissatisfaction with his life and the emergence of his alter ego, Tyler Durden.

Stream of Consciousness

A stream of consciousness approach can convey the character's thoughts in a raw, unfiltered manner, reflecting their mental state and inner turmoil.

Example: In "Requiem for a Dream," the fragmented and chaotic internal dialogue of the characters reflects their psychological decline and addiction.

Contrasting Internal and External Dialogue

Contrast internal dialogue with what the character says aloud. This can highlight their true feelings and conflicts, especially when they're hiding something from others.

Example: In "Dexter," Dexter Morgan's internal dialogue reveals his dark thoughts and true nature, which contrasts sharply with his calm and amiable external demeanor.

Flashbacks and Memories

Use internal dialogue to introduce flashbacks or memories, providing context and backstory that explain a character's current actions and emotions.

Example: In "Slumdog Millionaire," Jamal's internal dialogue and flashbacks to his childhood explain his motivations and how his life experiences help him answer the quiz questions.

Inner Monologues

An inner monologue can provide a deep dive into a character's psyche, allowing them to reflect on their experiences and emotions in a detailed and contemplative manner.

Example: In "Taxi Driver," Travis Bickle's inner monologues reveal his isolation, anger, and descent into madness, providing insight into his increasingly erratic behavior.

Juxtaposition with Visuals

Pair internal dialogue with visuals that either complement or contrast the character's thoughts. This can add layers of meaning and enhance the storytelling.

Example: In "American Beauty," Lester Burnham's internal dialogue about his mundane life is juxtaposed with visually striking images of his fantasies, highlighting his inner dissatisfaction.

Emotional Revelations

Use internal dialogue to reveal a character's deepest emotions, fears, and desires, adding depth and making them more relatable to the audience.

Example: In "Eternal Sunshine of the Spotless Mind," Joel's internal dialogue reveals his longing and heartbreak as he undergoes the procedure to erase his memories of Clementine.

Exploring Dilemmas and Decisions

Internal dialogue is effective for exploring a character's dilemmas and decision-making processes, showing their reasoning and internal conflicts.

Example: In "The Hunger Games," Katniss Everdeen's internal dialogue reveals her strategic thinking and moral dilemmas as she navigates the deadly arena.

Reflecting Character Growth

As the character evolves, their internal dialogue should reflect their growth and changing perspectives, showing how they've been affected by the story's events.

Example: In "The Shawshank Redemption," Andy Dufresne's internal dialogue evolves from despair to hope, reflecting his changing outlook on life and his eventual escape plan.

Subtext and Hidden Thoughts

Internal dialogue can reveal subtext, showing what a character truly thinks or feels beneath their outward actions and words.

Example: In "The Great Gatsby," Nick Carraway's internal dialogue often reveals his judgments and suspicions about the people around him, adding depth to his observations.

Building Suspense

Use internal dialogue to build suspense by revealing a character's fears or predictions about what might happen next, creating anticipation for the audience.

Example: In "Gone Girl," Amy's internal dialogue about her elaborate plan to frame Nick adds suspense and tension, as the audience gains insight into her manipulative mind.

Balancing Show and Tell

While internal dialogue is a form of telling, it should be balanced with showing through actions and visuals, ensuring the story remains dynamic and engaging.

Example: In "Stranger Than Fiction," Harold Crick's internal dialogue is balanced with visuals of his mundane life and the disruptions caused by the narrative voice, blending show and tell effectively.

Foreshadowing

Internal dialogue can foreshadow future events or conflicts, giving the audience hints about what's to come and adding layers of anticipation.

Example: In "A Clockwork Orange," Alex's internal dialogue foreshadows his violent tendencies and future conflicts, setting the stage for the story's unfolding events.

Expressing Regret and Reflection

Characters can use internal dialogue to express regret or reflect on past actions, providing insight into their remorse and potential for redemption.

Example: In "The Godfather Part II," Michael Corleone's internal reflections on his actions and decisions reveal his growing regret and the emotional toll of his ruthless pursuit of power.

Contrasting Internal Chaos with External Calm

Show a stark contrast between a character's chaotic internal dialogue and their calm exterior, highlighting their internal struggle and the facade they maintain.

Example: In "Black Swan," Nina's calm and controlled exterior contrasts with her frantic and paranoid internal dialogue, reflecting her psychological breakdown.

In summary, effectively revealing thoughts through internal dialogue involves using voiceover, stream of consciousness, contrasting internal and external dialogue, flashbacks and memories, inner monologues, juxtaposition with visuals, emotional revelations, exploring dilemmas and decisions, reflecting character growth, revealing subtext and hidden thoughts, building suspense, balancing show and tell, foreshadowing, expressing regret and reflection, and contrasting internal chaos with external calm. By focusing on these strategies, you can create rich, engaging internal dialogue that adds depth to your characters and enhances your screenplay.

Monologues: Crafting Powerful Soliloquies

Monologues and soliloquies are powerful tools in screenwriting that allow characters to express their innermost thoughts, emotions, and motivations directly to the audience. Crafting effective monologues requires careful attention to language, structure, and the character's voice. Here are strategies for creating compelling monologues and soliloquies.

Establishing Context

Set the context for the monologue by ensuring the audience understands why the character is speaking. The situation should warrant a deeper exploration of the character's thoughts and feelings.

Example: In "Hamlet," Hamlet's "To be, or not to be" soliloquy is set in a moment of profound existential crisis, providing the context for his deep philosophical musings.

Defining Purpose

A monologue should have a clear purpose, whether it's to reveal a character's inner conflict, express a deep-seated emotion, or advance the plot. Define what the monologue is meant to achieve.

Example: In "The Great Dictator," Charlie Chaplin's final speech serves to convey a powerful message about humanity, freedom, and unity, driving home the film's central themes.

Reflecting Character Voice

Ensure that the monologue reflects the character's unique voice and personality. The language, tone, and style should be consistent with how the character speaks throughout the story.

Example: In "Good Will Hunting," Will's monologue about the imperfections of love and relationships reflects his raw, honest, and often guarded nature, staying true to his character.

Building Emotional Arc

A powerful monologue often has an emotional arc, starting from one point and building towards a climax. This progression keeps the audience engaged and creates a more impactful experience.

Example: In "Network," Howard Beale's "I'm mad as hell" monologue starts with frustration and builds to an impassioned outcry, reflecting his growing anger and desperation.

Using Imagery and Metaphors

Rich imagery and metaphors can enhance a monologue, making it more vivid and memorable. These elements add depth and layers of meaning to the character's words.

Example: In "A Streetcar Named Desire," Blanche DuBois's monologue about her past is filled with poetic imagery and metaphors, revealing her fragility and longing for beauty.

Balancing Length and Pacing

Monologues should be long enough to explore the character's thoughts but not so long that they lose the audience's attention. Pay attention to pacing to maintain engagement.

Example: In "Pulp Fiction," Jules Winnfield's monologue about the Ezekiel 25:17 passage is concise yet powerful, delivering a significant character revelation without overstaying its welcome.

Incorporating Subtext

Subtext adds depth to a monologue, allowing the audience to infer more than what is explicitly stated. This can make the monologue more engaging and thought-provoking.

Example: In "American Beauty," Lester Burnham's monologue about his newfound freedom has layers of subtext about his midlife crisis and dissatisfaction with suburban life.

Highlighting Conflict and Resolution

A compelling monologue often explores an internal or external conflict, moving towards some form of resolution or revelation. This journey can be emotionally satisfying for the audience.

Example: In "12 Angry Men," Juror No. 8's monologue about reasonable doubt explores the conflict of justice versus prejudice, leading to a pivotal moment of resolution in the jury's deliberations.

Creating Authenticity

Ensure the monologue feels authentic and believable. The character's emotions and thoughts should resonate as genuine and true to their experiences and personality.

Example: In "Moonlight," Kevin's monologue to Chiron about their shared past and Kevin's own struggles feels deeply authentic, rooted in their personal history and emotions.

Addressing the Audience

In some cases, the character might break the fourth wall and address the audience directly. This can create a more intimate and engaging connection with the viewers.

Example: In "Ferris Bueller's Day Off," Ferris frequently addresses the audience directly, making them complicit in his adventures and providing insight into his carefree philosophy.

Using Silence and Pauses

Strategic use of silence and pauses can add weight to certain parts of a monologue, emphasizing important points and allowing the audience to absorb the character's words.

Example: In "The Shawshank Redemption," Red's parole hearing monologue uses pauses effectively, reflecting his disillusionment and the gravity of his words about institutionalization.

Evolving with the Plot

Monologues should align with the character's development and the plot's progression. They should reflect the character's current state and contribute to their arc.

Example: In "The Dark Knight," the Joker's monologues evolve with his chaotic plans, reflecting his philosophy and deepening the conflict with Batman.

Revealing Inner Thoughts

Soliloquies are particularly effective for revealing a character's innermost thoughts and struggles, providing insight into their motivations and emotions that other characters might not see.

Example: In "Breaking Bad," Walter White's soliloquies reveal his internal justifications and the transformation of his moral compass, giving the audience a deeper understanding of his descent into criminality.

Creating Memorable Lines

Crafting memorable lines or phrases within the monologue can make it more impactful and enduring in the audience's mind. These lines often encapsulate key themes or emotions.

Example: In "The Godfather," Michael Corleone's monologue about his family's criminal empire contains memorable lines that highlight the themes of power and loyalty.

Aligning with Themes

Ensure that the monologue aligns with the overall themes of the story, reinforcing the central messages and adding coherence to the narrative.

Example: In "Dead Poets Society," John Keating's monologues about seizing the day and the importance of poetry align with the film's themes of individualism and the power of art.

In summary, crafting powerful soliloquies and monologues involves establishing context, defining purpose, reflecting character voice, building an emotional arc, using imagery and metaphors, balancing length and pacing, incorporating subtext, highlighting conflict and resolution, creating authenticity, addressing the audience, using silence and pauses, evolving with the plot, revealing inner thoughts, creating memorable lines, and aligning with themes. By focusing on these strategies, you can create monologues that deeply resonate with the audience and enrich your screenplay.

Silence and Pauses: Using What's Not Said

Silence and pauses in dialogue are powerful tools that can add depth, tension, and emotional weight to a scene. They allow characters to communicate without words, often revealing more than spoken dialogue can. Here are strategies for effectively using silence and pauses in your screenplay.

Creating Tension

Silence can heighten tension, especially in scenes where conflict is brewing or a significant revelation is about to occur. The lack of dialogue can make the audience anticipate what will happen next.

Example: In "No Country for Old Men," the silent moments between Anton Chigurh and his victims create intense suspense, making the impending violence even more unnerving.

Reflecting Internal Conflict

Pauses and silence can reflect a character's internal conflict, allowing the audience to sense their hesitation, doubt, or turmoil without explicit dialogue.

Example: In "Breaking Bad," the moments of silence between Walter White and his wife Skyler convey their deepening rift and Walter's internal struggle with his criminal actions.

Building Anticipation

Strategic pauses before revealing critical information can build anticipation and keep the audience on edge, enhancing the impact of the revelation.

Example: In "The Dark Knight," the Joker's deliberate pauses during his monologues create suspense and make his eventual words more impactful.

Emphasizing Emotions

Silence can emphasize a character's emotional state, such as grief, shock, or contemplation, making the moment more poignant and relatable.

Example: In "Up," the silent montage of Carl and Ellie's life together powerfully conveys their love and loss, evoking deep emotions without a single word spoken.

Creating Realism

In real-life conversations, people often pause to think, react, or process their emotions. Incorporating these natural pauses can make dialogue feel more realistic and authentic.

Example: In "Manchester by the Sea," the awkward silences and pauses between characters reflect the real and raw nature of their grief and interpersonal dynamics.

Conveying Unspoken Thoughts

Silence can convey what characters are unwilling or unable to say aloud, hinting at unspoken thoughts and feelings that add layers to the narrative.

Example: In "Lost in Translation," the quiet moments between Bob and Charlotte convey their unspoken connection and the complexities of their emotions.

Highlighting Power Dynamics

Pauses and silence can highlight power dynamics in a scene, showing who is in control and who is feeling vulnerable or intimidated.

Example: In "The Godfather," the silent, intense moments between Michael Corleone and his adversaries often underscore his dominance and the tension in their interactions.

Using Non-Verbal Cues

Accompany silences with meaningful non-verbal cues, such as facial expressions, body language, or actions, to convey emotions and thoughts without dialogue.

Example: In "A Quiet Place," the characters' non-verbal communication, such as sign language and expressive glances, effectively conveys their fear and resolve in a world where silence is crucial for survival.

Allowing Time for Reflection

Pauses give characters and the audience time to reflect on significant events or revelations, adding depth and allowing the emotional weight to settle in.

Example: In "Schindler's List," the silent contemplation of Oskar Schindler as he realizes the impact of his actions provides a powerful moment of reflection and emotional resonance.

Indicating Reluctance or Fear

Silence can indicate a character's reluctance or fear to speak, revealing their vulnerability or the gravity of the situation.

Example: In "12 Years a Slave," the silences during Solomon Northup's experiences of brutality and dehumanization often speak louder than words, conveying the horror and his internal struggle.

Creating Contrast

Contrasting moments of silence with bursts of dialogue can make the spoken words more impactful and highlight the significance of what is being said.

Example: In "Pulp Fiction," the quiet moments before and after Jules's philosophical speech amplify the intensity and gravity of his words.

Enhancing Dramatic Impact

Well-placed pauses can enhance the dramatic impact of key moments, making the audience hang on to every word and action.

Example: In "The Social Network," the pauses during Mark Zuckerberg's depositions underscore the tension and gravity of the legal battles and personal betrayals being discussed.

Building Relationships

Silence can reveal the nature of relationships, whether it's comfortable silence between close friends or tense silence between adversaries.

Example: In "Before Sunrise," the comfortable silences between Jesse and Celine highlight their growing connection and mutual understanding.

Reflecting Cultural Norms

Incorporate cultural norms around silence and communication, as different cultures have different attitudes towards pauses in conversation, which can add authenticity to characters and settings.

Example: In "Lost in Translation," the cultural differences in communication styles between the American and Japanese characters are highlighted through their use of silence and pauses.

Conveying Desperation

Silence can convey a character's desperation or resignation, showing that they are at a loss for words or unable to express their feelings.

Example: In "Cast Away," the moments of silence as Chuck Noland contemplates his isolation and desperation on the deserted island powerfully convey his plight.

In summary, using silence and pauses effectively involves creating tension, reflecting internal conflict, building anticipation, emphasizing emotions, creating realism, conveying unspoken thoughts, highlighting power dynamics, using non-verbal cues, allowing time for reflection, indicating reluctance or fear, creating contrast, enhancing dramatic impact, building relationships, reflecting cultural norms, and conveying desperation. By focusing on these strategies, you can harness the power of what's not said to add depth, tension, and emotional resonance to your screenplay.

Dialogue Tags: Managing 'Said' and Alternatives

Dialogue tags are essential for clarifying who is speaking in a conversation. While "said" is the most common and unobtrusive tag, varying your tags can add nuance and emotion to dialogue. However, overusing alternatives can become distracting. Here are strategies for managing dialogue tags effectively in your screenplay.

Using 'Said' as a Default

"Said" is almost invisible to readers, making it a reliable default tag. It doesn't draw attention away from the dialogue and is useful for maintaining a smooth reading flow.

Example:

"I don't think this is a good idea," John said.

Incorporating Action Tags

Action tags replace or complement dialogue tags by describing what the character is doing while speaking. This adds context and can show emotions or actions.

Example:

"I don't think this is a good idea." John folded his arms across his chest.

Using Character Names and Pronouns

When a conversation involves only two characters, you can sometimes omit dialogue tags after establishing who is speaking. Alternatively, use character names or pronouns to clarify.

Example:

"I don't think this is a good idea," John said. "Why not?" Mary asked.

Varying Dialogue Tags

Occasionally use alternatives to "said" to convey specific emotions or tones, but do so sparingly to avoid distracting the reader.

Example:

"I don't think this is a good idea," John whispered.

Contextual Clues

Use the context of the conversation or setting to indicate who is speaking without relying on tags.

Example:

John looked around nervously. "I don't think this is a good idea."

Balancing Dialogue and Tags

Balance dialogue and tags to ensure clarity without overwhelming the reader with unnecessary tags or actions.

Example:

"I don't think this is a good idea," John said, glancing at the darkened alley. "It looks dangerous."

Expressing Emotion through Dialogue

Use the dialogue itself to convey emotion, reducing the need for explanatory tags.

Example:

"I don't think this is a good idea," John said, his voice trembling.

Avoiding Overly Complex Tags

Avoid complex or overly descriptive tags that can interrupt the flow of dialogue. Simplicity often works best.

Example:

"I don't think this is a good idea," John said nervously.

Using Tags for Pacing

Tags can be used to control the pacing of dialogue. Pauses and breaks can add tension or give the reader time to absorb important information.

Example:

"I don't think this is a good idea," John said. He paused, then added, "It looks dangerous."

Showing Character Relationships

Dialogue tags and actions can reveal relationships and dynamics between characters.

Example:

"I don't think this is a good idea," John said, looking to Mary for reassurance.

Integrating Internal Thoughts

Combine dialogue tags with internal thoughts to provide deeper insight into a character's mind.

Example:

"I don't think this is a good idea," John said. He couldn't shake the feeling that something was terribly wrong.

Alternating Tags and No Tags

Alternate between using tags and omitting them, especially in longer exchanges between two characters, to maintain clarity without becoming repetitive.

Example:

"I don't think this is a good idea," John said. "Why not?" "It looks dangerous."

Using Descriptive Verbs Sparingly

Descriptive verbs like "whispered," "shouted," or "muttered" can add variety but should be used sparingly to maintain impact.

Example:

"I don't think this is a good idea," John muttered.

Avoiding Redundancy

Ensure that the tag complements the dialogue rather than repeating information. If the dialogue already indicates how something is said, an additional descriptive tag may be unnecessary.

Example:

"I don't think this is a good idea," John said nervously. (Instead of: "I don't think this is a good idea," John said with nervousness in his voice.)

Using Body Language

Incorporate body language to convey emotions and actions, reducing the need for adverbs in dialogue tags.

Example:

"I don't think this is a good idea," John said, shifting his weight from one foot to the other.

Avoiding Adverb Overuse

While adverbs can be useful, overusing them can weaken your writing. Use strong verbs and context to convey the tone instead.

Example:

"I don't think this is a good idea," John said cautiously.

In summary, managing dialogue tags effectively involves using "said" as a default, incorporating action tags, using character names and pronouns, varying tags sparingly, providing contextual clues, balancing dialogue and tags, expressing emotion through dialogue, avoiding overly complex tags, using tags for pacing, showing character relationships, integrating internal thoughts, alternating tags and no tags, using descriptive verbs sparingly, avoiding redundancy, using body language, and avoiding adverb overuse. By focusing on these strategies, you can create clear, engaging, and natural dialogue in your screenplay.

Pacing Dialogue: Rhythm and Timing

Pacing dialogue effectively is crucial for maintaining the rhythm and flow of your screenplay. Proper pacing can heighten tension, convey emotions, and keep the audience engaged. Here are strategies for managing the rhythm and timing of dialogue.

Varying Sentence Lengths

Mix short, punchy sentences with longer, more descriptive ones to create a natural rhythm and keep the dialogue dynamic.

Example:

"I can't believe you did that." John paused, shaking his head. "Do you have any idea what this means for us? For the entire project?"

Using Pauses and Beats

Incorporate pauses and beats in the dialogue to add natural breaks, create tension, or emphasize a point. Use action lines or ellipses to indicate these pauses.

Example:

"I can't believe you did that..." John paused, taking a deep breath. "Do you have any idea what this means?"

Building Tension with Pacing

Use shorter, rapid exchanges during moments of high tension or conflict to create a sense of urgency and immediacy.

Example:

"We have to go. Now!" "But—" "No time. Move!"

Slowing Down for Reflection

Slow the pace with longer sentences and pauses when characters are reflecting, revealing important information, or experiencing deep emotions.

Example:

"I just... I don't know anymore," Mary said, her voice barely above a whisper. "Everything's changed. We've changed."

Balancing Dialogue and Action

Interlace dialogue with action to maintain a steady rhythm and prevent scenes from becoming too dialogue-heavy. Actions can also reveal character emotions and intentions.

Example:

"I can't believe you did that." John slammed his fist on the table, making the glasses rattle. "Do you have any idea what this means?"

Using Interruptions and Overlapping Speech

Incorporate interruptions and overlapping speech to create a sense of realism and urgency, especially in heated or chaotic scenes.

Example:

"We have to go. Now!" "But—" "No time. Move!"

Creating Natural Flow

Ensure the dialogue flows naturally by writing how people speak in real life. Avoid overly formal language unless it suits the character.

Example:

"Hey, what's up?" "Not much. Just thinking about what you said earlier."

Reflecting Character Dynamics

Pace the dialogue to reflect the dynamics between characters. Fast-paced, witty exchanges can indicate a close, playful relationship, while slower, measured dialogue can suggest formality or tension.

Example:

"Did you see that?" "Of course I did. Hard to miss." "You think it's serious?" "Very."

Building Suspense

Slow the pacing to build suspense, especially before revealing crucial information or during moments of uncertainty.

Example:

"I have to tell you something." John's voice trembled, and he took a deep breath before continuing. "It's about the project... and it's not good news."

Creating Emotional Impact

Use pauses and varied pacing to create emotional impact, allowing characters and the audience to process significant moments.

Example:

"She's gone," Mary said, her voice breaking. "I can't believe it... she's really gone."

Indicating Time Passing

Pacing can indicate the passage of time within a scene. Use longer, reflective dialogue to show contemplation or shorter, fragmented dialogue for rapid decision-making.

Example:

"We need to decide. Now." "I know, but..." "No buts. We're running out of time."

Revealing Information Gradually

Pace the dialogue to reveal information gradually, keeping the audience engaged and curious about what will happen next.

Example:

"There's something you need to know," John said. Mary frowned. "What is it?" "It's about the project... and it's not good news."

Using Silence

Strategic use of silence can add weight to dialogue, allowing important lines to resonate and giving the audience time to absorb what has been said.

Example:

"I can't believe you did that," John said. He paused, letting the words hang in the air. "Do you have any idea what this means?"

Echoing Real Conversations

Reflect real-life conversations by including hesitations, repetitions, and natural speech patterns to make the dialogue more relatable and engaging.

Example:

"I just... I don't know anymore," Mary said. "Everything's changed. We've changed."

Establishing Scene Rhythm

Match the dialogue pace to the scene's overall rhythm. Fast-paced dialogue suits action scenes, while slower dialogue works well for introspective or dramatic moments.

Example:

Action Scene: "Watch out!" "Where?" "Behind you!"

Dramatic Scene:

"I just... I don't know if I can do this anymore," Mary said, her voice breaking. "It's too much."

In summary, managing the rhythm and timing of dialogue involves varying sentence lengths, using pauses and beats, building tension with pacing, slowing down for reflection, balancing dialogue and action, using interruptions and overlapping speech, creating natural flow, reflecting character dynamics, building suspense, creating emotional impact, indicating time passing, revealing information gradually, using silence, echoing real conversations, and establishing scene rhythm. By focusing on these strategies, you can create engaging, dynamic, and emotionally resonant dialogue that enhances your screenplay's overall pacing.

Subtext in Relationships: Reading between the Lines

Subtext in dialogue allows characters to communicate underlying emotions, intentions, and tensions without stating them explicitly. It adds depth and complexity to relationships, making interactions more engaging and realistic. Here are strategies for using subtext to reveal the dynamics of relationships in your screenplay.

Creating Dual Meanings

Write dialogue that has a surface meaning but also implies something deeper. This allows characters to communicate their true feelings indirectly.

Example:

"I see you've been working late a lot," Mary said. John looked away. "Yeah, it's been busy at the office." (Underlying tension about potential infidelity or distance in the relationship)

Using Body Language

Pair dialogue with body language to convey subtext. A character's actions, facial expressions, and gestures can reveal what they are truly feeling or thinking.

Example:

"I'm fine," Sarah said, crossing her arms and avoiding eye contact. (Her body language suggests she is not fine at all)

Leveraging Tone and Inflection

The way a character says something can convey more than the words themselves. Tone, inflection, and emphasis can add layers of meaning.

Example:

"Sure, I trust you," Mark said, his voice dripping with sarcasm. (The sarcasm indicates that he actually does not trust the person)

Incorporating Silences and Pauses

Silences and pauses can speak volumes. The hesitation to respond, or a deliberate pause, can indicate discomfort, unspoken thoughts, or emotional weight.

Example:

"I love you," she said. He paused, then replied, "Me too." (The pause suggests uncertainty or lack of genuine feeling)

Using Indirect Responses

Characters can respond to questions or comments indirectly, avoiding the real issue or hinting at something deeper without addressing it head-on.

Example:

"Do you miss me?" she asked. "I've been keeping busy," he replied. (His response avoids the direct question, implying he may not want to admit his true feelings)

Implying History and Backstory

Dialogue can hint at a shared history or past events without explicitly stating them, allowing the audience to infer the context and underlying emotions.

Example:

"Not this again," she sighed. "You promised we wouldn't talk about it," he replied. (This exchange hints at a recurring issue or unresolved conflict in their past)

Revealing Contradictions

Characters might say one thing but mean another, or their words may contradict their actions, revealing subtext through inconsistency.

Example:

"I'm so happy for you," she said, forcing a smile. (Her forced smile contradicts her words, indicating jealousy or resentment)

Using Metaphors and Symbols

Metaphorical language and symbols can convey subtext, allowing characters to express complex emotions and ideas indirectly.

Example:

"This garden is a mess," he said, looking at the overgrown plants. "Yeah, it's been neglected," she replied. (The neglected garden symbolizes their relationship's state)

Hinting at Future Actions

Dialogue can hint at future actions or intentions, providing subtext about a character's plans or desires without directly stating them.

Example:

"Are you coming home tonight?" she asked. "We'll see how things go," he replied. (His response suggests uncertainty or reluctance about returning home)

Highlighting Power Dynamics

Subtext can reveal power dynamics in relationships, such as control, dominance, or submission, through subtle cues in dialogue and interactions.

Example:

"Can I go out with friends tonight?" she asked. "Let's talk about it later," he said, his tone dismissive. (His dismissal indicates control over her actions)

Embedding Foreshadowing

Use subtext to foreshadow future conflicts or revelations, hinting at what's to come without making it explicit.

Example:

"Everything's fine now, right?" he asked. "For now," she replied, her voice tinged with doubt. (Her doubt foreshadows potential trouble ahead)

Balancing Dialogue and Silence

Balance dialogue with moments of silence, where characters may struggle to find the right words, allowing their true feelings to simmer beneath the surface.

Example:

"I thought we were past this," he said. She remained silent, her eyes filling with tears. (Her silence indicates unresolved pain or conflict)

Using Repetition

Repetition of certain words or phrases can create subtext, emphasizing underlying emotions or tensions.

Example:

"Are you sure you're okay?" he asked. "I'm fine," she repeated, her voice shaky. (The repetition and shakiness suggest she is not fine)

Contrasting Public and Private Dialogue

Characters might speak differently in public versus private settings, revealing subtext through the contrast between their public facade and private reality.

Example:

In public: "We're doing great," he said, smiling. In private: "I don't know how much longer I can do this," he admitted. (The contrast reveals the true state of their relationship)

Employing Indirect Confrontation

Characters might confront each other indirectly, using veiled references or hypothetical situations to address underlying issues.

Example:

"If someone were to lie to their partner, do you think they could ever trust them again?" she asked. "I suppose it depends on the lie," he replied. (The indirect confrontation suggests a lack of trust in their relationship)

In summary, using subtext in relationships involves creating dual meanings, using body language, leveraging tone and inflection, incorporating silences and pauses, using indirect responses, implying history and backstory, revealing contradictions, using metaphors and symbols, hinting at future actions, highlighting power dynamics, embedding foreshadowing, balancing dialogue and silence, using repetition, contrasting public and private dialogue, and employing indirect confrontation. By focusing on these strategies, you can add depth and complexity to your characters' relationships, making your screenplay more engaging and realistic.

Deceptive Dialogue: Misdirection and Lies

Deceptive dialogue, where characters mislead, lie, or use misdirection, adds layers of intrigue and complexity to a screenplay. This technique can be used to develop characters, advance the plot, and create suspense. Here are strategies for crafting deceptive dialogue effectively.

Using Half-Truths

Characters can mix truth with lies to make their deception more believable. This can make it harder for others to detect the lie and adds nuance to the character's manipulation.

Example:

"I was at the office last night," John said. (He was at the office, but only briefly before going elsewhere)

Creating Ambiguity

Use ambiguous language that can be interpreted in multiple ways. This allows the character to deceive without directly lying.

Example:

"Did you see him yesterday?" she asked. "I saw someone who looked like him," he replied.

Employing Deflection

Characters can deflect questions or change the subject to avoid revealing the truth. This tactic keeps the other character off-balance and redirects attention.

Example:

"Where were you last night?" she asked. "Why are you always questioning me?" he shot back.

Exploiting Character Trust

Characters can exploit the trust others have in them to make their lies more convincing. This can deepen the betrayal when the truth is eventually revealed.

Example:

"You know you can trust me," he said earnestly. "I would never lie to you."

Using Evasion

Evasive answers can avoid direct lies while still deceiving. Characters may use vagueness or provide incomplete information.

Example:

"Did you finish the report?" the boss asked. "I've been working on it all day," she replied.

Setting Up Red Herrings

Introduce misleading clues or information through dialogue that diverts attention from the truth. This can create suspense and surprise.

Example:

"I heard the new guy has a shady past," he whispered.

Contradicting Non-Verbal Cues

Have a character's body language or actions contradict their words, creating dramatic irony where the audience knows the truth while other characters do not.

Example:

"I'm not worried at all," she said, but her trembling hands and nervous glances suggested otherwise.

Playing on Emotions

Use emotional appeals to make lies more convincing. Characters can exploit sympathy, guilt, or fear to manipulate others.

Example:

"Please believe me," he pleaded, tears welling up in his eyes. "I wouldn't do that to you."

Layering Lies

Characters can tell small lies to cover up a bigger lie, creating a web of deception that becomes more intricate and difficult to unravel.

Example:

"I was with Sarah," he said. (He wasn't, but mentioning a trusted friend makes the lie more credible)

Implanting False Memories

Characters can suggest events or details that create false memories, making others believe something that never happened.

Example:

"Remember when we saw that movie together last month?" she said. (They never saw the movie, but suggesting it as a memory makes it seem real)

Revealing Lies Gradually

Gradually reveal the deception through dialogue, building suspense and allowing the audience to piece together the truth over time.

Example:

"I thought you said you were at the office," she said. "I was, but then I had to run an errand," he replied, adding another layer to the lie.

Using Irony

Characters can use irony to lie, saying one thing while meaning another. This can be used to convey hidden truths to the audience while deceiving other characters.

Example:

"Of course I trust you," he said with a smirk. (His tone suggests the opposite)

Incorporating Confident Lies

Confident delivery can make lies more believable. Characters who lie with certainty and conviction are often more convincing.

Example:

"I saw him leave the building at eight," she said firmly. (Even though she didn't)

Leveraging Plausibility

Ensure that the lies told by characters are plausible within the story's context. Implausible lies can break immersion and be easily detected by both characters and the audience.

Example:

"I got stuck in traffic," he said. (In a city known for frequent traffic jams)

Creating Alibis

Characters can create detailed alibis to support their lies, adding layers of credibility and making it harder to uncover the truth.

Example:

"I was at the gym from six to eight, then I grabbed dinner at Joe's Diner. You can ask Joe; he saw me there," he said.

Utilizing Repetition

Repeating the lie can reinforce it, making it seem more credible each time it is mentioned. This can create a sense of inevitability around the deception.

Example:

"I've told you before, I was at the office. How many times do I need to say it?" he repeated.

Misleading Through Omissions

Characters can deceive by omitting crucial information, leading others to incorrect conclusions without directly lying.

Example:

"Did you tell her about the meeting?" "I told her we had a conversation," he said. (Omitting the details of the actual meeting)

Using False Accusations

Characters can deceive by accusing others of things they didn't do, deflecting suspicion from themselves.

Example:

"Why are you always so paranoid? Maybe you're the one hiding something," he accused.

Creating Tension through Silence

Strategic silences can imply agreement or disagreement, leaving room for interpretation and adding to the deception.

Example:

"Do you think he's telling the truth?" she asked. He remained silent, his lack of denial suggesting he might believe the lie.

In summary, crafting effective deceptive dialogue involves using half-truths, creating ambiguity, employing deflection, exploiting character trust, using evasion, setting up red herrings, contradicting non-verbal cues, playing on emotions, layering lies, implanting false memories, revealing lies gradually, using irony, incorporating confident lies, leveraging plausibility, creating alibis, utilizing repetition, misleading through omissions, using false accusations, and creating tension through silence. By focusing on these strategies, you can create rich, layered dialogue that adds depth and intrigue to your screenplay.

Dialogue that Builds Mystery

Creating a sense of mystery through dialogue is a powerful way to engage your audience and keep them invested in your story. Effective mysterious dialogue can intrigue, provide subtle clues, and set up compelling questions that drive the narrative forward. Here are strategies for crafting dialogue that builds mystery.

Asking Rhetorical Questions

Characters can ask rhetorical questions that hint at deeper mysteries or unknowns, prompting the audience to think and speculate.

Example:

"Why would someone go to all this trouble?" she murmured, staring at the cryptic note.

Dropping Hints and Clues

Sprinkle subtle hints and clues throughout the dialogue, encouraging the audience to piece together the puzzle over time.

Example:

"Did you notice the unusual symbol on the envelope? I've seen it somewhere before, but I can't remember where."

Using Ambiguous Language

Incorporate ambiguous or vague language that can be interpreted in multiple ways, leaving room for speculation and uncertainty.

Example:

"There's more to this town than meets the eye," he said with a knowing smile.

Withholding Information

Have characters deliberately withhold information or speak in incomplete sentences, creating a sense of secrecy and curiosity.

Example:

"I know something you don't," he said, trailing off. "But you're not ready to hear it yet."

Foreshadowing

Use foreshadowing in dialogue to hint at future events or revelations, creating anticipation and suspense.

Example:

"You think this is the end? It's only the beginning," she warned, her eyes glinting with a hidden truth.

Contradictory Statements

Characters can make contradictory statements that leave the audience questioning what's true and what's false.

Example:

"He's always been reliable… except for that one time. But let's not talk about that."

Creating Unresolved Tensions

Introduce unresolved tensions or conflicts between characters through dialogue, suggesting deeper issues that need to be uncovered.

Example:

"You still haven't told me the whole story, have you?" she asked, her voice tinged with suspicion.

Embedding Secrets

Characters can refer to secrets or past events without fully explaining them, adding layers of intrigue.

Example:

"Remember what happened last summer? We can't let that happen again."

Using Cryptic Statements

Craft cryptic statements that are open to interpretation, prompting the audience to think about their meaning and significance.

Example:

"The answer lies where the shadows meet," he whispered, before disappearing into the night.

Reflecting Internal Conflicts

Dialogue that hints at a character's internal conflicts or hidden agendas can add mystery to their motives and actions.

Example:

"I wish I could tell you the truth, but it's too dangerous," he said, his eyes filled with torment.

Leveraging Silence

Strategic use of silence or pauses in dialogue can add tension and suggest that there's more left unsaid.

Example:

"Do you trust him?" she asked. He hesitated, then simply replied, "I don't know."

Misdirection

Use misdirection in dialogue to lead the audience and characters down the wrong path, creating surprises and twists.

Example:

"I'm sure the key is in the attic," he said confidently, knowing it was actually hidden elsewhere.

Creating Layers of Truth

Introduce layers of truth where characters reveal parts of the story, but not the whole truth, encouraging the audience to dig deeper.

Example:

"Yes, I was there that night. But I didn't see everything."

Introducing Mysterious Characters

Introduce characters who are enigmatic and whose motives are unclear, adding to the overall sense of mystery.

Example:

"He just showed up one day, claiming to know things about everyone. No one knows where he came from."

Alluding to Hidden Connections

Characters can allude to hidden connections or relationships, suggesting deeper ties and secrets to be uncovered.

Example:

"There's a reason we've all been brought together, but that's not something I can explain just yet."

Leveraging Unanswered Questions

Allow characters to ask questions that remain unanswered, prompting the audience to seek answers alongside them.

Example:

"Who sent this message? And why now?"

Building Suspense through Dialogue

Use dialogue to build suspense, suggesting that something significant is about to happen or be revealed.

Example:

"Everything changes tonight. Be ready."

Highlighting Inconsistencies

Characters can point out inconsistencies or oddities that suggest something isn't quite right, adding to the mystery.

Example:

"Why would she say she was at the party when no one remembers seeing her?"

Embedding Symbolism

Incorporate symbolic language or references that have deeper meanings, prompting the audience to think critically.

Example:

"The old lighthouse hasn't shone its light in years, but some say it's still guiding lost souls."

In summary, crafting dialogue that builds mystery involves asking rhetorical questions, dropping hints and clues, using ambiguous language, withholding information, foreshadowing, creating contradictory statements, embedding secrets, using cryptic statements, reflecting internal conflicts, leveraging silence, using misdirection, creating layers of truth, introducing mysterious characters, alluding to hidden connections, leveraging unanswered questions, building suspense, highlighting inconsistencies, and embedding symbolism. By focusing on these strategies, you can create engaging and intriguing dialogue that keeps your audience invested in uncovering the mysteries of your story.

Dialogue in Flashbacks: Past and Present Interactions

Using flashbacks effectively in your screenplay can add depth to characters and provide essential backstory. Dialogue within flashbacks should be crafted to clearly distinguish past events from the present while maintaining narrative coherence. Here are strategies for creating effective dialogue in flashbacks that enhances both past and present interactions.

Establishing Time Shifts

Clearly signal the transition between past and present to avoid confusion. Visual cues, changes in setting, or dialogue tags can help establish the time shift.

Example:

(Present) "I still remember the day everything changed," John said, his eyes distant. (Flashback) "You can do it, John! Just believe in yourself," his coach's voice echoed in the gym.

Using Consistent Character Voices

Ensure that characters' voices remain consistent across time periods, even if their language or attitudes evolve. This maintains continuity and helps the audience recognize them.

Example:

(Present) "You've always been stubborn," Sarah said with a smile. (Flashback) "You never listen, do you?" Sarah's younger self snapped.

Reflecting Character Development

Show how characters have changed over time by contrasting their past and present dialogue. This highlights their growth and adds depth to their arcs.

Example:

(Present) "I've learned to let go," Mary said calmly. (Flashback) "I can't forgive them! Never!" a younger Mary screamed, tears streaming down her face.

Revealing Key Backstory

Use flashbacks to reveal crucial backstory that informs the present narrative. Ensure the dialogue in flashbacks provides context and adds layers to current events.

Example:

(Present) "Why are you so afraid of commitment?" Lisa asked. (Flashback) "I'll never leave you," his mother promised, moments before walking out the door forever.

Maintaining Emotional Continuity

Ensure the emotional tone of flashbacks aligns with the present narrative. This continuity helps the audience understand the impact of past events on current emotions.

Example:

(Present) "It still hurts," Mark admitted, his voice breaking. (Flashback) "I promise, nothing will change," his best friend said, just before moving away.

Using Flashbacks to Answer Questions

Introduce flashbacks that answer questions raised in the present narrative. This technique creates a sense of discovery and satisfaction for the audience.

Example:

(Present) "Why did you quit music?" she asked. (Flashback) "I can't play anymore," he told his bandmates, cradling his injured hand.

Incorporating Symbolism

Use symbolic dialogue in flashbacks to add layers of meaning and connect past and present. Symbolic elements can resonate across time periods, deepening the narrative.

Example:

(Present) "Do you remember the song we used to sing?" she asked. (Flashback) "This song will always bring us back together," he said, strumming the guitar.

Highlighting Changes in Relationships

Show how relationships have evolved over time by contrasting past and present interactions. This highlights dynamics and the passage of time.

Example:

(Present) "We used to be so close," she said wistfully. (Flashback) "I'll always be here for you," her friend said, giving her a tight hug.

Creating Dramatic Irony

Use flashbacks to create dramatic irony, where the audience knows more about past events than the characters in the present. This adds tension and engagement.

Example:

(Present) "I trust him completely," she said confidently. (Flashback) "If she ever finds out, it'll destroy her," he whispered to his accomplice.

Reflecting Themes

Ensure flashback dialogue reflects the overarching themes of your story. This helps unify the narrative and adds depth to both past and present interactions.

Example:

(Present) "Sometimes, you have to let go," he said thoughtfully. (Flashback) "Hold on to what you love, no matter what," his father had advised.

Using Natural Transitions

Transition smoothly between past and present by using visual or auditory cues, like a character's gaze shifting to a significant object, or a sound that triggers the memory.

Example:

(Present) She stared at the old photograph on the mantel. (Flashback) "Smile for the camera!" her mother laughed as they posed for the picture.

Developing Parallel Narratives

Create parallel narratives where events in the past mirror or contrast with the present. This technique enriches the storytelling and highlights connections.

Example:

(Present) "I have to find my own path," he said. (Flashback) "You have to follow your own dreams, no matter what," his mentor advised.

Balancing Dialogue and Action

Ensure that flashback scenes balance dialogue with action, providing a fuller picture of past events and how they relate to current situations.

Example:

(Present) "Why do you hate that place so much?" she asked. (Flashback) As he ran through the burning building, he shouted, "I'll never set foot here again!"

Using Flashbacks for Character Insight

Use flashbacks to provide insight into a character's motivations, fears, and desires. This adds depth and complexity to their present actions.

Example:

(Present) "I don't think I can go through with it," he said, hesitating at the door. (Flashback) "You're not good enough," his coach had yelled during his last performance.

In summary, creating effective dialogue in flashbacks involves establishing time shifts, using consistent character voices, reflecting character development, revealing key backstory, maintaining emotional continuity, answering present questions, incorporating symbolism, highlighting relationship changes, creating dramatic irony, reflecting themes, using natural transitions, developing parallel narratives, balancing dialogue and action, and providing character insight. By focusing on these strategies, you can craft flashback dialogues that enrich your narrative and deepen the connections between past and present interactions.

Dialogue in Dream Sequences: Surreal and Symbolic

Dream sequences can add layers of meaning and symbolism to your screenplay, revealing a character's subconscious thoughts and emotions. Crafting dialogue for these sequences requires a blend of surreal and symbolic elements to capture the dreamlike quality. Here are strategies for creating effective dialogue in dream sequences.

Incorporating Symbolism

Use symbolic language and imagery that reflect the character's inner thoughts and emotions. Symbols can represent fears, desires, and unresolved conflicts.

Example:

"You're lost, aren't you?" the figure in the fog said. "Just like in the maze of your own mind."

Employing Surreal Elements

Incorporate surreal elements that defy logic and reality, reflecting the fluid and unpredictable nature of dreams.

Example:

"Why are you wearing that?" she asked, pointing to his clown suit. "Because you never take me seriously," he replied, his voice echoing.

Creating Disjointed Dialogue

Dream dialogue can be disjointed and fragmented, mimicking the often incoherent nature of dreams. This can add to the surreal atmosphere.

Example:

"I can't find the door," she said, spinning around. "There are no doors here," the voice replied from nowhere. "Only windows to your soul."

Using Repetition

Repetition of words or phrases can create a haunting and memorable effect, emphasizing key themes or emotions.

Example:

"Run," the voices chanted. "Run and never look back."

Blurring Time and Space

Dialogue in dreams can blur the lines between past, present, and future, reflecting the fluidity of time in the subconscious mind.

Example:

"You were here before," the child said, though she had never seen him before. "You will be here again."

Layering Multiple Meanings

Dialogue in dreams can have multiple layers of meaning, reflecting the complexity of the character's inner world.

Example:

"Are you afraid of the dark?" the shadow asked. "I'm afraid of what hides in it," he replied.

Using Metaphorical Language

Metaphors can convey deep emotional truths and abstract concepts in a dreamlike manner.

Example:

"Your heart is a locked box," she said, holding an ornate key. "Only you know where the key is hidden."

Creating Characters as Symbols

Characters in dream sequences can represent different aspects of the protagonist's psyche, such as fears, desires, or unresolved issues.

Example:

"Why are you here?" he asked the stranger. "I am the part of you that you hide," the stranger replied.

Incorporating Non-Linear Dialogue

Dream dialogue can be non-linear, jumping from one topic to another without logical connections, mirroring the erratic nature of dreams.

Example:

"Do you remember the night?" she asked. "The moon was blue," he replied, though she had asked about a different night altogether.

Using Ethereal Voices

Dream sequences can feature ethereal or disembodied voices that add to the surreal atmosphere.

Example:

"Who's there?" she called out. "You know who I am," the voice whispered from all directions.

Exploring Hidden Desires

Dialogue in dreams can reveal hidden desires and subconscious thoughts that the character might not express in waking life.

Example:

"Why don't you just say it?" the mirror image taunted. "You want to leave everything behind."

Reflecting Emotional States

The tone and content of dream dialogue should reflect the character's emotional state, whether it's fear, confusion, longing, or joy.

Example:

"Everything is falling apart," he said, as the walls around him crumbled. "Maybe it's time to rebuild," she replied from the rubble.

Playing with Language

Use poetic, abstract, or nonsensical language to enhance the dreamlike quality of the dialogue.

Example:

"The stars are singing tonight," she said, her words drifting like stardust.

Creating Opposites and Contradictions

Include contradictory statements and opposites to create a sense of confusion and surrealism.

Example:

"You're here and not here," he said, holding her hand. "I see you, but you're invisible."

Introducing Incongruous Elements

Mix incongruous elements in dialogue to highlight the dream's surreal nature.

Example:

"Why is there a river in the living room?" she asked, wading through the water. "Because you never learned to swim," the fish replied.

Reflecting Inner Conflict

Dialogue can reveal inner conflicts and dilemmas that the character faces, often in a symbolic or exaggerated manner.

Example:

"I don't know which path to take," he said, standing at the crossroads. "The one less traveled, or the one that's safe?" the owl asked.

Using Unreliable Narrators

Characters in dreams can act as unreliable narrators, providing misleading or cryptic information.

Example:

"This is the truth," the figure said, though everything around him suggested otherwise.

In summary, crafting dialogue in dream sequences involves incorporating symbolism, employing surreal elements, creating disjointed dialogue, using repetition, blurring time and space, layering multiple meanings, using metaphorical language, creating characters as symbols, incorporating non-linear dialogue, using ethereal voices, exploring hidden desires, reflecting emotional states, playing with language, creating opposites and contradictions, introducing incongruous elements, reflecting inner conflict, and using unreliable narrators. By focusing on these strategies, you can create surreal and symbolic dialogue that enhances the dreamlike quality of your screenplay and provides deeper insights into your characters' subconscious minds.

Adapting Dialogue for Different Genres

Adapting dialogue to fit different genres is crucial for maintaining the tone, style, and expectations of your screenplay. Each genre has unique conventions and characteristics that should be reflected in the way characters speak. Here are strategies for adapting dialogue to suit various genres.

Action

Action movies thrive on fast-paced, concise, and impactful dialogue. Characters often speak in short, direct sentences that reflect urgency and tension.

Example:

"We've got five minutes before it blows. Move!"

Romance

Romantic dialogue tends to be more emotional, expressive, and sometimes poetic. Characters often discuss feelings, desires, and relationships.

Example:

"I've loved you since the moment we met. I can't imagine my life without you."

Comedy

Comedy dialogue relies heavily on timing, wit, and humor. It often includes puns, jokes, and playful banter.

Example:

"Are you sure this is a good idea?" "No, but I'm an optimist. What could go wrong?"

Horror

Horror dialogue is often tense, suspenseful, and filled with fear or dread. Characters may speak in whispers, scream, or express anxiety.

Example:

"Did you hear that? I think we're not alone in here."

Science Fiction

Science fiction dialogue often includes technical jargon, speculative concepts, and futuristic slang. It can also explore philosophical ideas and moral dilemmas.

Example:

"We need to recalibrate the quantum stabilizer before we can initiate the warp drive."

Fantasy

Fantasy dialogue often has a formal or archaic tone, especially in high fantasy settings. Characters may use elaborate descriptions and speak in a grandiose manner.

Example:

"By the ancient laws of our land, I vow to protect this realm with my life."

Drama

Drama dialogue is typically realistic and emotionally charged. It focuses on character development, relationships, and internal conflicts.

Example:

"I can't keep pretending everything is okay. We need to talk about what's really going on."

Thriller

Thriller dialogue is often fast-paced, filled with suspense, and strategically reveals information to build tension. It can be cryptic and intense.

Example:

"You have 24 hours to find the package, or they die. No more warnings."

Historical

Historical dialogue should reflect the time period in which the story is set. It often includes period-specific language, formal speech, and cultural references.

Example:

"Pray, my lord, grant me the boon of your counsel."

Mystery

Mystery dialogue often involves questioning, clues, and red herrings. Characters might engage in cryptic conversations that hint at deeper secrets.

Example:

"Everyone has a motive, but only one of us had the opportunity. Who was it?"

Western

Western dialogue is often characterized by its rugged, straightforward, and sometimes laconic style. It reflects the harsh, frontier setting and the no-nonsense attitudes of the characters.

Example:

"This town ain't big enough for the both of us."

Musical

Musical dialogue often includes rhythmic, poetic, or lyrical elements, as characters may transition from spoken words to song.

Example:

"I've been waiting for this moment, to tell you how I feel. It's like a dream come true, everything is so real."

Crime

Crime dialogue is often gritty, terse, and filled with slang. It reflects the underworld settings and the tough, often morally ambiguous characters.

Example:

"You wanna know who did it? You gotta pay up first."

Adventure

Adventure dialogue is often spirited, enthusiastic, and filled with a sense of wonder and excitement. Characters may discuss exploration, discovery, and daring feats.

Example:

"Pack your bags! We're setting out at dawn for the lost city of gold."

Noir

Noir dialogue is characterized by its cynical, hard-boiled tone. It often includes sharp, witty exchanges and a sense of fatalism.

Example:

"Dames like her are trouble. But what can I say? Trouble's my middle name."

Fantasy Comedy

In a genre that combines fantasy with comedy, the dialogue should balance the whimsical elements of fantasy with humor and wit.

Example:

"Did you really turn the king into a frog?" "Well, he was getting a bit too ribbit-tious for my taste."

Romantic Comedy

Romantic comedy dialogue blends the emotional expressiveness of romance with the humor and playfulness of comedy.

Example:

"You know, falling for you was like tripping over my own feet." "Was it love at first fall?"

Psychological Thriller

Psychological thriller dialogue is often intense, introspective, and filled with tension. It explores characters' minds and the psychological aspects of fear and suspense.

Example:

"You think you know what's real? That's your first mistake." **Superhero** Superhero dialogue often includes grandiose, inspirational speeches and a sense of duty or destiny. It can also incorporate humor and wit. *Example:**

"With great power comes great responsibility."

Parody

Parody dialogue mimics and exaggerates the conventions of other genres for comedic effect. It often includes satire and absurdity.

Example:

"Do you expect me to talk?" "No, Mr. Bond, I expect you to laugh at this ridiculous plot twist."

Animated Films

Dialogue in animated films is often lively, engaging, and tailored for all ages. It can include humor, whimsy, and clear emotional expression.

Example:

"Come on, let's go on an adventure!" "Right behind you, buddy! Just let me grab my cape."

Sci-Fi Dialogue: Creating New Worlds

Crafting dialogue for science fiction involves not only telling a compelling story but also immersing the audience in a new and often unfamiliar world. Here are strategies for creating effective sci-fi dialogue that helps to build and enrich your fictional universe.

Incorporating Technological Jargon

Use specific and believable technological terms and jargon to ground your world in a sense of realism. However, balance it to avoid overwhelming the audience with too much technical detail.

Example:

"We need to recalibrate the quantum stabilizer before we can initiate the warp drive."

Exploring Ethical and Philosophical Themes

Science fiction often delves into ethical and philosophical questions. Characters can reflect on these themes through their dialogue, adding depth to the narrative.

Example:

"If we create artificial intelligence with emotions, do we also inherit the responsibility for their well-being?"

Creating Futuristic Slang

Develop unique slang or phrases that reflect the culture and time period of your sci-fi world. This adds authenticity and immersion.

Example:

"That new hover car is totally stellar, man!"

Using Expository Dialogue Wisely

While expository dialogue is necessary to explain complex scientific concepts, integrate it naturally into the conversation to avoid info-dumping.

Example:

"How does this neural interface work?" "It links directly to your synaptic pathways, allowing you to control the ship with your thoughts."

Reflecting Socio-political Structures

Dialogue can reveal the socio-political landscape of your world, including hierarchies, power dynamics, and societal norms.

Example:

"In the outer colonies, we don't have the luxury of debating ethics. It's survival first, laws second."

Balancing Realism and Imagination

Combine realistic dialogue with imaginative concepts to make your world both believable and wondrous.

Example:

"Have you ever seen a supernova up close? It's like watching a star give birth to a new universe."

Introducing Alien Cultures

When dealing with alien species, use dialogue to convey their unique culture, language, and perspective without making them incomprehensible.

Example:

"To us, time is a circle, not a line. Every moment exists simultaneously," the alien ambassador explained.

Highlighting Advanced Science and Technology

Characters should talk about advanced scientific concepts and technologies naturally, reflecting their everyday familiarity with such advancements.

Example:

"Transfer the data to my neural implant. I need to analyze it before the meeting."

Showing Adaptation to Environment

Dialogue can reflect how characters have adapted to their environment, whether it's a space station, a different planet, or a post-apocalyptic Earth.

Example:

"Remember to adjust your oxygen mask before stepping outside. The atmosphere here is toxic."

Evolving Human Interactions

Show how human interactions have evolved in your sci-fi world, whether through advanced communication methods or altered social norms.

Example:

"Let's sync our thoughts before we proceed. It's faster than talking."

Building Tension with Unknowns

Use dialogue to build tension around unknown scientific phenomena or mysterious elements of your world.

Example:

"We've detected an anomaly in sector seven. No one knows what it is, but it's disrupting our instruments."

Describing Alien Landscapes

Characters can describe alien landscapes or environments, helping to paint a vivid picture of the setting.

Example:

"The sky here is a perpetual twilight, and the forests glow with bioluminescent flora."

Creating New Social Customs

Invent new social customs or rituals that characters reference or explain, reflecting the unique culture of your sci-fi world.

Example:

"It's tradition to share a memory before negotiations begin. It builds trust."

Exploring Identity and Consciousness

Discuss themes of identity, consciousness, and humanity through dialogue, especially in relation to AI, cloning, or genetic modification.

Example:

"If my memories were transferred to a clone, is that clone still me?"

Utilizing Flashbacks and Memories

Characters can recall past events or experiences that provide context and background for the current story.

Example:

"I remember the first time I saw Earth from space. It was a blue gem in an endless void."

Reflecting on Time and Space

Dialogue can reflect the vastness and complexity of time and space, often with a sense of wonder or existential reflection.

Example:

"Traveling through a wormhole is like bending reality. What takes a moment here could span centuries on the other side."

Incorporating Multilingual Dialogue

In a diverse sci-fi universe, characters might switch between languages or use a common intergalactic language, adding to the richness of the world.

Example:

"Activate the translator matrix. I need to understand what they're saying."

Using Subtext and Implications

Employ subtext to suggest deeper layers of meaning or conflict without explicit explanation, adding mystery and depth.

Example:

"They say the colony on Mars went silent for a reason. Best not to ask too many questions."

In summary, adapting dialogue for science fiction involves incorporating technological jargon, exploring ethical and philosophical themes, creating futuristic slang, using expository dialogue wisely, reflecting socio-political structures, balancing realism and imagination, introducing alien cultures, highlighting advanced science and technology, showing adaptation to environments, evolving human interactions, building tension with unknowns, describing alien landscapes, creating new social customs, exploring identity and consciousness, utilizing flashbacks and memories, reflecting on time and space, incorporating multilingual dialogue, and using subtext and implications. By focusing on these strategies, you can create rich, immersive dialogue that helps build and define your sci-fi world.

Fantasy Dialogue: Enchanting and Epic Speech

Crafting dialogue for fantasy worlds requires a touch of the magical and the majestic. The dialogue should reflect the enchanting nature of the setting, the epic scale of the story, and the diverse cultures and characters within it. Here are strategies for creating effective fantasy dialogue.

Using Archaic and Formal Language

Incorporate archaic or formal language to give your dialogue an old-world, timeless feel. This can help establish the setting and tone of your fantasy world.

Example:

"Hark! The prophecy doth speak of a hero who shall rise from the shadows."

Incorporating Myths and Legends

Characters in a fantasy world often reference myths, legends, and prophecies. This adds depth to the world-building and provides a sense of history.

Example:

"According to the ancient scrolls, only the one with a pure heart can wield the Sword of Light."

Using Rich Descriptive Language

Fantasy dialogue should be vivid and descriptive, painting a picture of the world and its wonders.

Example:

"The emerald hills stretch beyond the horizon, where dragons once roamed the skies."

Creating Unique Cultural Speech Patterns

Develop distinct speech patterns and dialects for different cultures and races within your fantasy world. This adds authenticity and variety to the dialogue.

Example:

"The Elves speak in melodic tones, their words like a gentle breeze through the leaves."

Incorporating Magic and Enchantment

Characters should speak of magic and enchantment naturally, as if it is a normal part of their world. This helps immerse the audience in the fantasy setting.

Example:

"With a flick of her wand, she summoned the winds to carry her message across the realm."

Using Symbolism and Metaphor

Fantasy dialogue often uses symbolism and metaphor to convey deeper meanings and themes.

Example:

"Beware the serpent that lies in wait, for its fangs bring not just death, but eternal darkness."

Crafting Grandiose and Heroic Speech

Epic fantasy often features grandiose and heroic speeches that inspire and rally characters. These speeches should be powerful and stirring.

Example:

"Rise, my friends! Today we fight not just for our lives, but for the future of all we hold dear!"

Reflecting Hierarchies and Titles

Respect the hierarchical structures and titles within your fantasy world. Characters should address each other according to their rank and status.

Example:

"My liege, the armies of the north are at our doorstep. We must prepare for battle."

Highlighting Quests and Journeys

Fantasy dialogue often revolves around quests and journeys. Characters discuss their goals, challenges, and the mystical elements they encounter.

Example:

"We must travel to the enchanted forest and retrieve the Crystal of Eternity before the next full moon."

Incorporating Ancient Languages

Introduce fragments of ancient or mystical languages to add an air of mystery and authenticity to your fantasy world.

Example:

"Eldarion, ai mána meldo, elen sila lumenn' omentielvo."

Using Prophecies and Omens

Prophecies and omens are staples of fantasy literature. They can drive the plot and add an element of fate and destiny.

Example:

"The seer's vision foretold a child born under a blood moon would bring about the kingdom's salvation."

Expressing Loyalty and Betrayal

Themes of loyalty and betrayal are common in fantasy stories. Dialogue should reflect these intense emotional experiences.

Example:

"I swore an oath to protect you, my king. I would rather die than see you harmed."

Describing Magical Creatures and Beings

Characters should speak about magical creatures and beings with wonder, fear, or familiarity, depending on their experiences.

Example:

"The griffins guard the sacred mountain. Only those deemed worthy may pass."

Incorporating Rituals and Traditions

Fantasy worlds often have unique rituals and traditions. Characters' dialogue should reflect their participation in and respect for these customs.

Example:

"During the Festival of Lights, we honor the spirits of our ancestors with song and dance."

Conveying Wisdom and Knowledge

Characters, especially mentors or sages, often impart wisdom and knowledge through their dialogue, guiding the heroes on their journey.

Example:

"Wisdom is not found in the pages of books alone, but in the trials and tribulations of life."

Using Elevated Diction

Elevated diction adds a sense of grandeur and seriousness to the dialogue, suitable for epic moments and important declarations.

Example:

"As the dawn breaks, so shall our resolve. We march to victory or to valiant death!"

Employing Poetic Devices

Use poetic devices such as alliteration, assonance, and rhythm to make the dialogue more lyrical and enchanting.

Example:

"Through forests dark and mountains high, our path is lit by moonlit sky."

Creating Mystical and Enigmatic Dialogue

Characters like wizards, seers, and mystical beings can speak in riddles and enigmatic phrases, adding layers of mystery.

Example:

"Seek the one who sees without eyes and speaks without words; only then shall you find the truth."

Maintaining Consistency

Ensure that the dialogue is consistent with the established rules and tone of your fantasy world. This maintains immersion and believability.

Example:

In a world where magic is common, characters should discuss spells and enchantments as everyday occurrences rather than surprises.

By focusing on these strategies, you can create captivating and immersive dialogue that brings your fantasy world to life.

Continuing to craft captivating fantasy dialogue, we will explore more techniques and examples to further enhance the enchanting and epic quality of your screenplay.

Interweaving Personal and Epic Narratives

Balance personal character moments with the grand scale of epic narratives. Personal dialogue can ground the story while epic dialogue elevates it.

Example:

Personal: "I never knew my father, but I will honor his legacy." Epic: "Our ancestors fought for this land, and we shall defend it with our lives!"

Creating Legendary Backstories

Dialogue can be used to weave legendary backstories and history, adding depth to characters and the world.

Example:

"Long ago, the first king of Eldoria forged this realm with his dragon-fire sword."

Reflecting Diverse Species and Races

Different species and races should have distinct ways of speaking, reflecting their unique cultures and perspectives.

Example:

Elf: "The forest whispers secrets to those who listen." Dwarf: "There's no problem a good hammer can't fix."

Utilizing Pledges and Vows

Fantasy characters often make solemn pledges and vows that carry significant weight. These can add to the epic feel and demonstrate commitment.

Example:

"I vow upon my honor and the spirits of my ancestors to protect you until my last breath."

Describing Otherworldly Phenomena

Characters should describe otherworldly phenomena with wonder and reverence, enhancing the magical atmosphere.

Example:

"The stars aligned in a celestial dance, casting their ethereal glow upon the enchanted lake."

Embedding Political Intrigue

Incorporate political intrigue and courtly dialogue to reflect the complex power dynamics within kingdoms and realms.

Example:

"The council has convened, my lord. They whisper of rebellion and seek to undermine your rule."

Exploring Prophetic Dialogue

Use prophetic dialogue to hint at future events and add an air of destiny and inevitability.

Example:

"When the twin moons align, the chosen one shall rise to reclaim the throne."

Incorporating Mythical Artifacts

Dialogue can include references to mythical artifacts and their significance, adding layers of mystery and importance.

Example:

"The Amulet of Dawn has been lost for centuries. Its power is said to rival that of the gods."

Creating Emotional Resonance

Ensure that dialogue captures the emotional weight of the story, especially in moments of triumph, loss, and sacrifice.

Example:

"Our victory came at a great cost. We shall honor the fallen with every breath we take."

Utilizing Epic Similes and Metaphors

Employ epic similes and metaphors to create vivid imagery and convey the grandeur of the fantasy world.

Example:

"Her beauty was like the first light of dawn, radiant and pure, breaking the eternal night."

Exploring Internal Conflict

Characters can voice their internal conflicts through introspective dialogue, adding depth to their journeys.

Example:

"Every step I take brings me closer to my destiny, yet further from the life I once knew."

Describing Epic Battles

Dialogue during and after battles should reflect the chaos, bravery, and consequences of warfare.

Example:

"Hold the line! For our homes, for our families!"

Highlighting Ancient Wisdom

Characters like wizards, sages, and elders can share ancient wisdom and teachings through their dialogue.

Example:

"Patience, young one. The river of time flows in its own course. We cannot hasten its current."

Conveying the Mystique of Nature

Nature in fantasy worlds often holds a mystical quality. Characters should reflect this in their dialogue.

Example:

"The mountains breathe with the whispers of the ancients, and the rivers sing songs of forgotten lore."

Utilizing Character-Specific Vocabulary

Give each character a distinct vocabulary that reflects their background, profession, and personality.

Example:

A warrior might speak of honor and battles, while a scholar might reference ancient texts and wisdom.

Employing Foreboding Dialogue

Characters can use foreboding dialogue to build tension and hint at impending doom or challenges.

Example:

"A storm is coming, one that will test our courage and strength like never before."

Incorporating Dramatic Monologues

Dramatic monologues can highlight key moments and provide insight into a character's thoughts and motivations.

Example:

"For too long, I have wandered in the shadows, seeking redemption. Today, I step into the light to reclaim my fate."

Reflecting Themes of Destiny and Fate

Dialogue should often touch on themes of destiny and fate, reinforcing the epic nature of the fantasy narrative.

Example:

"It was written in the stars that you would rise, a beacon of hope in our darkest hour."

Balancing Light and Dark Themes

Ensure that dialogue reflects the balance of light and dark themes within your story, highlighting the struggles and triumphs of your characters.

Example:

"In the heart of darkness, we found a spark of hope that guided us back to the light." In summary, continuing to craft enchanting and epic fantasy dialogue involves interweaving personal and epic narratives, creating legendary backstories, reflecting diverse species and races, utilizing pledges and vows, describing otherworldly phenomena, embedding political intrigue, exploring prophetic dialogue, incorporating mythical artifacts, creating emotional resonance, utilizing epic similes and metaphors, exploring internal conflict, describing epic battles, highlighting ancient wisdom, conveying the mystique of nature, utilizing character-specific vocabulary, employing foreboding dialogue, incorporating dramatic monologues, reflecting themes of destiny and fate, and balancing light and dark themes. By focusing on these strategies, you can create immersive and captivating dialogue that enriches your fantasy world and engages your audience.

Horror Dialogue: Building Fear and Suspense

Crafting dialogue for horror requires a delicate balance of building fear, creating suspense, and revealing just enough information to keep the audience on edge. Here are strategies for creating effective horror dialogue that intensifies the atmosphere and keeps the audience hooked.

Using Uncertainty and Ambiguity

Incorporate vague and ambiguous dialogue that leaves room for interpretation, making the audience and characters unsure of what's happening.

Example:

"Did you hear that? I think something's out there."

Employing Short, Choppy Sentences

Short, choppy sentences can convey panic and urgency, heightening the tension.

Example:

"We need to go. Now!"

Revealing Information Slowly

Drip-feed information through the dialogue to build suspense gradually. Characters can discover and reveal crucial details bit by bit.

Example:

"I found something in the basement. It's... I think it's a map."

Using Silence and Pauses

Strategic silences and pauses in dialogue can create tension and make the audience anxious about what might happen next.

Example:

"Where did you say you saw it?" (long pause) "Right behind you."

Creating Contradictory Statements

Characters can make contradictory statements that add to the confusion and fear, leaving others (and the audience) unsure of what to believe.

Example:

"He was here. I swear it." "But the door was locked. How could he have gotten in?"

Incorporating Whispers and Soft Voices

Characters speaking in whispers or hushed tones can create an intimate and eerie atmosphere, making the audience lean in and listen more closely.

Example:

"Keep your voice down. It's listening."

Highlighting Fear and Paranoia

Dialogue should reflect the characters' growing fear and paranoia, making the audience feel their anxiety and uncertainty.

Example:

"I can't shake the feeling that we're being watched."

Using Descriptive and Sensory Language

Include descriptive and sensory language in dialogue to create vivid, unsettling images in the audience's mind.

Example:

"The walls were covered in a sticky, red substance. It smelled like iron."

Foreshadowing

Use dialogue to foreshadow future events or threats, creating a sense of impending doom.

Example:

"I've heard stories about this place. No one who enters ever comes out the same."

Creating Isolated Characters

Characters can express feelings of isolation and helplessness through their dialogue, intensifying the horror.

Example:

"No signal. We're completely cut off from the outside world."

Reflecting Desperation

Desperation in dialogue can make the characters' fear more palpable and urgent.

Example:

"We have to find a way out of here. We can't stay in this house any longer."

Incorporating Unreliable Narrators

Characters who are unreliable or have questionable sanity can add layers of complexity and doubt to the dialogue.

Example:

"I know what I saw. You have to believe me, even if it sounds crazy."

Using Sudden Outbursts

Sudden outbursts of emotion or fear can break the tension and create shocking moments.

Example:

"Get away from me!" she screamed, pushing him aside.

Describing Supernatural Elements

Dialogue should reflect the characters' encounters with supernatural elements, heightening the sense of fear and the unknown.

Example:

"It wasn't a person. It was something else... something not human."

Creating a Sense of Dread

Characters can express a sense of dread and foreboding, making the audience anticipate that something bad is going to happen.

Example:

"I've got a bad feeling about this. We shouldn't be here."

Utilizing Dramatic Irony

Let the audience know something that the characters do not, creating dramatic irony that builds suspense.

Example:

"Don't worry. Everything's fine." (While the audience sees a shadow creeping behind the character)

Reflecting Trauma and Flashbacks

Dialogue can reflect past trauma or flashbacks, revealing how previous experiences influence current fears.

Example:

"I've seen this before. It happened to my brother. He didn't make it out alive."

Using Symbolic Language

Incorporate symbolic language and references that hint at deeper, more sinister meanings.

Example:

"The crows always gather here at dusk. They say it's because of the spirits."

Ending with Cliffhangers

Conclude dialogues with cliffhangers or unresolved questions to keep the audience in suspense.

Example:

"What's that noise?" (Blackout)

In summary, crafting effective horror dialogue involves using uncertainty and ambiguity, employing short, choppy sentences, revealing information slowly, using silence and pauses, creating contradictory statements, incorporating whispers and soft voices, highlighting fear and paranoia, using descriptive and sensory language, foreshadowing, creating isolated characters, reflecting desperation, incorporating unreliable narrators, using sudden outbursts, describing supernatural elements, creating a sense of dread, utilizing dramatic irony, reflecting trauma and flashbacks, using symbolic language, and ending with cliffhangers. By focusing on these strategies, you can create dialogue that builds fear and suspense, keeping your audience on the edge of their seats.

Romance Dialogue: Creating Chemistry

Creating chemistry between characters in a romance involves crafting dialogue that conveys attraction, emotional connection, and the nuances of a developing relationship. Here are strategies for creating effective romance dialogue that builds chemistry and engages the audience.

Using Playful Banter

Incorporate light-hearted teasing and playful banter to show characters' attraction and comfort with each other.

Example:

"You think you can beat me at chess?" "Watch and learn, sweetheart."

Building Tension through Subtext

Use subtext to hint at deeper feelings and desires, creating a layer of tension and anticipation.

Example:

"Do you always look at me like that?" "Like what?" "Like you're seeing something no one else does."

Expressing Vulnerability

Allow characters to show vulnerability and share personal stories or insecurities, deepening their connection.

Example:

"I never told anyone this, but I'm scared of being alone." "You don't have to be. Not anymore."

Creating Intimate Moments

Dialogue in quiet, intimate moments can build emotional closeness and reveal the characters' growing affection.

Example:

"Your laugh is my favorite sound." "Really? I always thought it was too loud." "It's perfect."

Using Compliments and Flattery

Sincere compliments and flattery can show admiration and appreciation, strengthening the bond between characters.

Example:

"You have the most beautiful eyes I've ever seen." "Coming from you, that means a lot."

Highlighting Shared Interests and Values

Dialogue that highlights shared interests and values can establish a foundation for the relationship and create a sense of compatibility.

Example:

"I can't believe you love hiking too. What's your favorite trail?" "Definitely the Blue Ridge. The views are breathtaking."

Reflecting Mutual Respect

Show mutual respect and admiration in the dialogue, emphasizing the healthy and supportive nature of the relationship.

Example:

"I'm really proud of you for going after your dreams." "Thank you. Your support means everything to me."

Building Sexual Tension

Use flirtatious dialogue and suggestive comments to build sexual tension and anticipation.

Example:

"Is it just me, or is it getting hot in here?" "Maybe it's just us."

Creating Emotional Highs and Lows

Incorporate emotional highs and lows in the dialogue to reflect the complexity and intensity of romantic relationships.

Example:

"I can't imagine my life without you." "And I can't bear the thought of losing you."

Using Personal Nicknames

Personal nicknames can add a layer of intimacy and familiarity, showing a special bond between characters.

Example:

"Hey, Sunshine, how was your day?" "Better now that you're here, Moonbeam."

Reflecting Inner Conflict

Characters can express their inner conflicts and doubts about the relationship, adding depth and realism.

Example:

"What if this doesn't work out?" "Then we'll face it together, whatever happens."

Incorporating Physical Touch

Dialogue that describes or alludes to physical touch can enhance the sense of closeness and attraction.

Example:

"Your hand fits perfectly in mine." "It's like they were made for each other."

Sharing Future Dreams and Plans

Discussing future dreams and plans can show the characters' commitment and hope for a shared future.

Example:

"Where do you see us in five years?" "Hopefully, in a little house by the sea, just you and me."

Using Metaphors and Similes

Metaphors and similes can make romantic dialogue more poetic and expressive.

Example:

"Being with you is like coming home after a long journey."

Expressing Jealousy and Possessiveness

Jealousy and possessiveness, when handled carefully, can add tension and show the depth of a character's feelings.

Example:

"I saw the way he looked at you." "You have nothing to worry about. It's you I love."

Building to a Confession of Love

Gradually build up to a confession of love, using dialogue that shows the characters' growing feelings and realizations.

Example:

"I don't know how to say this, but... I think I'm falling for you." "I've been waiting to hear those words."

Highlighting Sacrifices

Dialogue that reflects the sacrifices characters are willing to make for each other can deepen the emotional impact.

Example:

"I'd give up anything to be with you." "You don't have to. We'll find a way together."

Creating Moments of Shared Laughter

Shared laughter can build a sense of camaraderie and joy, enhancing the chemistry between characters.

Example:

"Remember that time we got lost in the city?" "And ended up at that crazy carnival? How could I forget?"

Using Silence Effectively

Strategic use of silence in dialogue can add depth and emotional weight, allowing characters to communicate without words.

Example:

"I..." "Shh. You don't have to say anything. I know."

In summary, creating chemistry in romance dialogue involves using playful banter, building tension through subtext, expressing vulnerability, creating intimate moments, using compliments and flattery, highlighting shared interests and values, reflecting mutual respect, building sexual tension, creating emotional highs and lows, using personal nicknames, reflecting inner conflict, incorporating physical touch, sharing future dreams and plans, using metaphors and similes, expressing jealousy and possessiveness, building to a confession of love, highlighting sacrifices, creating moments of shared laughter, and using silence effectively. By focusing on these strategies, you can create engaging and heartfelt dialogue that brings your romantic relationships to life.

Comedy Dialogue: Timing and Wit

Crafting effective comedy dialogue requires sharp timing, clever wit, and a deep understanding of character dynamics. Here are strategies for creating dialogue that delivers laughs and keeps your audience engaged.

Utilizing Timing and Pacing

Comedy often relies on timing. Proper pacing and well-placed pauses can enhance the comedic impact of dialogue.

Example:

"I thought you said you were a vegetarian." "I am. I'm just really bad at it."

Creating Unexpected Twists

Surprise your audience with unexpected twists in dialogue that subvert their expectations.

Example:

"Why are you wearing a suit?" "It's laundry day. This is all I have left."

Employing Sarcasm and Irony

Sarcasm and irony can add layers of humor, especially when characters deliver lines with a deadpan expression.

Example:

"Oh great, another meeting. Just what I needed to make my day complete."

Using Wordplay and Puns

Wordplay and puns can be a clever way to inject humor into dialogue. The trick is to use them sparingly and ensure they fit naturally within the conversation.

Example:

"I can't believe you broke my favorite mug." "Don't worry, it's a mug-nificent opportunity to buy a new one."

Exaggeration and Hyperbole

Characters can use exaggeration and hyperbole to make their points more dramatically and humorously.

Example:

"I'm so hungry I could eat a horse. A small one. Maybe a pony."

Highlighting Character Flaws

Highlighting characters' flaws and eccentricities can lead to humorous situations and exchanges.

Example:

"I'm not clumsy. The floor just hates me."

Creating Relatable Humor

Humor that taps into universal experiences or everyday situations can resonate strongly with the audience.

Example:

"Why does the Wi-Fi always go out right when I'm about to win a game?" "It's the universe telling you to get a life."

Playing with Double Entendres

Double entendres can add a layer of sophistication to your humor, appealing to audiences who appreciate clever wordplay.

Example:

"Are you coming to the party tonight?" "I'm on the fence." "Be careful. That's how splinters happen."

Developing Running Gags

Running gags or recurring jokes can create a sense of continuity and payoff when revisited throughout the narrative.

Example:

"Is that your infamous lucky tie?" "Lucky? It's brought me nothing but strange looks and bad coffee."

Creating Contrast with Serious Situations

Humor can be heightened by placing it in contrast with more serious or tense situations.

Example:

"We're trapped in an elevator with no cell service." "Great, now I have to talk to you. My worst nightmare."

Using Visual Humor and Physical Comedy

Incorporate visual humor and physical comedy in conjunction with dialogue to create a more dynamic comedic effect.

Example:

"I'm fine. Totally fine." (As character says this, they knock over a vase, slip on the water, and fall)

Highlighting Miscommunication

Misunderstandings and miscommunication can lead to humorous exchanges and situations.

Example:

"Can you pass the salt?" "Sure. Where are you going?"

Leveraging Awkwardness and Social Faux Pas

Awkward situations and social faux pas can be a rich source of humor, especially if the character is oblivious to their own missteps.

Example:

"Nice to meet you. I'm a hugger." (The other person awkwardly extends a hand for a handshake)

Employing Rapid-Fire Dialogue

Fast-paced, rapid-fire exchanges can create a lively, energetic humor dynamic.

Example:

"Did you see that?" "See what?" "That!" "What?" "Never mind, it's gone."

Breaking the Fourth Wall

Occasionally breaking the fourth wall can add a meta-humor element, engaging the audience directly.

Example:

"Of course this is happening. Why wouldn't it be? It's not like things were going well before." (Glances at the camera)

Using Callback Jokes

Callback jokes refer back to earlier lines or situations, creating a sense of continuity and rewarding attentive audiences.

Example:

Earlier in the story: "I'll bet you five bucks you'll be late." Later: "Looks like I owe you five bucks."

Highlighting Incongruity

Pointing out incongruous or absurd elements in a situation can be highly effective for humor.

Example:

"We're going on a diet." "Right after we finish this cake?" "Of course. No sense in wasting food."

Incorporating Cultural References

Use cultural references that your audience will understand and appreciate, but be mindful of ensuring they remain relevant over time.

Example:

"Trying to solve this is like trying to figure out the ending of 'Lost.'"

Exploring Satire and Parody

Satire and parody allow you to humorously critique societal norms, genres, or specific subjects.

Example:

"Oh, look! Another superhero movie. Because we definitely don't have enough of those."

In summary, creating effective comedy dialogue involves utilizing timing and pacing, creating unexpected twists, employing sarcasm and irony, using wordplay and puns, exaggeration and hyperbole, highlighting character flaws, creating relatable humor, playing with double entendres, developing running gags, creating contrast with serious situations, using visual humor and physical comedy, highlighting miscommunication, leveraging awkwardness and social faux pas, employing rapid-fire dialogue, breaking the fourth wall, using callback jokes, highlighting incongruity, incorporating cultural references, and exploring satire and parody. By focusing on these strategies, you can craft witty and engaging dialogue that brings humor and energy to your screenplay.

Drama Dialogue: Emotional Depth

Creating dialogue that conveys emotional depth in a drama requires a nuanced understanding of characters, relationships, and the human condition. Effective dramatic dialogue should reveal inner conflicts, convey intense emotions, and drive the narrative forward. Here are strategies for crafting emotionally resonant dialogue in drama.

Exploring Inner Conflict

Characters should express their internal struggles and dilemmas through dialogue, revealing their vulnerabilities and complexities.

Example:

"I don't know if I can forgive you. Every time I look at you, I see the betrayal."

Using Subtext

Subtext allows characters to convey deeper meanings and emotions beneath the surface of their words, adding layers to the dialogue.

Example:

"I'm really happy for you." (When the character is actually feeling jealous or hurt)

Expressing Vulnerability

Allow characters to show vulnerability, making them more relatable and authentic.

Example:

"I've always been afraid of failing. Every time I try, I hear my father's voice telling me I'm not good enough."

Incorporating Silence and Pauses

Strategic use of silence and pauses can emphasize the weight of the dialogue, allowing emotions to resonate.

Example:

"I... I need some time to think." (Pause) "Take all the time you need."

Reflecting Realistic Conversations

Ensure dialogue feels natural and realistic, reflecting how people genuinely speak, including interruptions, hesitations, and unfinished thoughts.

Example:

"It's just... I mean... I thought we were okay. But now..."

Using Monologues

Monologues can provide a deep dive into a character's psyche, allowing them to articulate their inner thoughts and emotions.

Example:

"Every morning, I wake up and wonder if today will be any different. If today, I'll find a reason to smile."

Highlighting Relationships

Dialogue should reflect the dynamics and complexities of relationships, showing how characters interact and affect each other.

Example:

"You're the only person who knows me, really knows me. And that's why it hurts so much that you lied."

Creating Tension and Conflict

Conflict is at the heart of drama. Use dialogue to heighten tensions and reveal the stakes involved.

Example:

"You think you can just walk back into my life after all these years? It doesn't work that way."

Using Descriptive Language

Descriptive language can paint a vivid picture of emotions and settings, enhancing the mood and tone of the scene.

Example:

"The room felt like a tomb, cold and suffocating, filled with the ghosts of unspoken words."

Revealing Backstory

Dialogue can subtly reveal backstory, providing context and depth to characters' current actions and emotions.

Example:

"You weren't there when Mom died. You have no idea what I went through."

Creating Emotional Highs and Lows

Balance moments of intense emotion with quieter, reflective dialogue to create a dynamic emotional landscape.

Example:

"I can't do this anymore. I'm tired." (Softly) "I know. But we have to keep going. For them."

Expressing Regret and Forgiveness

Dialogue around regret and forgiveness can be deeply moving, showing characters grappling with their past actions and seeking redemption.

Example:

"I'm sorry for everything. I wish I could take it all back."

Highlighting Personal Growth

Characters should evolve, and their dialogue should reflect this growth, showing how they change over the course of the story.

Example:

"I used to think I needed someone to complete me. But now, I realize I'm enough on my own."

Using Symbolism and Metaphors

Symbolic language and metaphors can add depth and resonance to dialogue, conveying complex emotions and themes.

Example:

"You're like a storm. Beautiful, powerful, and completely unpredictable."

Reflecting Cultural and Social Contexts

Dialogue should reflect the cultural and social contexts of the characters, adding authenticity and depth to their interactions.

Example:

"In our family, we don't talk about feelings. We just keep going, no matter what."

Incorporating Dramatic Irony

Dramatic irony can enhance the emotional impact of dialogue, where the audience knows more than the characters, creating a poignant contrast.

Example:

"It's just a routine check-up. I'm sure it's nothing serious." (Knowing the character has a serious illness)

Expressing Hope and Despair

Balance expressions of hope and despair to create a rich emotional tapestry, reflecting the ups and downs of the human experience.

Example:

"Even in the darkest times, I believe there's a chance for something better."

Creating Relatable Emotions

Ensure that the emotions conveyed in dialogue are relatable and grounded in real human experiences, allowing the audience to connect deeply with the characters.

Example:

"I'm terrified of being alone. But I'm even more terrified of being with someone who doesn't really see me."

Exploring Ethical and Moral Dilemmas

Characters can grapple with ethical and moral dilemmas through their dialogue, adding depth and complexity to the narrative.

Example:

"Doing the right thing isn't always easy. Sometimes, it feels impossible. But we have to try."

In summary, creating emotionally resonant drama dialogue involves exploring inner conflict, using subtext, expressing vulnerability, incorporating silence and pauses, reflecting realistic conversations, using monologues, highlighting relationships, creating tension and conflict, using descriptive language, revealing backstory, creating emotional highs and lows, expressing regret and forgiveness, highlighting personal growth, using symbolism and metaphors, reflecting cultural and social contexts, incorporating dramatic irony, expressing hope and despair, creating relatable emotions, and exploring ethical and moral dilemmas. By focusing on these strategies, you can craft dialogue that adds emotional depth and complexity to your screenplay, engaging your audience and enriching your narrative.

Action Dialogue: Urgency and Brevity

Creating effective dialogue for action scenes requires a focus on urgency, brevity, and clarity. The dialogue should enhance the fast-paced nature of action sequences while maintaining the tension and driving the plot forward. Here are strategies for crafting dialogue that captures the essence of action-packed moments.

Using Short, Punchy Sentences

Keep sentences short and to the point to reflect the urgency and rapid pace of action scenes.

Example:

"Move! Now!"

Conveying Urgency

Characters should speak with a sense of urgency, emphasizing the immediate need for action or decision-making.

Example:

"We've got to get out of here before it's too late."

Giving Clear Instructions

Action scenes often require clear instructions to ensure everyone understands what needs to be done quickly.

Example:

"Cover me! I'll disarm the bomb."

Reflecting Tension and Stress

Dialogue should reflect the tension and stress of the situation, with characters showing signs of pressure.

Example:

"Stay focused. We can't afford any mistakes."

Using Commands and Directives

Commands and directives keep the dialogue assertive and action-oriented, ensuring swift responses.

Example:

"Get down!"

Reacting to Immediate Threats

Characters should react to immediate threats or changes in the environment, keeping the dialogue dynamic and responsive.

Example:

"Watch out! Incoming!"

Incorporating Brevity and Efficiency

Efficiency in language is key; characters should use the fewest words necessary to convey their message.

Example:

"Got it?" "Got it."

Highlighting Stakes

Dialogue should remind the audience of the stakes involved, emphasizing the high risk and potential consequences.

Example:

"If we don't stop them, thousands will die."

Using Urgent Questions

Urgent questions can convey the need for immediate information or decision-making.

Example:

"How much time do we have?"

Reflecting Physical Activity

Dialogue should reflect the physical activity and movement of the characters, often delivered between breaths or grunts.

Example:

"Keep running! Don't look back!"

Showing Determination

Characters' determination and resolve should be evident in their dialogue, highlighting their commitment to the task.

Example:

"We're not leaving anyone behind."

Creating Rhythmic Cadence

Match the rhythm of the dialogue to the pacing of the action, creating a seamless flow between speech and movement.

Example:

"On my count. Three, two, one. Go!"

Using Tactical Language

Incorporate tactical or strategic language, especially for characters with military or specialized training.

Example:

"Secure the perimeter. No one gets in or out."

Reflecting Urgent Problem-Solving

Characters often need to solve problems on the fly, with dialogue reflecting quick thinking and adaptability.

Example:

"The bridge is out. We need another way across!"

Incorporating Shouts and Exclamations

Shouts and exclamations can enhance the intensity of the scene and convey immediate reactions.

Example:

"Hold the line!"

Using Interrupted Speech

Characters might interrupt each other or be interrupted by events, reflecting the chaotic nature of action scenes.

Example:

"We have to—" (Explosion) "Get down!"

Emphasizing Critical Moments

Highlight critical moments with pointed dialogue that underscores their importance.

Example:

"This is our only shot. Make it count."

Reflecting Team Dynamics.

Show the dynamics of a team under pressure, with dialogue that emphasizes cooperation and coordination.

Example:

"I need cover fire. You, take the left flank."

Incorporating Defiant Speech

Defiant or rallying speech can inspire characters and heighten the stakes of the action.

Example:

"We're not giving up. Not now, not ever."

Balancing Dialogue and Action

Ensure dialogue complements the physical action, without overshadowing or slowing it down.

Example:

"Get the door!" (Action: Character rushes to secure the door while another holds off enemies)

In summary, crafting effective action dialogue involves using short, punchy sentences, conveying urgency, giving clear instructions, reflecting tension and stress, using commands and directives, reacting to immediate threats, incorporating brevity and efficiency, highlighting stakes, using urgent questions, reflecting physical activity, showing determination, creating rhythmic cadence, using tactical language, reflecting urgent problem-solving, incorporating shouts and exclamations, using interrupted speech, emphasizing critical moments, reflecting team dynamics, incorporating defiant speech, and balancing dialogue and action. By focusing on these strategies, you can create dynamic and engaging dialogue that enhances the intensity and pace of your action scenes.

Thriller Dialogue: Tension and Twists

Thriller dialogue is all about creating suspense, building tension, and delivering unexpected twists. It should keep the audience on the edge of their seats, always guessing and eager for the next revelation. Here are strategies for crafting effective thriller dialogue that enhances tension and delivers impactful twists.

Creating Suspenseful Conversations

Build suspense by having characters discuss or hint at looming threats and dangers.

Example:

"Something's not right. I can feel it in my bones."

Using Ambiguity and Vagueness

Characters can speak in ambiguous terms, leaving key details out and allowing the audience to fill in the gaps with their imagination.

Example:

"There are things you don't know. Things you wouldn't believe."

Incorporating Subtext

Subtext adds layers of meaning to dialogue, making what's unsaid just as important as what is said.

Example:

"Have you spoken to the police?" "Why would I do that?"

Delivering Information Slowly

Reveal crucial information bit by bit, keeping the audience hooked and wanting more.

Example:

"I found something. But you're not going to like it."

Using Red Herrings

Introduce misleading clues or statements that divert attention from the true plot, keeping the audience guessing.

Example:

"I think the gardener saw something. Maybe we should talk to him."

Employing Dramatic Pauses

Strategic pauses can heighten tension, making the audience anticipate what will be said next.

Example:

"Do you know who did it?" (Long pause) "Yes. I do."

Highlighting Desperation and Urgency

Characters often face desperate situations in thrillers. Their dialogue should reflect their urgency and high stakes.

Example:

"We have to move now! There's no time to waste."

Incorporating Threats and Ultimatums

Threats and ultimatums raise the stakes and add a sense of immediate danger.

Example:

"You have 24 hours to deliver, or your family pays the price."

Using Misdirection

Characters can mislead others intentionally, adding complexity and unexpected turns to the plot.

Example:

"Meet me at the old warehouse at midnight." (Later reveals it was a trap)

Building Psychological Tension

Dialogue can reflect the psychological tension between characters, especially in cat-and-mouse scenarios.

Example:

"You think you're safe? Think again."

Creating Cliffhangers

End scenes or dialogues with cliffhangers, leaving the audience in suspense.

Example:

"I know who the killer is. It's—" (Cut to black)

Exploring Inner Conflicts

Characters should express their inner conflicts, adding depth and complexity to their motivations and actions.

Example:

"I don't know if I can trust you anymore. But I don't have a choice."

Incorporating Revelations

Revelations and confessions should be shocking and unexpected, altering the course of the story.

Example:

"It was me. I've been working with them all along."

Reflecting Manipulation and Deception

Characters in thrillers often manipulate and deceive each other. Their dialogue should reflect these tactics.

Example:

"You can trust me. I'm on your side." (While secretly planning a betrayal)

Highlighting Moral Dilemmas

Characters in thrillers often face moral dilemmas. Their dialogue should reflect their struggle with these choices.

Example:

"If saving one means losing many, can you still live with yourself?"

Using Foreshadowing

Subtly foreshadow future events through dialogue, creating anticipation and tension.

Example:

"Remember, not everything is as it seems."

Reflecting High Stakes

Ensure dialogue consistently reflects the high stakes involved in the story, keeping the tension high.

Example:

"If we fail, it's not just our lives on the line. It's everyone's."

Incorporating Tense Confrontations

Characters should have tense confrontations that bring underlying conflicts to the surface.

Example:

"You think you can control everything. But you're wrong."

Creating Dynamic Power Shifts

Dialogue should reflect the shifting power dynamics between characters, especially in high-stakes scenarios.

Example:

"You're not in charge here anymore. I am."

Revealing Hidden Agendas

Characters often have hidden agendas. Dialogue should hint at or reveal these secrets in impactful ways.

Example:

"I've been playing you from the start. Every move you made was exactly what I wanted."

Tension and Twists

Continuing to enhance the suspense and unpredictability of thriller dialogue, we will explore additional techniques and examples to deepen the tension and deliver unexpected twists.

Creating Mysterious Introductions

Introduce characters with mysterious or ambiguous dialogue, making the audience question their motives and backgrounds.

Example:

"People call me many things, but you can call me a friend. For now."

Using Coded Messages and Riddles

Characters can communicate through coded messages or riddles, adding an element of intrigue and mystery.

Example:

"Follow the path where the shadows meet. Only then will you find what you seek."

Revealing Unreliable Information

Characters may provide unreliable or conflicting information, keeping the audience guessing about the truth.

Example:

"He said he was there all night, but the security footage says otherwise."

Incorporating Interrogations

Interrogation scenes can heighten tension and reveal crucial information. The power dynamics in these scenes should be evident in the dialogue.

Example:

"Where were you last night?" "I already told you, I don't remember!"

Using Flashbacks and Reveals

Use dialogue to trigger flashbacks or reveal past events that are critical to understanding the present situation.

Example:

"Remember that night in Paris? It wasn't an accident."

Highlighting Dual Identities

Characters with dual identities or hidden lives can create compelling twists and tension through their dialogue.

Example:

"You think you know me, but the person you see is just a mask."

Reflecting Paranoia

Dialogue can reflect a character's growing paranoia, making the audience question what is real and what is imagined.

Example:

"They're watching us. I can feel their eyes on me all the time."

Creating Ambiguous Endings

End dialogues or scenes with ambiguity, leaving the audience uncertain and eager for more information.

Example:

"Did you find what you were looking for?" "Maybe. Or maybe it found me."

Using Power Plays and Manipulation

Characters can engage in power plays and manipulation, using dialogue to assert dominance or control over others.

Example:

"You're in over your head. Walk away while you still can."

Incorporating Betrayals

Betrayals can be revealed through shocking dialogue, turning the story on its head and heightening the drama.

Example:

"It was you. You've been betraying us all along."

Reflecting Desperation and Last Chances

Characters often face last-chance scenarios in thrillers. Their dialogue should reflect the desperation and finality of these moments.

Example:

"This is our only shot. We can't afford to fail."

Building Confessions

Slowly build up to confessions, using dialogue to peel back layers of deceit and reveal the truth.

Example:

"I didn't mean for it to happen. But once it started, I couldn't stop."

Highlighting Escape Plans

Characters devising escape plans or last-ditch efforts can create tension and urgency in the dialogue.

Example:

"We need to get out of here. Now. Here's the plan."

Reflecting Isolation and Hopelessness

Isolation and a sense of hopelessness can be conveyed through dialogue, emphasizing the dire circumstances characters face.

Example:

"There's no one coming to save us. We're on our own."

Exploring Trust and Distrust

Dialogue can explore themes of trust and distrust, with characters questioning each other's loyalty and intentions.

Example:

"Can I trust you?" "You don't have a choice."

Incorporating Countdown Timers

Use dialogue to introduce countdown timers or deadlines, creating a ticking clock that heightens tension.

Example:

"We have ten minutes before the bomb goes off. Move!"

Creating Ambiguous Loyalties

Characters with ambiguous loyalties can add layers of intrigue and unpredictability to the dialogue.

Example:

"I'm not here for them. I'm here for me."

Using Confrontations and Showdowns

Confrontations and showdowns between characters can be intense and climactic, with dialogue reflecting the high stakes.

Example:

"This ends here. One way or another."

Highlighting Moral Ambiguity

Characters in thrillers often operate in morally grey areas. Their dialogue should reflect this ambiguity and complexity.

Example:

"Sometimes, you have to do bad things for good reasons. Can you live with that?"

Using Layered Dialogue

Layer dialogue with multiple meanings or implications, making conversations rich and complex.

Example:

"You've always been good at hiding things." "You have no idea how good."

Reflecting Conflicting Emotions

Characters can express conflicting emotions through their dialogue, adding depth to their psychological state.

Example:

"I hate you for what you did, but I can't stop loving you."

Incorporating Sudden Realizations

Characters can have sudden realizations or epiphanies in the middle of conversations, shifting the direction of the dialogue and the story.

Example:

"Wait a minute... If he was there, then he couldn't have... Oh my God, we've been wrong all along."

Using Deceptive Calmness

Characters speaking with a deceptive calmness can create a chilling effect, hinting at underlying menace.

Example:

"I'm not angry. I'm just disappointed. And you know how dangerous that can be."

Creating False Security

Give characters a false sense of security through dialogue, only to shatter it with an unexpected twist.

Example:

"Everything's under control. You're safe now." (Alarm blares)

Highlighting Dual Meanings

Use dialogue that can be interpreted in different ways, adding layers of meaning and tension.

Example:

"It's funny how things come full circle, isn't it?"

Revealing Double Agents

Introduce or reveal double agents through dialogue, adding an element of betrayal and surprise.

Example:

"You think you're so clever, don't you?" "Clever enough to know you're working for them."

Incorporating Psychological Manipulation

Characters can manipulate each other psychologically, using dialogue to play mind games and create tension.

Example:

"Are you sure you're not imagining things? Sometimes the mind plays tricks on us."

Reflecting Fatalistic Attitudes

Characters with fatalistic attitudes can convey a sense of inevitable doom, heightening the suspense.

Example:

"It doesn't matter what we do. It's already too late."

Using Misdirection in Conversations

Characters can misdirect each other in conversations, leading to unexpected revelations or twists.

Example:

"I'm looking for someone." "Really? Who?" "You."

Creating Enigmatic Responses

Characters can give enigmatic or cryptic responses, leaving others (and the audience) puzzled and intrigued.

Example:

"What are you hiding?" "More than you can imagine."

Building to Explosive Revelations

Slowly build up to explosive revelations, using dialogue to create a crescendo of tension.

Example:

"I've been lying to you. From the very beginning."

Incorporating Memory and Flashbacks

Characters can discuss memories or flashbacks, revealing critical information and adding depth to the narrative.

Example:

"Do you remember that night? The one we promised never to talk about?"

Using Non-Sequiturs

Introduce non-sequiturs in dialogue to create disorientation and unease, reflecting a fractured or unstable state of mind.

Example:

"Pass the salt, would you?" "We're all going to die."

Creating Layered Motives

Characters can have layered motives that are revealed through dialogue, adding complexity to their actions and decisions.

Example:

"I didn't do it for the money. I did it because I wanted to watch you suffer."

Incorporating Dark Humor

Dark humor can add a unique tension to thriller dialogue, providing relief while maintaining the overall suspense.

Example:

"Well, this is just great. Trapped in a basement with a killer on the loose. Perfect end to a perfect day."

Exploring Ethical Dilemmas

Characters grappling with ethical dilemmas can reveal their inner conflicts and add depth to the narrative.

Example:

"If saving her means sacrificing them, can I still do it?"

Using Cliffhanger Statements

End scenes or dialogues with cliffhanger statements, keeping the audience in suspense.

Example:

"I know who the mole is. It's—"

Incorporating Foreshadowing

Foreshadow future events through dialogue, creating anticipation and a sense of impending doom.

Example:

"Mark my words, this isn't over. Not by a long shot."

Enhancing thriller dialogue involves using layered dialogue, reflecting conflicting emotions, incorporating sudden realizations, using deceptive calmness, creating false security, highlighting dual meanings, revealing double agents, incorporating psychological manipulation, reflecting fatalistic attitudes, using misdirection in conversations, creating enigmatic responses, building to explosive revelations, incorporating memory and flashbacks, using non-sequiturs, creating layered motives, incorporating dark humor, exploring ethical dilemmas, using cliffhanger statements, and incorporating foreshadowing. By focusing on these strategies, you can maintain high tension, deliver unexpected twists, and keep your audience thoroughly engaged in your thriller narrative.

Historical Dialogue: Authenticity and Accuracy

Creating authentic and accurate historical dialogue requires thorough research, a keen ear for period-appropriate language, and an understanding of the social and cultural context of the time. Here are strategies for crafting dialogue that immerses the audience in a historical setting while maintaining authenticity and accuracy.

Researching Period Language

Thoroughly research the language, slang, idioms, and expressions of the time period to ensure the dialogue is authentic.

Example:

"Pray, sir, might I inquire as to the time?"

Using Formal and Polite Speech

Depending on the historical period, speech was often more formal and polite compared to modern-day language.

Example:

"It is an honor to make your acquaintance, Lady Elizabeth."

Reflecting Social Hierarchies

Dialogue should reflect the social hierarchies and relationships of the time, including titles, ranks, and forms of address.

Example:

"Yes, Your Grace, I shall attend to it at once."

Incorporating Historical Events and Figures

Reference historical events, figures, and customs to ground the dialogue in its specific historical context.

Example:

"Have you heard the latest news from the front? General Washington's troops have claimed a decisive victory."

Avoiding Anachronisms

Ensure that words, phrases, and concepts that were not used or known in the period are avoided to maintain authenticity.

Example:

Avoid: "Let's grab a coffee and brainstorm." Instead: "Shall we take tea and discuss our plans?"

Capturing the Rhythm and Cadence

Capture the rhythm and cadence of speech from the era, which may involve longer sentences and a different structure.

Example:

"It is with great regret that I must inform you of the unfortunate demise of our dear friend."

Reflecting Historical Attitudes and Beliefs

Characters' dialogue should reflect the attitudes, beliefs, and norms of the time, even if they differ from contemporary views.

Example:

"It is widely believed that a lady's virtue is her most prized possession."

Using Period-Appropriate Titles and Terms of Address

Use correct titles and terms of address for different social classes and relationships.

Example:

"Good day, Mr. Darcy."

Incorporating Dialects and Accents

When appropriate, incorporate dialects and accents to add authenticity, but ensure it remains readable and not overly distracting.

Example:

"Ye ken we'll be late if we dinna leave soon."

Reflecting Historical Gender Roles

Dialogue should reflect the gender roles and expectations of the time, providing authenticity and context.

Example:

"As a woman, it is not my place to speak out in the council, but I must voice my concerns."

Using Historical Jargon and Technical Terms

Incorporate jargon and technical terms relevant to the professions, trades, and activities of the time.

Example:

"Fetch the apothecary; we require his expertise in concocting a remedy for this ailment."

Showing Historical Conflict and Tension

Dialogue can reflect historical conflicts and tensions, such as class struggles, political unrest, or cultural clashes.

Example:

"The peasants are revolting against the lord's taxes; it will not be long before the city is in chaos."

Incorporating Literary and Artistic References

Characters might reference contemporary literature, art, and cultural works of their time.

Example:

"Have you read the latest pamphlet by Mr. Paine? His words are truly revolutionary."

Reflecting Historical Etiquette and Manners

Ensure dialogue reflects the etiquette and manners of the period, which often governed social interactions strictly.

Example:

"Please, allow me to escort you to the ballroom, Miss Bennett."

Using Appropriate Emotional Expression

Characters' expressions of emotion should be true to the time period, which might involve more restrained or formal ways of showing feelings.

Example:

"I am deeply honored by your kind words, and I assure you they are reciprocated."

Reflecting Historical Education and Literacy

Characters' language should reflect their level of education and literacy, which varied widely in different historical periods and social classes.

Example:

A noble might say, "Indeed, the stars align most fortuitously for our endeavors." A peasant might say, "The stars are good for us, they are."

Balancing Authenticity with Readability

While striving for authenticity, ensure the dialogue remains accessible and engaging for modern readers.

Example:

Authentic: "I must beg your pardon, but it is imperative that we depart forthwith."

Balanced: "I'm sorry, but we need to leave immediately."

Incorporating Religious and Superstitious Beliefs

Reflect the religious and superstitious beliefs prevalent in the time period through characters' dialogue.

Example:

"God willing, we shall have a bountiful harvest this year."

Using Historical Similes and Metaphors

Incorporate similes and metaphors that would be familiar and relevant to the period.

Example:

"Her beauty shines like the morning sun upon dewdrops."

In summary, crafting authentic and accurate historical dialogue involves researching period language, using formal and polite speech, reflecting social hierarchies, incorporating historical events and figures, avoiding anachronisms, capturing the rhythm and cadence of the era, reflecting historical attitudes and beliefs, using period-appropriate titles and terms of address, incorporating dialects and accents, reflecting historical gender roles, using historical jargon and technical terms, showing historical conflict and tension, incorporating literary and artistic references, reflecting historical etiquette and manners, using appropriate emotional expression, reflecting historical education and literacy, balancing authenticity with readability, incorporating religious and superstitious beliefs, and using historical similes and metaphors. By focusing on these strategies, you can create immersive and engaging historical dialogue that enhances the authenticity and accuracy of your narrative.

Writing for Ensemble Casts: Multiple Voices

Writing for an ensemble cast requires balancing multiple characters, ensuring each has a distinct voice, and weaving their narratives together seamlessly. Here are strategies for creating compelling and dynamic dialogue for ensemble casts.

Establishing Distinct Voices

Give each character a unique voice that reflects their personality, background, and role in the story.

Example:

Anna: "We must stick to the plan. It's the only way." Tom: "Plans are overrated. Let's just see what happens."

Balancing Screen Time

Ensure that each character has enough dialogue and screen time to develop their story arc and contribute to the overall narrative.

Example:

Scene 1: Focus on Anna's leadership. Scene 2: Shift to Tom's spontaneity. Scene 3: Introduce Sarah's empathy.

Creating Interwoven Storylines

Intertwine the characters' storylines, allowing their interactions to drive the plot forward and create cohesion.

Example:

Anna and Tom argue about the plan while Sarah tries to mediate, revealing different aspects of their personalities.

Reflecting Relationships

Dialogue should reflect the various relationships between characters, whether they are friends, rivals, or lovers.

Example:

Anna: "You never take anything seriously, Tom!" Tom: "And you're always too serious, Anna. Maybe we balance each other out."

Using Group Dynamics

Showcase the dynamics of the group, including conflicts, alliances, and shifting loyalties.

Example:

Anna: "We need to vote on this." Sarah: "I'm with Anna. We need a plan." Tom: "You two can vote. I'll be over there, improvising."

Maintaining Individual Arcs

Each character should have their own arc that contributes to the overall story but also stands alone as a complete journey.

Example:

Anna's arc: Learning to trust others. Tom's arc: Understanding the value of planning. Sarah's arc: Finding her voice as a mediator.

Highlighting Different Perspectives

Characters should bring different perspectives to the table, reflecting their unique experiences and viewpoints.

Example:

Anna: "We have to think long-term." Tom: "I'm just trying to survive the next five minutes." Sarah: "Can we please find a middle ground?"

Using Conflict to Drive Dialogue

Conflict is a natural part of ensemble casts. Use it to create tension and reveal character traits.

Example:

Anna: "If you had listened to me, we wouldn't be in this mess!" Tom: "And if you had loosened up, we might have actually enjoyed ourselves."

Creating Moments of Unity

Balance conflicts with moments of unity where the ensemble comes together, showcasing their strength as a group.

Example:

Anna: "We might not always agree, but we need to stick together." Tom: "For once, I agree with Anna. Let's do this."

Reflecting Social and Cultural Contexts

Ensure the dialogue reflects the social and cultural contexts of each character, adding depth and authenticity.

Example:

Anna, the disciplined leader: "We have to stick to protocol." Tom, the rebellious spirit: "Protocols are made to be broken." Sarah, the empathetic mediator: "Can we find a way that respects both views?"

Incorporating Subplots

Subplots involving different characters can enrich the narrative and provide additional layers to the main plot.

Example:

Anna's subplot: Struggling with family expectations. Tom's subplot: Seeking adventure and freedom. Sarah's subplot: Balancing her personal and group responsibilities.

Using Humor and Wit

Inject humor and wit into the dialogue to lighten the mood and build rapport between characters.

Example:

Tom: "What's the worst that could happen?" Anna: "Do you really want a list?"

Showing Character Growth

Dialogue should reflect the characters' growth and changes over the course of the story.

Example:

Early in the story: Anna: "Stick to the plan, no deviations." Later in the story: Anna: "Okay, Tom, what's your idea?"

Reflecting Group Evolution

As the ensemble evolves, their dialogue should reflect their changing dynamics and strengthened bonds.

Example:

Anna: "I never thought I'd say this, but maybe Tom's right." Tom: "See, miracles do happen."

Using Overlapping Dialogue

In scenes with multiple characters, use overlapping dialogue to create a realistic and dynamic flow of conversation.

Example:

Anna: "We need to—" Tom: "—figure this out quickly." Sarah: "Everyone, calm down!"

Incorporating External Threats

External threats can bring the ensemble together or drive them apart, depending on how they respond.

Example:

Anna: "The storm's getting worse. We need to find shelter." Tom: "There's an old cabin nearby. Follow me." Sarah: "I hope it's still standing."

Developing Unique Speech Patterns

Give each character a distinct speech pattern or catchphrase that sets them apart.

Example:

Anna: "By the book." Tom: "Go with the flow." Sarah: "Let's find a balance."

Reflecting Inner Conflicts

Characters' inner conflicts can be revealed through their dialogue, adding depth to their personalities.

Example:

Anna: "I can't afford to fail. Everyone's counting on me." Tom: "You're too hard on yourself, Anna. It's okay to ask for help."

Using Climactic Dialogues

In climactic moments, use powerful and emotionally charged dialogue to heighten the stakes and impact.

Example:

Anna: "This is it. We either succeed together, or we fail alone." Tom: "Then let's make sure we succeed."

By focusing on these strategies, you can create rich and dynamic ensemble dialogue that brings your characters to life and drives your narrative forward.

Contemporary Dialogue: Reflecting Modern Speech

Writing contemporary dialogue involves capturing the essence of how people communicate today. This means reflecting current linguistic trends, cultural references, and social dynamics in a way that feels authentic and relatable. Here's how you can achieve that in your screenplay.

Understanding Modern Speech Patterns

Contemporary dialogue often mirrors the way people speak in real life, including the use of contractions, slang, and informal expressions. Pay attention to how people interact in your target demographic and reflect that in your writing.

Example:

"Can't believe you're late again," said Sam, rolling his eyes. "Seriously, it's like you don't even try."

Incorporating Slang and Colloquialisms

Use current slang and colloquial expressions to make characters sound authentic. However, be cautious not to overdo it; slang can quickly become dated.

Example:

"Dude, that's totally lit," exclaimed Alex, grinning. "Where'd you get that?"

Reflecting Technological Influences

Modern dialogue often incorporates references to technology and social media, as these are integral to contemporary life. This can include mentions of apps, online culture, or digital communication styles.

Example:

"Did you see her post on Instagram?" Jenna asked, scrolling through her phone. "It's everywhere."

Utilizing Informal and Casual Speech

Contemporary dialogue tends to be more informal and conversational. Avoid overly formal language unless it suits a specific character or context.

Example:

"I'm so not in the mood for this," said Mark. "Can we just, like, not?"

Including Interruptions and Overlaps

People often talk over each other and interrupt in real conversations. Reflect this in your dialogue to capture the spontaneity and realism of modern speech.

Example:

Lisa: "I don't think—" Paul: "Wait, let me finish." Lisa: "No, but—" Paul: "Seriously, just listen!"

Using Modern Humor and References

Integrate contemporary humor and cultural references to keep the dialogue relevant and engaging. This includes jokes, memes, or references to current events.

Example:

"Man, this is like the worst season finale ever," said Chris. "I mean, who writes this stuff?"

Showing Social Media Influence

Characters might discuss or be influenced by social media trends, viral content, or online personas. Reflect this influence in their interactions and conversations.

Example:

"Everyone's talking about that new TikTok challenge," Emily said. "I've seen it everywhere."

Capturing Diverse Speech Patterns

Contemporary dialogue should reflect the diversity of voices in modern society, including different accents, sociolects, and speech styles.

Example:

"I'm tellin' ya, that's not how it works around here," said Maria, her accent coloring her words.

Reflecting Changing Attitudes and Norms

Modern dialogue should acknowledge evolving social attitudes and norms, such as inclusivity, mental health awareness, and environmental concerns.

Example:

"Have you ever thought about going vegan?" asked Jordan. "It's a game-changer for the planet."

Using Dialogue to Reveal Trends

Current dialogue can reflect ongoing societal trends or issues, giving insight into characters' lives and perspectives.

Example:

"I'm just so over the hustle culture," said Taylor. "It's like everyone's just burning out."

Crafting Dialogue for Different Demographics

Tailor dialogue to fit the specific age group, profession, or social background of your characters to ensure it feels authentic.

Example:

For teenagers: "That's so fetch," said Jessica. "Seriously, you need to catch up." For professionals: "We need to pivot our strategy," said Marcus. "The current model isn't working."

Integrating Current Phrases and Expressions

Incorporate phrases that are popular in contemporary vernacular, but be cautious to avoid clichés.

Example:

"Let's just keep it 100," said Ava. "We need to be honest about what's happening."

Reflecting Regional Variations

Different regions have unique ways of speaking. If your characters come from different places, include regional variations in their dialogue.

Example:

Northeastern: "You guys wanna grab a slice?" Southern: "Y'all come over for some sweet tea."

Avoiding Overuse of Jargon

While contemporary dialogue often includes technical or industry-specific jargon, be mindful not to overuse it to the point where it alienates the audience.

Example:

"Let's optimize our workflow using Agile methodologies," said Rachel. "It'll streamline the process."

Highlighting Generational Speech Differences

Different generations often have distinct ways of speaking. Reflect these differences to create authentic character interactions.

Example:

Older character: "Back in my day, we did things differently." Younger character: "Yeah, but that's ancient history. We've moved on."

Balancing Modernity with Timelessness

While it's important to reflect contemporary speech, also ensure that dialogue doesn't become so tied to specific trends that it feels dated quickly.

Example:

"Everything's moving so fast," said Jamie. "Sometimes I just need to unplug and breathe."

Crafting Dialogue for Diverse Platforms

Characters may interact across various communication platforms, from face-to-face conversations to text messages and video calls. Reflect these modes in your dialogue.

Example:

Text message: "Can't wait to see you later! 😊" Phone call: "Hey, are you still coming tonight?" Face-to-face: "So glad you could make it! How was your day?"

Using Realistic Dialogue in Diverse Settings

Ensure dialogue reflects the environment and context in which it's delivered, whether it's a casual hangout, a professional meeting, or a high-stakes confrontation.

Example:

Casual hangout: "Let's just chill and watch some Netflix." Professional meeting: "We need to address the budgetary concerns." High-stakes confrontation: "You have no idea what you're getting into!"

Balancing Dialogue with Visual Storytelling

Remember that dialogue is just one part of storytelling. Ensure it complements and enhances the visual elements of your screenplay.

Example:

As Sarah speaks about her frustration, the camera zooms in on her clenched fists and tense expression, emphasizing her emotions.

Ensuring Consistency with Character Voice

Even in contemporary dialogue, maintain consistency with each character's voice and personality. Ensure that modern expressions fit their established speech patterns.

Example:

For a tech-savvy character: "Let's just run a quick data analysis and see where we stand." For a more laid-back character: "I'm just gonna roll with it and see what happens."

Refreshing Dialogue with Contemporary References

Update dialogue with fresh, contemporary references to keep it relevant and engaging.

Example:

"Have you heard about the latest streaming platform?" asked Mia. "It's got all the shows everyone's talking about."

Integrating Contemporary Themes

Reflect current social issues and themes in your dialogue, making it more relevant and thought-provoking.

Example:

"I'm really concerned about climate change," said Ella. "We need to start making a difference now."

Creating Authenticity in Everyday Conversations

Capture the rhythm and flow of everyday conversations to make your dialogue feel natural and genuine.

"Hey, what's up?" said Jordan. "Not much, just hanging out. You?"

In summary, writing contemporary dialogue involves understanding modern speech patterns, incorporating slang and technological influences, using informal language, reflecting social media impacts, capturing diverse speech styles, and balancing authenticity with the natural flow of conversation. By focusing on these elements, you can create dialogue that resonates with today's audience and feels fresh and relevant.

Adapting Dialogue from Source Material

Adapting dialogue from source material, such as novels, plays, or historical events, is a nuanced process that requires careful consideration to ensure that the essence of the original content is preserved while making it suitable for the screen. Here's how to approach this adaptation effectively:

Understanding the Source Material

Before you adapt dialogue, thoroughly understand the source material. This involves recognizing the themes, character motivations, and the context of the dialogue in the original work. The goal is to retain the original's intent and impact while making it fit the visual and auditory nature of film or television.

Example: If adapting a novel, consider how the internal monologues and descriptive passages can be transformed into visually and audibly engaging dialogue.

Maintaining Character Voice

Ensure that the characters' voices remain consistent with how they are portrayed in the source material. This involves preserving their unique speech patterns, idiosyncrasies, and personality traits.

Example: If a character in a novel is known for their witty and verbose dialogue, keep that same style in the screenplay, but adapt it to fit the pacing and format of a screenplay.

Condensing and Simplifying

Screenplay dialogue tends to be more concise and direct than prose. While adapting, condense lengthy monologues and descriptive passages into succinct, impactful lines of dialogue. Focus on capturing the core message and emotions rather than every detail.

Example: A lengthy soliloquy in a play might be trimmed to a powerful, brief statement that conveys the same sentiment on screen.

Adapting for Visual Storytelling

Dialogue in screenplays must complement visual storytelling. Convert narrative descriptions and internal thoughts into dialogue that can be delivered through actors and integrated with visual elements.

Example: In a novel, a character's inner conflict might be expressed through detailed narrative. In a screenplay, this internal struggle can be shown through interactions with other characters and dialogue that reveals their emotional state.

Respecting the Original Tone and Style

While adapting, respect the tone and style of the source material. Ensure that the dialogue maintains the original's mood, whether it's dramatic, comedic, or reflective.

Example: If adapting a dark, intense drama, ensure the dialogue retains its gravity and depth, even if it is condensed or modified for the screen.

Incorporating Modern Language

If the source material is dated, update the dialogue to make it more accessible to contemporary audiences while preserving the original's meaning and tone.

Example: Historical dialogue can be updated with modern language while maintaining the original context and character dynamics.

Balancing Adaptation with Originality

While it's crucial to stay true to the source material, don't be afraid to make adjustments for the screen. This might include altering dialogue to better suit the medium, pacing, or character development in the film or television adaptation.

Example: A line that works well in a novel might need to be altered to fit a different pacing or to fit the rhythm of the scene in a screenplay.

Addressing Dialogue Flow

Consider how dialogue flows in the source material and adapt it to fit the natural rhythm of screen dialogue. This might involve reworking the dialogue for smoother exchanges and pacing suitable for visual media.

Example: A dialogue exchange in a novel might need to be restructured to ensure it flows well and maintains tension in a screenplay.

Ensuring Accessibility and Engagement

Adapt dialogue to be engaging and accessible for the screen audience. This means ensuring that the dialogue is clear, relatable, and dynamic.

Example: Complex or abstract ideas in a novel might need to be simplified or presented through more dynamic dialogue in a screenplay to keep viewers engaged.

Maintaining Authenticity

Ensure that any changes made during adaptation do not compromise the authenticity of the characters or the original story. The adapted dialogue should still feel true to the source material's essence.

Example: A character's signature catchphrase or distinctive way of speaking should be retained to preserve their authenticity and recognisability.

Collaborating with the Original Creators

If possible, collaborate with the original creators or rights holders of the source material. Their insights can help ensure that the adaptation remains faithful to their vision while making necessary adjustments for the screen.

Example: Working with an author on adapting their novel can provide valuable feedback on maintaining the integrity of the characters and story.

Balancing Dialogue with Visuals and Sound

Consider how the adapted dialogue will interact with visual and sound elements in the film or television adaptation. Ensure that the dialogue complements and enhances these elements rather than overshadowing them.

Example: Dialogue in a scene with intense action might need to be concise and impactful, fitting seamlessly with the visual and auditory elements of the scene.

Testing and Refining Dialogue

Test the adapted dialogue through readings or rehearsals to ensure it works effectively in the context of the screenplay. Make adjustments as needed to ensure that it resonates well with both actors and audiences.

Example: Conducting table reads can reveal how the dialogue flows and whether it effectively conveys the intended emotions and themes.

Adapting Dialogue for Different Genres

When adapting dialogue from source material, consider how the genre of the adaptation might influence the dialogue. Different genres have unique conventions and expectations for dialogue.

Example: Dialogue in a historical drama might need to be more formal, while a contemporary comedy might benefit from more casual and witty exchanges.

Retaining Iconic Lines

If the source material contains iconic or memorable lines, find ways to incorporate these into the adaptation. These lines can serve as a nod to fans of the original work and add authenticity to the adaptation.

Example: Famous lines from a classic novel can be adapted verbatim or slightly modified to fit the screenplay while retaining their impact.

Balancing Fidelity and Innovation

Strive to balance fidelity to the original dialogue with innovation to suit the screen medium. The goal is to create a screenplay that honors the source material while making it engaging and effective for a visual audience.

Example: A novel's rich, descriptive dialogue can be distilled into impactful, visually-oriented lines that capture the same essence.

In summary, adapting dialogue from source material requires a deep understanding of the original work, careful condensation and simplification, and thoughtful integration with screen storytelling. By balancing fidelity to the source with the needs of the screen medium, you can create a compelling and faithful adaptation that resonates with both existing fans and new audiences.

Editing Dialogue: Cutting and Polishing

Editing dialogue is a crucial step in crafting a screenplay that feels sharp, engaging, and authentic. This process involves not just trimming unnecessary lines but also refining dialogue to enhance its impact and clarity. Here's a comprehensive guide to cutting and polishing dialogue to ensure it resonates with audiences and serves the story effectively:

Evaluating Dialogue for Relevance

Begin by assessing each piece of dialogue for its relevance to the story and characters. Every line should serve a purpose, whether it's advancing the plot, revealing character traits, or building tension. Remove lines that don't contribute meaningfully to these elements.

Example: If a character's monologue doesn't advance the plot or reveal something crucial about them, consider trimming or cutting it entirely.

Ensuring Dialogue Advances the Plot

Dialogue should propel the story forward. Evaluate whether each conversation or line adds to the progression of the plot. If a dialogue exchange doesn't move the story forward, it may be a candidate for revision or removal.

Example: An extended conversation about a minor subplot that doesn't impact the main story can be shortened or eliminated.

Eliminating Redundancy

Watch for repetitive dialogue that restates information or emotions already conveyed. Redundancy can make scenes feel slow and less engaging. Trim or rework lines that simply reiterate points.

Example: If two characters discuss the same issue in different scenes, consolidate their dialogue to avoid repetition and maintain pacing.

Refining for Clarity and Impact

Dialogue should be clear and impactful. Rework lines that are ambiguous or convoluted. Aim for precision in word choice and sentence structure to ensure that the audience understands the intended message and feels the desired emotional impact.

Example: Complex or abstract dialogue might need simplification to ensure it is accessible and effective for the audience.

Balancing Dialogue with Pacing

The rhythm of dialogue affects the overall pacing of a scene. Fast-paced dialogue can heighten tension, while slower, more reflective dialogue can build emotional depth. Edit dialogue to maintain the intended pace and keep the scene engaging.

Example: In a high-tension scene, quick, sharp exchanges can enhance urgency, while longer, introspective lines might slow the pace for dramatic effect.

Creating Natural Flow

Dialogue should flow naturally and mimic real conversation. Edit lines to ensure they feel organic and avoid sounding stilted or overly formal. Characters should speak in a way that feels authentic to their personalities and relationships.

Example: Characters with a close relationship might use more casual, relaxed language compared to characters with a more formal or distant relationship.

Improving Dialogue for Character Voice

Each character should have a distinct voice that reflects their personality, background, and current emotional state. Rework lines that sound too similar between characters or don't align with their established voice.

Example: A character known for their witty banter should have dialogue that reflects their sharpness, while a more serious character's lines should be correspondingly sober.

Trimming Excessive Dialogue

Cut any dialogue that feels excessive or unnecessary. In screenwriting, brevity is key. Ensure that each line is essential and contributes to the scene's objective, character development, or emotional tone.

Example: A character's lengthy exposition can often be condensed to a few impactful lines that achieve the same effect without bogging down the scene.

Enhancing Subtext

Dialogue often carries subtext—implied meaning beneath the surface. Ensure that subtext is clear and effective. Edit dialogue to strengthen underlying themes and character motivations without making them overtly obvious.

Example: Instead of a character explicitly stating their fear, use subtextual dialogue that hints at their anxiety through their choice of words and tone.

Polishing for Consistency

Consistency is crucial in dialogue, especially in longer works. Ensure that character voices, tones, and speech patterns remain consistent throughout the screenplay. This helps maintain the believability of the characters and story.

Example: A character who speaks in a particular dialect or mannerism should do so consistently, and any changes should be motivated by the narrative.

Integrating with Action and Visuals

Dialogue should complement the action and visual elements of a scene. Ensure that dialogue doesn't overshadow or conflict with visual storytelling. Edit dialogue to seamlessly integrate with the visuals and enhance the overall impact of the scene.

Example: If a scene involves intense action, dialogue should be concise and direct to match the fast pace of the visuals.

Testing Dialogue

Read dialogue aloud or conduct table reads to gauge its effectiveness. Hearing the dialogue spoken can reveal issues with flow, clarity, and impact that might not be apparent in written form. Make adjustments based on these readings to refine the dialogue.

Example: During a table read, actors might highlight lines that feel awkward or unnatural, providing insight into necessary revisions.

Maintaining Emotional Resonance

Ensure that dialogue maintains its emotional resonance after editing. Dialogue should still convey the intended emotions and connect with the audience on a personal level. Make sure that cuts or changes don't diminish the emotional impact.

Example: If a character's pivotal line is altered, ensure that the revised line retains the same emotional weight and significance.

Considering Feedback

Incorporate feedback from others, such as script readers, directors, or actors. Fresh perspectives can offer valuable insights into dialogue effectiveness and suggest improvements that enhance the overall screenplay.

Example: Feedback might reveal dialogue that doesn't land as intended or suggest ways to enhance character interactions.

Finalizing Dialogue

After cutting and polishing, conduct a final review to ensure that all dialogue is cohesive, engaging, and aligned with the screenplay's overall tone and style. Make any last-minute adjustments to ensure that the dialogue shines in the final draft.

Example: A final review might involve ensuring that dialogue transitions smoothly between scenes and that all character voices are distinct and true to their development.

In summary, editing dialogue involves a careful balance of trimming excess, refining clarity, and ensuring natural flow while preserving character voices and emotional impact.

Testing Dialogue: Reading Aloud and Feedback

Testing dialogue is a vital step in the screenwriting process, allowing you to ensure that your dialogue not only reads well on the page but also sounds natural and effective when spoken. This process involves reading dialogue aloud and seeking feedback from others to refine and perfect your script. Here's how to approach this critical phase:

Reading Dialogue Aloud

Reading your dialogue aloud is one of the most effective ways to test its quality. This exercise helps you catch issues with flow, pacing, and naturalness that may not be obvious when reading silently. Here's how to do it effectively:

Solo Read-Through: Start by reading your dialogue out loud to yourself. This helps you hear how the words sound and identify any awkward or unnatural phrasing. Pay attention to the rhythm of the dialogue and how it fits with the overall scene.

Character Voices: While reading, try to use distinct character voices to get a sense of how each character's dialogue fits their personality. This can help you identify inconsistencies in character voice or unnatural speech patterns.

Pacing and Flow: Listen for any lines that disrupt the pacing or feel too slow or rushed. Dialogue should have a natural rhythm, matching the tension and mood of the scene. Adjust any lines that feel clunky or out of sync.

Emotional Impact: Assess whether the dialogue conveys the intended emotions. If a line is meant to be humorous, dramatic, or tense, ensure it delivers the right emotional effect when spoken.

Clarity: Ensure that the dialogue is clear and understandable. If any lines are confusing or ambiguous, rewrite them to enhance clarity without sacrificing subtlety.

Conducting Table Reads

Table reads involve gathering a group of actors or friends to read through your script. This method provides valuable insights into how dialogue plays out in a real-world setting. Here's how to make the most of a table read:

Organize the Read-Through: Arrange a table read with a diverse group of readers who can bring different perspectives to your script. This group can include actors, fellow writers, or anyone familiar with script analysis.

Assign Roles: Provide scripts with roles assigned to each participant. This allows you to hear how the dialogue sounds in context and how characters interact with one another.

Observe Reactions: Pay attention to the readers' reactions as they perform the dialogue. Note any areas where they stumble, react with confusion, or appear disengaged. These reactions can highlight dialogue issues that need addressing.

Record the Session: If possible, record the table read to review later. Listening to the recording can reveal nuances you might miss during the live session, such as pacing issues or inconsistencies in character voices.

Encourage Feedback: Ask participants for their feedback on the dialogue. Encourage them to share their impressions on character voices, flow, and any lines that feel out of place. This feedback can provide fresh perspectives and help refine your script.

Gathering Constructive Feedback

Feedback from others is crucial for identifying areas for improvement in your dialogue. Here's how to gather and use feedback effectively:

Choose the Right Reviewers: Select reviewers who have experience with screenwriting or who can provide valuable insights into dialogue. These might include fellow writers, directors, or actors.

Be Open to Criticism: Approach feedback with an open mind. Constructive criticism is meant to help you improve your script, so be willing to consider suggestions and make necessary revisions.

Focus on Common Themes: Look for recurring themes or issues in the feedback you receive. If multiple reviewers point out similar problems, it's likely an area that needs attention.

Ask Specific Questions: When seeking feedback, ask specific questions about aspects of the dialogue, such as clarity, character voice, and emotional impact. This targeted approach can help you address particular concerns.

Revise and Test Again: After incorporating feedback, revisit the dialogue and test it again through reading aloud or another table read. Repeated testing ensures that revisions enhance the dialogue and address any lingering issues.

Final Adjustments

After testing and receiving feedback, make final adjustments to your dialogue. Here's what to focus on during this stage:

Refine Language: Polish any lines that need tweaking to improve clarity or impact. Ensure that every word and phrase serves a purpose and enhances the overall dialogue.

Maintain Consistency: Ensure that all dialogue remains consistent with character voices, tone, and the story's pacing. Consistency is key to maintaining a coherent and engaging script.

Enhance Emotional Resonance: Make sure that the dialogue effectively conveys the intended emotions and supports character development. Emotional resonance is crucial for connecting with the audience.

Final Proofread: Conduct a final proofread to catch any remaining errors or inconsistencies. This final check ensures that your dialogue is polished and ready for submission or production.

In summary, testing dialogue through reading aloud and gathering feedback is essential for refining and perfecting your script. This process helps you ensure that your dialogue is engaging, natural, and effective, ultimately enhancing the overall quality of your screenplay.

Rewriting Dialogue: Iteration and Improvement

Rewriting dialogue is a fundamental part of the screenwriting process. It's about refining your script to ensure that each line serves its intended purpose and contributes to the overall story. Here's a comprehensive guide to effectively iterating and improving dialogue:

Understanding the Need for Rewriting

Dialogue often undergoes several revisions before it reaches its final form. Understanding why and when to rewrite is key to improving your script:

Clarity and Impact: Sometimes, dialogue may be unclear or fail to have the desired impact. Rewriting helps clarify the meaning and strengthen the emotional or dramatic effect.

Character Consistency: Characters may initially speak in ways that don't fully align with their established personalities. Rewriting allows you to fine-tune dialogue to better reflect each character's voice and development.

Pacing and Flow: Dialogue can affect the pacing of a scene. If a conversation feels too slow or rushed, rewriting can help adjust the rhythm to enhance the scene's flow.

Authenticity: Realistic dialogue is crucial for audience engagement. Rewriting helps ensure that the dialogue feels natural and true to life, avoiding clichés or unnatural phrasing.

Techniques for Effective Rewriting

Identify Weak Spots: Review your dialogue for any lines that feel awkward, forced, or out of character. Mark these areas for revision. Consider both individual lines and overall dialogue patterns.

Simplify and Streamline: Simplify complex or verbose dialogue. Aim for brevity and clarity, ensuring each line conveys its intended meaning without unnecessary embellishment.

Enhance Subtext: Dialogue often works best when it's not just about what's being said, but what's being left unsaid. Rewriting can enhance subtext, allowing characters to communicate deeper meanings through their words.

Adjust Tone and Voice: Ensure that the tone and voice of the dialogue match the scene's mood and each character's personality. Rewriting may involve adjusting language, tone, and speech patterns to fit these elements.

Strengthen Emotional Impact: Revisit dialogue to ensure it effectively conveys the desired emotions. Revise lines to enhance their emotional resonance and make them more impactful.

Dialogue Tags and Beats: If your dialogue is accompanied by action or description, make sure it complements and enhances the spoken words. Rewriting might involve adjusting or adding dialogue tags and beats to improve clarity and rhythm.

Iterative Process

Write Multiple Drafts: Rewriting often involves multiple drafts. After making initial revisions, set the script aside and return with fresh eyes. This distance helps you view the dialogue more objectively.

Seek Feedback: Share your revised dialogue with trusted readers or collaborators. Their feedback can provide new perspectives and highlight areas for further improvement.

Test in Context: Read the revised dialogue within the context of the scene or the entire script. Ensure that the changes fit seamlessly and enhance the overall narrative.

Refine Through Rehearsals: If possible, test the dialogue in a rehearsal setting with actors. Their performances can reveal additional nuances and areas for refinement.

Common Issues and Solutions

Dialogue Feels On-the-Nose: Characters may speak in ways that are too direct or explicit. Rewriting should involve finding ways to convey information or emotions more subtly, allowing for subtext and interpretation.

Character Voice Overlap: Characters may sound too similar, making it hard to distinguish their voices. Focus on refining individual speech patterns and language to make each character's voice distinct and authentic.

Expository Dialogue: Dialogue that delivers too much information can feel forced. Rewriting should aim to weave exposition naturally into conversations, maintaining the flow and keeping the audience engaged.

Unnatural Flow: Dialogue that feels stilted or unnatural can disrupt the scene's pacing. Rewriting should focus on making conversations more fluid and realistic, ensuring they reflect natural speech patterns.

Lack of Conflict or Tension: Dialogue that lacks conflict or tension can make scenes feel flat. Rewriting should introduce or heighten conflicts through sharp, engaging dialogue that drives the scene forward.

Final Considerations

Consistency: Ensure that revised dialogue remains consistent with the character's development and the story's themes. Consistency is crucial for maintaining a cohesive narrative.

Polish and Proofread: Conduct a final proofread to catch any remaining errors or inconsistencies. A polished script is essential for professional presentation and readability.

Stay Open to Change: Be prepared to make further revisions as needed. Dialogue rewriting is an iterative process, and ongoing improvements can lead to a more compelling and effective script.

Dialogue in Adaptations: Staying True to the Original

When adapting a story from one medium to another, such as from a novel or play to a screenplay, the dialogue is a crucial element that requires careful attention. The goal is to stay true to the original work while crafting dialogue that fits the new format and resonates with a different audience. Here's a guide on how to achieve that balance:

Understanding the Source Material

Deep Analysis: Before starting the adaptation, deeply analyze the source material. Understand the nuances of the original dialogue—its tone, style, and purpose. Consider how dialogue contributes to character development, plot progression, and thematic elements.

Character Voice: Pay attention to how each character speaks in the original work. Their speech patterns, language, and dialogue style are key to capturing their essence. Ensure that these elements are preserved in the adaptation, adjusting only where necessary to fit the new medium.

Plot and Themes: Identify the central plot points and themes conveyed through dialogue in the source material. Ensure that these core elements are maintained in the adaptation, even if the dialogue needs to be modified.

Adapting Dialogue to Screen

Condensing and Streamlining: Dialogue in novels or plays often includes detailed descriptions and internal monologues that aren't suitable for the screen. Condense and streamline the dialogue to fit the visual and auditory nature of film or television. Focus on essential information and emotions while cutting redundant or overly verbose lines.

Visual and Auditory Context: Unlike written narratives, screenplays rely on visual and auditory storytelling. Adapt the dialogue to complement the visual elements and actions. Show rather than tell where possible, using dialogue to enhance the scenes rather than convey information that can be shown visually.

Naturalistic Speech: Dialogue in screenplays should sound natural and conversational. Adapt the dialogue to ensure it fits the rhythm and flow of spoken language. Avoid overly formal or literary language unless it is consistent with the character's voice.

Character Dynamics: In adapting dialogue, maintain the relationships and dynamics between characters. Ensure that their interactions remain true to the original, even if the dialogue needs to be rephrased or shortened.

Balancing Fidelity and Creativity

Preserve Key Moments: Identify key dialogue moments that are pivotal to the plot or character development. Preserve these moments as much as possible, making adjustments only to fit the screenplay format.

Creative Adjustments: While staying true to the original, allow for creative adjustments that enhance the screenplay. This might include altering dialogue for pacing, clarity, or dramatic effect. Balance fidelity with creativity to ensure that the adaptation resonates with both fans of the original and new audiences.

Modernization: If the original dialogue is dated, consider updating it to reflect contemporary language and sensibilities while retaining the essence of the characters and story. Ensure that modernization doesn't compromise the integrity of the original work.

Dialogue Adaptation Techniques

Dialogue Compression: Use techniques like dialogue compression to convey the same meaning in fewer words. Focus on the core message and emotions, and eliminate any extraneous details.

Sub-textual Adaptation: Adapt dialogue to capture the underlying subtext and themes of the original work. Ensure that the emotional and thematic weight of the dialogue is preserved, even if the exact wording changes.

Character Consistency: Ensure that the adapted dialogue remains consistent with the characters' personalities and development. Characters should speak in ways that reflect their motivations, backgrounds, and relationships.

Scene Transitions: Adapt dialogue to smoothly transition between scenes. Ensure that dialogue helps to bridge gaps and maintain narrative flow, avoiding abrupt shifts or disjointed conversations.

Testing and Feedback

Table Readings: Conduct table readings of the adapted screenplay to test the dialogue. Listen to how it sounds when spoken aloud and make adjustments as needed. This helps to identify any awkward phrasing or unnatural flow.

Feedback from Source Material Experts: Seek feedback from individuals familiar with the original work. Their insights can help ensure that the adapted dialogue stays true to the source material while fitting the new format.

Audience Reaction: Consider testing the screenplay with a sample audience, including fans of the original work. Their reactions can provide valuable feedback on how well the adapted dialogue resonates with the intended audience.

Final Considerations

Respect for Original Work: Always approach adaptations with respect for the original work. Ensure that the essence of the original dialogue is preserved and that the adaptation honors the author's intent.

Creative Flexibility: Be prepared to make creative adjustments to the dialogue as needed. The adaptation process often involves balancing fidelity with the demands of the new medium.

Consistency across the Script: Ensure that adapted dialogue is consistent throughout the screenplay. All dialogue should align with the characters' development, plot progression, and thematic elements.

In summary, adapting dialogue from one medium to another involves a careful balance between staying true to the original work and making necessary adjustments for the new format. By understanding the source material, preserving key moments, and creatively adapting dialogue, you can create a screenplay that honors the original while resonating with a new audience.

Collaborating on Dialogue: Writers and Actors

When crafting dialogue for the screen, collaboration between writers and actors is essential to achieve the most compelling and authentic results. Both parties bring unique perspectives and skills to the table, and their cooperation can elevate the quality of the dialogue, enhance character portrayals, and ensure that the script resonates with audiences. Here's how writers and actors can work together effectively on dialogue:

Understanding the Roles

Writers' Perspective:

Crafting the Dialogue: Writers create dialogue with specific intentions, including character development, plot advancement, and thematic expression. They design dialogue to convey emotions, reveal character traits, and drive the narrative.

Maintaining Structure: Writers focus on the structure and flow of the screenplay. They consider how dialogue fits into scenes, contributes to pacing, and interacts with visual elements.

Actors' Perspective:

Bringing Characters to Life: Actors interpret dialogue through their performances, adding nuance, emotion, and depth. They embody characters and use dialogue to express internal states and reactions.

Delivering Authenticity: Actors strive to make dialogue sound natural and believable, reflecting real human interactions and experiences.

Effective Collaboration Techniques

Early Involvement:

Workshops and Readings: Involve actors in early workshops and table readings. This provides them with the opportunity to engage with the dialogue and provide feedback on how it feels in practice.

Script Discussions: Engage in discussions with actors about the script's dialogue before shooting begins. Understanding their perspectives and interpretations can lead to a more refined and authentic portrayal.

Feedback and Adaptation:

Actor Insights: Encourage actors to share their insights on the dialogue. They may suggest changes to better reflect their character's voice or to enhance believability.

Writer Flexibility: Writers should be open to feedback and willing to adapt dialogue if it improves the overall performance. Be willing to make revisions that serve the story and characters better.

Balancing Creativity:

Maintaining Core Intent: While being open to actor suggestions, ensure that the core intent and structure of the dialogue remain intact. The dialogue should still align with the writer's vision for the story and characters.

Collaborative Creativity: Foster a creative environment where both writers and actors can experiment with different ways of delivering lines. This collaboration can lead to fresh and innovative dialogue.

Enhancing Performance through Dialogue

Character Voice:

Consistency: Ensure that dialogue is consistent with the character's voice and development. Actors should feel confident that the dialogue reflects their character's personality and journey.

Depth and Complexity: Writers can provide actors with background information and context that enriches their understanding of the character and the dialogue. This depth can lead to more nuanced performances.

Emotional Resonance:

Emotional Accuracy: Collaborate to ensure that the emotional tone of the dialogue matches the scene's intent. Actors can provide valuable feedback on how dialogue impacts their emotional performance.

Adjustments for Authenticity: Be prepared to adjust dialogue to enhance emotional resonance. Small changes can make a significant difference in how dialogue is received by audiences.

Practical Tips for Writers and Actors

Open Communication:

Regular Check-ins: Maintain regular communication throughout the production process. Writers and actors should discuss any concerns or adjustments related to dialogue.

Constructive Feedback: Provide and receive feedback constructively. Focus on how changes can improve the dialogue and overall performance.

Understanding Context:

Scene Context: Writers should provide actors with context for each scene, including the emotional stakes and character motivations. This helps actors deliver dialogue in line with the scene's objectives.

Actor Input: Actors should consider the broader context of the dialogue within the screenplay. Understanding how their performance fits into the overall narrative can guide their delivery.

Workshops and Rehearsals:

Rehearsals: Use rehearsals to experiment with different interpretations of the dialogue. This collaborative process allows writers and actors to explore various delivery options and refine the script.

Feedback Sessions: Schedule feedback sessions where actors can discuss their experiences with the dialogue and suggest improvements. Writers can then incorporate relevant changes.

Addressing Challenges

Conflicting Visions:

Finding Common Ground: When conflicting visions arise, focus on finding common ground. Both writers and actors should work together to resolve differences while keeping the story's integrity intact.

Compromise and Adaptation: Be willing to compromise and adapt dialogue as necessary. The goal is to achieve a performance that is true to the character and serves the story effectively.

Maintaining Authenticity:

Balancing Artistic Vision: Strive to balance the writer's artistic vision with the actor's need for authenticity. Dialogue should feel genuine and true to the character while aligning with the writer's intentions.

Adapting for Performance:

Performance Adjustments: Be prepared to make final adjustments to dialogue based on actors' performances. Sometimes, what works on the page may need to be refined for the screen.

Collaborating on dialogue requires a dynamic and open exchange between writers and actors. By understanding each other's roles, engaging in constructive feedback, and balancing creativity with authenticity, both parties can create dialogue that is compelling, believable, and impactful. Effective collaboration not only enhances character portrayals but also contributes to the overall success of the screenplay, ensuring that the dialogue resonates with audiences and supports the narrative's goals.

Final Thoughts on Dialogue: Making It Memorable

As we reach the end of our exploration into writing dialogue for screenplays, it's time to reflect on what truly makes dialogue memorable and impactful. Dialogue is more than just words on a page; it's a crucial element that breathes life into characters, drives the plot forward, and leaves a lasting impression on audiences. Here are some final thoughts on crafting dialogue that stands out and resonates long after the credits roll.

1. Embrace Authenticity

Authenticity is the cornerstone of memorable dialogue. Characters should speak in ways that are true to their experiences, personalities, and backgrounds. Authentic dialogue reflects real-life conversations, capturing the nuances of how people actually communicate. This doesn't mean that every line must be literal; instead, it should be grounded in truth, allowing characters to express themselves in ways that feel genuine.

2. Prioritize Subtext

Subtext is the hidden layer beneath the surface of dialogue. It's what characters mean, rather than what they say outright. Crafting dialogue with rich subtext adds depth and complexity to interactions, making conversations more engaging and thought-provoking. By allowing characters to speak around the issue, hint at their true feelings, or imply more than they say, you can create dialogue that resonates on multiple levels.

3. Focus on Unique Voices

Each character should have a distinct voice that sets them apart from others. This uniqueness can be achieved through speech patterns, vocabulary, and tone. A well-defined voice not only helps to differentiate characters but also enriches their individuality and adds layers to their personalities. Consider how their backgrounds, experiences, and attitudes influence the way they speak, and use these elements to make their dialogue distinctive.

4. Balance Dialogue with Action

Dialogue should complement, not overshadow, the action. Effective dialogue moves the story forward and reveals character while seamlessly integrating with the visual and physical aspects of the screenplay. Ensure that conversations are purposeful and that they enhance or reflect the ongoing action. This balance helps maintain pacing and keeps the narrative engaging.

5. Infuse Dialogue with Emotion

Emotion is a driving force in memorable dialogue. Whether it's joy, anger, sadness, or fear, emotional depth in dialogue can profoundly impact the audience. Characters' emotions should be conveyed through their words, delivery, and interactions. Use dialogue to explore and express the full range of human emotions, and allow moments of vulnerability or intensity to shine through.

6. Craft Dialogue with Purpose

Every line of dialogue should serve a specific purpose, whether it's advancing the plot, revealing character, or underscoring themes. Avoid filler or unnecessary conversations that don't contribute to the narrative. Ensure that dialogue is concise, impactful, and aligned with the overall story arc. Purposeful dialogue keeps the audience engaged and invested in the characters and their journeys.

7. Embrace the Power of Silence

Sometimes, what is left unsaid can be as powerful as the dialogue itself. Silence, pauses, and non-verbal cues can convey tension, contemplation, or emotional weight. Use silence strategically to complement dialogue and allow characters to process or react to what's been said. This interplay between spoken words and silence can add layers of meaning and depth to scenes.

8. Iterate and Refine

The process of writing dialogue is iterative. Don't be afraid to revise and refine your dialogue as you develop the screenplay. Read it aloud, test it in rehearsals, and seek feedback to ensure it flows naturally and resonates with its intended impact. Iteration helps to polish dialogue, making it sharper and more effective.

9. Consider Genre and Tone

Dialogue should align with the genre and tone of the screenplay. Whether you're writing a comedy, drama, thriller, or sci-fi, the style and substance of dialogue should match the overall mood and expectations of the genre. Each genre has its conventions and stylistic nuances, so tailor your dialogue accordingly to fit the context.

10. Reflect on the Impact

Finally, think about the lasting impact you want your dialogue to have. Memorable dialogue often contains lines or exchanges that stay with the audience long after they've left the theater or turned off the screen. Aim to create dialogue that is thought-provoking, emotionally resonant, and capable of sparking reflection or conversation.

Writing memorable dialogue is an art form that requires attention to detail, an understanding of character and context, and a dedication to authenticity and emotional depth. As you craft your dialogue, keep these principles in mind to create conversations that engage, entertain, and leave a lasting impression. Dialogue is not just about conveying information; it's about creating connections, exploring emotions, and making a mark on your audience. With thoughtful consideration and creative finesse, your dialogue can truly shine and make your screenplay unforgettable.

The Importance of Your Voice and Your Legacy

As we wrap up this exploration of dialogue for screenwriters, it's crucial to reflect on a more personal and profound aspect of the craft: the importance of your unique voice and the legacy you leave behind. Dialogue, while a technical skill, is also deeply intertwined with your individuality as a writer and the lasting impact you aim to create through your work. Let's delve into why your voice matters and how it contributes to the legacy you build as a storyteller.

Your Unique Voice

Every writer possesses a unique voice—a distinct style, perspective, and approach to storytelling that sets them apart from others. This voice is not just about the words you choose but also about how you convey emotions, themes, and character interactions through dialogue. Your voice is the fingerprint of your creativity, the signature that makes your work instantly recognizable.

Embracing and nurturing your voice is essential because it defines your storytelling identity. When you write with authenticity and confidence, your dialogue reflects your personal insights, experiences, and worldview. This authenticity resonates with audiences, creating a deeper connection between your characters and viewers. It's through your unique voice that you can offer fresh perspectives, challenge conventions, and bring something new to the screenwriting landscape.

The Power of Individuality

In a world brimming with stories and voices, standing out requires embracing your individuality. Your voice allows you to infuse dialogue with originality and nuance, making your work memorable and impactful. Whether you write with humor, poignancy, or intensity, your unique voice adds a distinct flavor to your dialogues, distinguishing your scripts from others.

Consider how iconic screenwriters like Quentin Tarantino, Aaron Sorkin, or Nora Ephron have made their mark through their distinct voices. Their dialogue is instantly recognizable because it embodies their personal style and sensibilities. Your voice, too, has the power to shape how your stories are perceived and remembered.

Building a Legacy

As you craft dialogue and weave narratives, you're not only creating stories but also building a legacy. The impact of your work extends beyond immediate audiences to future generations of viewers, writers, and storytellers. Your legacy is shaped by the themes you explore, the characters you create, and the dialogues you craft.

Your dialogue can contribute to your legacy in several ways:

Cultural Impact: Dialogue that addresses universal themes or captures the zeitgeist of a particular era can have a lasting cultural impact. Think of memorable lines or exchanges from classic films that have become part of popular culture. Your words have the potential to influence and resonate with audiences long after they're first heard.

Inspiring Others: By writing with passion and authenticity, you inspire others to find and embrace their voices. Your work can serve as a beacon for aspiring screenwriters, showing them the importance of personal expression and the value of crafting dialogue that reflects one's true self.

Setting Standards: Your dialogue can set new standards in storytelling, pushing the boundaries of what's possible in terms of character development, thematic exploration, and emotional depth. By contributing innovative and thought-provoking dialogue, you help shape the future of screenwriting and storytelling.

Personal Fulfillment: Ultimately, the legacy you build through your dialogue is a reflection of your personal journey and achievements. Crafting dialogue that you're proud of and that resonates with others brings a sense of fulfillment and accomplishment, knowing that your voice has made a meaningful contribution to the world of storytelling.

Leaving a Lasting Impact

As you continue to write and refine your craft, keep in mind the legacy you wish to create. Focus on the stories you want to tell, the characters you want to bring to life, and the dialogues that will define your work. Embrace your voice, make bold choices, and strive to create dialogue that is not only engaging but also transformative.

In the end, your dialogue is a testament to who you are as a writer and a storyteller. It reflects your passions, values, and vision. By staying true to your voice and crafting dialogue with intention and heart, you ensure that your work leaves a lasting impact on audiences and contributes to the rich tapestry of storytelling.

So, as you move forward in your screenwriting journey, remember the importance of your voice and the legacy you are creating. Write with confidence, authenticity, and purpose. Your dialogue has the power to captivate, inspire, and endure—leaving a mark that speaks to the essence of who you are as a writer and storyteller.

I hope you found information and inspiration you can use for your next project. If you liked this book, please leave a review where you bought it. Thank you from the author.